The Blood-Drenched Sea

The Blood-Drenched Sea

Ships at War in the Ancient Mediterranean

Alfred S. Bradford

 PRAEGER®

An Imprint of ABC-CLIO, LLC

Santa Barbara, California • Denver, Colorado

Library of Congress Cataloging-in-Publication Data

Names: Bradford, Alfred S., author.
Title: The blood-drenched sea : ships at war in the ancient Mediterranean / Alfred S. Bradford.
Description: Santa Barbara, California : Praeger, an imprint of ABC-CLIO, LLC, [2019] | Includes bibliographical references and index.
Identifiers: LCCN 2019015039 (print) | LCCN 2019020362 (ebook) | ISBN 9781440871030 (ebook) | ISBN 9781440871023 (hard copy : alk. paper)
Subjects: LCSH: Naval history, Ancient. | Mediterranean Region—History, Naval. | Naval battles—Mediterranean Region—History—To 1500. | Ships, Ancient—Mediterranean Region. | Mediterranean Sea—Navigation—History.
Classification: LCC V55.M44 (ebook) | LCC V55.M44 B73 2019 (print) | DDC 359.00937—dc23
LC record available at https://lccn.loc.gov/2019015039

ISBN:978-1-4408-7102-3 (print)
     978-1-4408-7103-0 (ebook)

23 22 21 20 19   1 2 3 4 5

This book is also available as an eBook.

Praeger
An Imprint of ABC-CLIO, LLC

ABC-CLIO, LLC
147 Castilian Drive
Santa Barbara, California 93117
www.abc-clio.com

This book is printed on acid-free paper ∞

Manufactured in the United States of America

To Carl Malmstrom
My Friend

Contents

Maps and Illustrations   xi

Preface: Wars at Sea   xiii

Introduction: The Blue on the Map   xv

Part One   Turmoil in the Eastern Mediterranean   1

Chapter 1   The First to Risk Their Lives upon the Water   3

Chapter 2   The Minoans and the First "Thalassocracy"   5

Chapter 3   The Collapse of Civilization   9

Chapter 4   The Assault on Egypt   12

Chapter 5   Greek Colonization in the East   16

Part Two   The Spread of Hellenism   21

Chapter 6   How to Build a Boat in the Eighth Century BCE   23

Chapter 7   Greek Colonization in the West   24

Chapter 8   A Typical Foundation Story   29

Chapter 9   Ramming   31

Chapter 10   The Trireme   36

Chapter 11   Polycrates: King, Tyrant, Pirate   41

Part Three   The Persian Wars   47

Chapter 12   Darius and the Greeks   49

Chapter 13   The First Naval Assault on Athens   54

Chapter 14   "Flee to the Ends of the Earth"   59

Chapter 15   "Pray to the Winds"   63

Chapter 16   "Brave Sons of Greece, Advance!"   68

Chapter 17   "Lead the Army"   73

Part Four   The Peloponnesian Wars   77

Chapter 18   Yoke Mates   79

Chapter 19   "A Bad Day for Greece"   84

Chapter 20   The Strong Do What They Want   92

Chapter 21   "Thrice Nine Days"   98

Chapter 22   Athens at Bay   106

Part Five   The Rise of Superpowers   117

Chapter 23   Hanging by a Thread   119

Chapter 24   Conon the Athenian   125

Chapter 25   Giant Men, Giant Ships   131

Part Six   The Roman Domination   141

Chapter 26   Rowing on Land   143

Chapter 27   Sacred Chickens   149

Chapter 28   The First Illyrian War, 229–228 BCE   156

Chapter 29   A Different Kind of War   159

Chapter 30   The First Macedonian War   167

Chapter 31   Greeks Will Be Free   175

Chapter 32   Thirst for Gold   182

Part Seven   The Roman Empire   189

Chapter 33   I Shall Crucify You   191

Chapter 34   Three Million Killed, Enslaved, Pacified   197

Chapter 35   Son of a God   204

Chapter 36   The Long Peace   212

Chapter 37   Decline and Fall   215

Conclusion   219

Notes   223

Classical Sources Cited and/or Translated (by the Author)   239

Bibliography   241

Index   245

Maps and Illustrations

Maps

Greece West   xviii

Greece East   xix

Greater Greece   xx

Persian Wars   xxi

Italy   xxii

Syracuse Sketch Map   xxiii

Roman Empire   xxiii

Piraeus   xxiv

Illustrations

1   Early representation of a capsized war vessel (beak and eye). The fish represent the sea, but also the fate of the drowned sailors (as the fragment shown in Illustration 2 demonstrates).   2

2   A fish devouring a corpse. This painting, and others on other vases, clearly depicts the corpse's phallus, which may be simply anatomical, but also may depict a common physical reaction to violent death.   2

3   Phase One. The ship of the sea peoples is under attack by Egyptian archers. The crew members, whose armament consists of swords and spears, have little chance to respond. The enemy soldiers are distinguished by their "feathered" helmets and the enemy ship by the bird- (duck-) headed prows.   13

4   Phase Two. Another ship of a different sea people is under
        attack. The mast of the ship has been grappled, and the ship
        is beginning to capsize.   14

5   Phase Three. The sea people's ship has capsized. There are
        no survivors.   14

6   The Aristonothos vase. This painting appears to depict
        a pirate ship attacking an armed merchant or a foreign
        (possibly Etruscan) warship.   22

7   A schematic of a trireme with the Lenormant relief
        superimposed.   39

8   Trireme tactics.   48

9   The Kerameikos vase. An amphibious assault.   78

10   Illustrations 10–17 depict battles at sea, boarding, and
        the landing of troops. Illustration 10 shows a geometric
        fragment of a ship battle.   114

11   Athenian fragment (from a krater) of a sea battle with
        dead upon the deck.   114

12   The Dipylon vase. Men straining at the oars.   114

13   Attic geometric (8th century BCE). Either a boarding battle
        or a raid.   115

14   The Paris and Helen ship (spouted krater from Thebes).
        The ship is probably not a bireme, but rather reflects
        the artist's attempt to show both sets of oarsmen.   115

15   This painting (a krater from Thebes) may be an artist's
        attempt to depict a penteconter, a long ship packed
        with oarsmen.   115

16   The cup is shaped like a ship with a boar's snout. Compare
        the ships' prows. A wild boar from a vase painting is
        included for comparison.   116

17   The rowing schemes of a quinquereme and a trireme.   116

18   Black-figured Hydria. This painting makes clear that
        boarding was done bow to bow.   118

19   "Who is safe?" Black-figure painting (540–500 BCE)
        of a pirate ship attacking a merchant.   142

20   Detail of the pirate ship.   142

21   Liberna from the column of Trajan.   190

Preface: Wars at Sea

This book, *The Blood-Drenched Sea,* contains the naval battles and wars fought in the ancient Mediterranean from the first scenes on the walls of an Egyptian mortuary temple depicting Egypt's defeat of a massive seaborne invasion in 1191 BCE to the invasion and destruction of the Roman Empire. Herein are the ships, crews, and leaders who determined the course of ancient history, along with the wars and battles, told through artifacts, extant literary and visual sources, and modern reconstructions—the Minoan sea domain; the legendary sack of Troy; the wandering of Odysseus and the expansion of Greeks throughout the Mediterranean; the great Athenian victory over the Persians at Salamis; the Athenian sea empire, ruined by one superstitious man; and the three wars between Rome and Carthage that cost the Romans hundreds of thousands of lives and vast wealth.

The Romans brought the whole of the Mediterranean under their control and then fought each other in destructive civil wars until Octavian settled the question of the new empire by winning the sea battle at Actium. The book concludes with the fall of the Roman Empire followed by a brief sketch of the subsequent history of oared warships and the tactic of ramming. This one-volume history puts seemingly isolated events in a larger context: for instance, the first wave of Greek colonization is usually treated as a separate subject, a peaceful settlement of unoccupied territory; but seen in context, it becomes a part of the violent movement of the so-called "sea peoples" who ravaged and resettled the Eastern Mediterranean.

The purpose of this account is to present the reader with the events as experienced—as far as possible—by the participants. I hope my book will reach everyone interested in the ancient world, naval history, war, and the sea. It is a fascinating story.

All translations of Greek and Latin passages are my own.

Introduction: The Blue on the Map

The blue on a map of the Mediterranean world represents the lifeblood flowing through the body of Hellas, for Hellas is less the acropolises, the mountains, and the tiny plains than it is the ports, shipyards and docks, the round ships and the long ships, penteconters, biremes, triremes, and the whole network of communities interconnected by sea.

Greeks traveled everywhere by sea, they carried merchandise—some traders regularly voyaged over one thousand miles—and, with the merchandise, they carried their culture: the *Iliad* and the *Odyssey*; the songs of individuality by Archilochus and Sappho; the beginnings of scientific theory; ethical philosophy (carried by Plato from Athens to Syracuse); and books brought from all over the Greek world to the library in Alexandria. Greeks delighted in tales of the sea, tales of the foolish pirates transformed into dolphins by Dionysus, whom they had kidnapped; tales of that earliest explorer/adventurer, Jason, who went on a quest to the Black Sea to recover the Golden Fleece and discovered everything an adventurous spirit could wish, exotic places (and creatures), gold, and a barbaric—and beautiful—princess; and, especially, they delighted in tales of Odysseus, "the many-sided, who saw the cities of numerous men (and understood their hearts). At sea he suffered many pains in his soul, struggling to preserve the lives and the homecoming of his comrades. . . ."

If the Greeks did not quite believe, like the buccaneers of later fame, that they could pluck gold from the trees of foreign lands, nonetheless, they knew that one voyage could provide wealth enough to last them the rest of their lives, if they survived. As Hesiod wrote, "It is a horrible death, to die among the waves, but money means life to poverty-stricken men." Ancient wrecks litter the floor of the Mediterranean, although, ironically, not wrecks of triremes, or other warships, because, even punctured by a ram, triremes did not sink to the bottom (little good that that did their crews).

The Greeks divided the sailing year into winter (*cheimon*) and summer (*theros*), the "bad" season and the "good" season. The most favorable part of the summer sailing season ran from late May to mid-September, but hardier—perhaps foolhardy—sailors ventured out to the sea during a more extended season, which stretched from the beginning of March to the second week of November. From early July to the end of August, the Etesian (west) winds hastened on ships sailing from the west, but hindered traffic from the east. Still, even in the best of weather, ships' captains did not like losing sight of land—they, and their steersmen and navigators, took their route from the stars, the currents, the winds, dead reckoning of their position and speed, but, preferably, by recognizing landmarks along the coasts. Winter is characterized by uncertain, and dangerous, weather when the Romans labeled the sea "closed" (*mare clausum*). Coasting was still possible, but transmarine travel was avoided, and war at sea was suspended.

Even at the height of the sailing season, conditions could be wildly unpredictable. Homer relates that Nestor and Menelaus, returning from Troy, crossed the open sea from Lesbos to Euboea in one night (after a favorable sacrifice). Four days later, Nestor reached Argos and from there had an easy voyage around the Peloponnesus to his palace in Pylos, but Menelaus was delayed at Sunion (the promontory of Attica) by the funeral of his helmsman. That few days' delay changed the situation totally—he was blown off course, the fleet was split in two, one half was wrecked on the Cretan shore, and the other half (with Menelaus) was blown to Egypt (where Menelaus turned the misfortune to his advantage by looting the countryside).

Storms could be horrible, the horror exaggerated by the belief that the god of the sea, Poseidon, was directing the storm at you personally, as, in the *Odyssey,* he did at Odysseus:

> Poseidon gathered the clouds, took his trident in his hand, and stirred up the waters. All the storms gathered from every direction and with the clouds he hid the earth and ocean. Night rose out of the heavens. East and West, North and South, the winds blew, and a mighty wave rolled. And Odysseus felt his knees give way and he was terrified.
>
> . . .
>
> A huge, towering wave rushed on him, broke over him, and spun the boat. The terrible, twisting winds snapped the mast halfway up, the whole rigging fell into the sea, and the helm was torn from his hands. He fell far from the boat, plunged under the water, and struggled for a long time to reach the surface, so great was the force of the waves, but, finally, he broke the surface and spit out the bitter water as streams of it ran down his head. Despite all, he still knew where his boat was, he fought against the waves, reached the boat, and seated himself in the middle—he barely escaped death. The great wave bore him here and there, just as the North Wind scatters seeds over the ground, for the wind churned the sea now here, now there.

Then Poseidon set upon him a terrible, towering wave, which smashed the boat to pieces and hurled Odysseus into the sea; he clung to an oar like a man clinging to a bucking bronco. Even when the storm abated and Odysseus finally floated close to shore, his troubles were not over, for the waves were carrying him toward the rocks, where he expected that he would be dashed to pieces.

Such were the perils these intrepid voyagers faced.

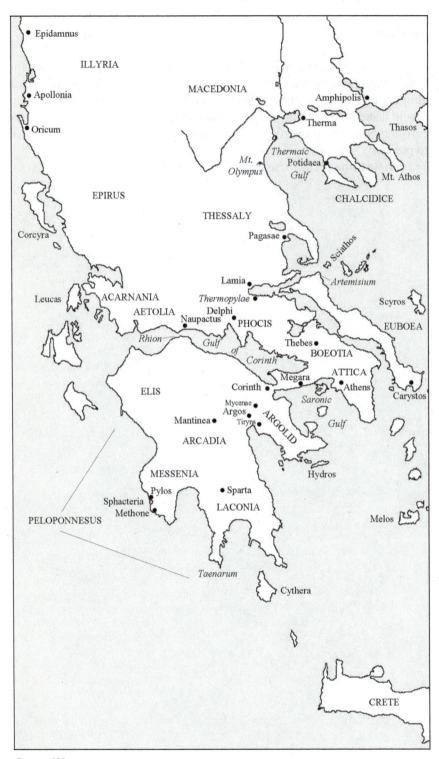

Greece West

Greece East

Greater Greece

Persian Wars

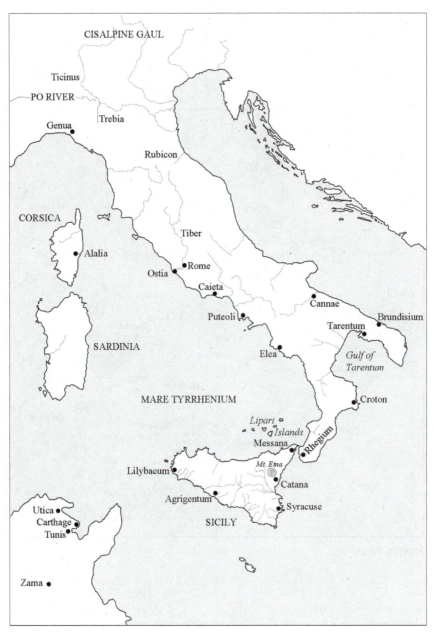

Italy

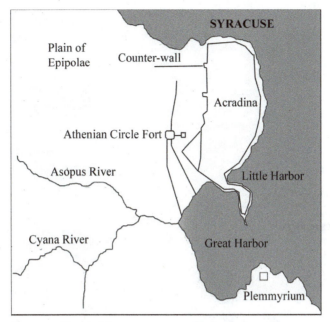

Syracuse Sketch Map

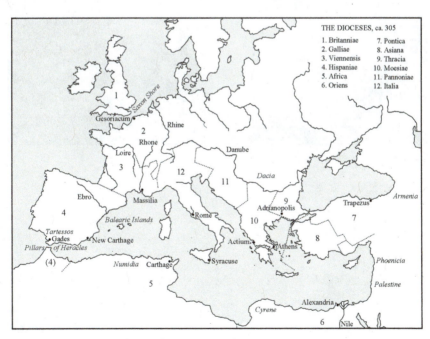

Roman Empire

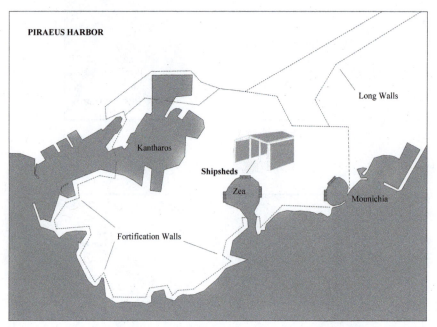

PIRAEUS HARBOR

Long Walls

Kantharos

Shipsheds

Zea

Mounichia

Fortification Walls

Piraeus

PART 1

Turmoil in the Eastern Mediterranean

Illustration 1. Early representation of a capsized war vessel (beak and eye). The fish represent the sea, but also the fate of the drowned sailors (as the fragment shown in Illustration 2 demonstrates). (Adapted and redrawn by Alfred S. Bradford)

Illustration 2. A fish devouring a corpse. This painting, and others on other vases, clearly depicts the corpse's phallus, which may be simply anatomical, but also may depict a common physical reaction to violent death. (Adapted and redrawn by Alfred S. Bradford)

The First to Risk Their Lives upon the Water

The names of the first courageous souls who dared to trust their lives to water-craft are not known to us, but these individuals, wherever they reached the end of land and gazed across an expanse of water at a distant shore, were seized with the desire to discover what was there (or they were driven to escape what lay behind them). The individuals may not be known, but the consequences are—after human beings arrived in Southeast Asia about twenty-five thousand years ago, they spread across the seas to the islands within their view, and then, as their proficiency increased, across the open ocean to the farthest uninhabited places on earth including Australia and parts of the coasts of North and South America.

In the last expansion of human beings across the globe (about thirty-five hundred years ago), they settled the islands of Oceania, which spreads across an area larger than the continent of Africa. The people in their new lands traded with the people who stayed behind. The materials they traded, originating from the newly settled islands, are found scattered across the lands they departed. The people of the Aegean, for instance, over eight millennia ago, transported obsidian from the tiny island of Melos across no less than 120 kilometers (75 miles) of sea to Greece, to Cyprus, to Crete, and to numerous other Aegean islands.

In the very beginning, people propelled themselves across rivers or straits on a simple flotation device: a single, unfinished log; a bundle of reeds; or grasses enclosed in a hide. However, as they encountered wider expanses of water, or wished to travel upon a river, they fastened logs together into rafts or they fashioned canoes by burning or carving out a single log; and, at some point, instead of propelling these craft with their hands and feet, an innovator invented the paddle, while others invented more sophisticated boats.

The most common type of vessel throughout the Mediterranean and Europe was a boat fashioned from a bag of sewn hides into which was inserted a frame. (The earliest representation of such a boat—a rock carving from Kvalsund about six thousand years old—depicts two hunters closing in on a swimming reindeer.) Canoes were favored by northern North American Indians who sewed strips of birch bark together into a waterproof sack and then inserted a keel and ribs. Boats woven from reeds were preferred by the people living along the Nile. Whether reed, bark, or hide, the nature of these raw materials required the craftsmen to finish the exterior first, in what is known as the "shell-first" method (as opposed to the "frame-first" method); through antiquity, even as the materials changed, "shell-first" remained the standard method of ship construction.

Egyptians used the Nile reeds to weave simple boats for local use and more elaborate boats for longer trips. Egypt, the "gift of the Nile," was constrained by its geography to communicate by boat; and for that, after the invention of sails (by 3100 BCE), the Nile was perfect: its current carried boats to the north and prevailing winds blew them back south again. When Egyptians ventured into the Mediterranean and needed larger boats to import the cedars of Lebanon and other products bought with Egyptian gold, they simply increased the size of their reed boats, sometimes with disastrous results, which one pharaoh (of the mid-third millennium) attempted to ameliorate by encasing his transports in netting.

The expansion of maritime trade required the Egyptians to build harbors and shipyards in Egypt and forts and warships to protect their prosperous trade from pirates. In the mid-second millennium, the famous conqueror Thutmose III established a chain of forts and harbors along the eastern shore of the Mediterranean for the protection of Egyptian trade and the rapid transportation of Egyptian troops. On one expedition reaching to the Euphrates River, he records an event in the marshes of Niy. "My Majesty killed a herd of one hundred-twenty elephants there. Never has anything like this been done by a king since the god received the white crown. I say this with no boasting or exaggeration." Consequent to this little excursion, Thutmose encountered new people, one of whom—a people previously unknown to him—he records as *the people of the isles in the middle of the sea.*

These people—the first, according to Greek chronographers, to rule the sea—were the Minoans.

CHAPTER TWO

The Minoans and the First "Thalassocracy"

Sadly, we don't know who the Minoans were, where they lived before they came to Crete, what language they spoke, or even what they called themselves. We call them "Minoans" as a tribute to the legendary "King Minos," who in the *Odyssey* was said to reside in the mighty Cretan city of Cnossos and who was so important that every nine years Zeus set aside time to confer with him. What we do know about them derives, first, from contemporary chronicles of the ancient Near East; second, from legends of the Greeks; and, third, and most spectacularly, from excavations conducted by Sir Arthur Evans in the late nineteenth and early twentieth centuries.

From the chronicles, we learn that Minoan artisans plied their trade all over the Near East and Egypt and that Minoan sailors were renowned for their knowledge of the art of navigation. (In Ugarit, a city in northern Syria, people believed that their craftsman god Kothar-wa-Khasis had come from Crete to teach them navigation.)

According to the legend of Athens's great hero Theseus, the Athenians were compelled by Minos to pay him a tribute of seven young men and seven young women every ninth year. Two times Minos had had the captive youths and maidens brought to Cnossus and thrown into the labyrinth for the pleasure of his son, the bestial Minotaur; but on the third (and ultimate) occasion that Minos exacted his tribute, Theseus volunteered to go himself. He won the love of the princess, Ariadne; used her help to kill the Minotaur (and escape from the labyrinth); and after rather heartlessly abandoning the princess, returned in triumph to Athens. Later, when another son of Minos threatened revenge, Theseus secretly collected a fleet, invaded Crete, and sacked Cnossus.

The fifth-century Athenian historian Thucydides, who investigated the distant past of Greece, would have been able to visit the "triaconter, with which Theseus sailed to Crete." As the timbers had rotted—over the course of nine centuries!—the planks had been conscientiously replaced by the Athenians to preserve the ship and thus entertain philosophers with the conundrum: When did the ship of *Theseus* cease to be the *ship* of Theseus, if, in fact, it ever did? Thucydides wrote, "Minos was the most ancient ruler (of whom we know) to have possessed a fleet and to have ruled the greater part of the Greek Sea and the Cyclades. He expelled the Carians [a non-Greek people], colonized most of the islands, installed his sons as rulers and drove the pirates from the sea." In sum, the chronicles and legends reflect a civilization widely known for its naval prowess and ingenuity (even if its ingenuity did not quite rise to the heights of the wings of Icarus).

The excavations conducted by Sir Arthur Evans revealed a civilization that had endured for six centuries, reached its height around thirty-seven hundred years ago, and accorded with the bits and pieces of the legends and chronicles. Minoan civilization revolved around palaces without fortifications. These palaces were ablaze with light and color; their walls were decorated with remarkably beautiful frescoes—an art form the Minoans perfected. The exuberant frescoes, augmented with vase paintings, reveal a great deal about the Minoans: their love of the natural beauty of seascapes and marine animals; their costume (men in kilts and women in dresses with the bosom sometimes bare); their preferences in foods; their sense of confidence and security arising from their dominance on land and sea; their vitality; and their pride in the ships that gave them power.

The ruins reveal, as well, a startling correspondence to the legends of Greece: sprawling palaces so complex that they can hardly be described as other than *labyrinthine*; the prominence of the symbol of the double-headed axe, the *labrys*, a tool with a special—though to us unknown—significance in Minoan culture and the root of the non-Greek word "labyrinth;" and, in one of the most beautiful frescoes, there is a scene involving a bull, a maiden clutching its horns, and another maiden poised to catch a youth vaulting over the bull's back.

Minoan art on Crete is free of martial scenes—no warriors, no implements of war, no military action—but frescoes found in Minoan Thera do depict such scenes: a seaborne invasion, three naked corpses floating in the water, and armed soldiers advancing upon an unsuspecting town. We will not be far from the truth if we believe that these frescoes represent common Minoan actions and that the Minoans' dominance of the sea allowed them to do to others what others could not do to them.

Theran frescoes depict Minoan ships in detail (augmented by seals and other representations); the ships are crescent-shaped and equipped with both sails and oars—the sails and masts would be stored, while the crew rowed.

Originally, perhaps, Minoan ships had been long and narrow, suitable for paddling—and small boats were still paddled—and designed more for quick piratical raids (as in the frescoes) than for trade. With such ships, the Minoans lived their lives free from the threat of an attack from the sea; and yet they were far from secure because of devastating earthquakes, which regularly destroyed their palaces (although the Minoans did rebuild after each disaster). In the later seventeenth century, however, the Minoan civilization on Thera was wiped out by a catastrophic earthquake and volcanic explosion.

The Minoans had no naval rivals in the eastern Mediterranean until the Mycenaeans (Homer's Achaeans) entered Greece in the sixteenth century as a part of the greater movement of the Indo-European chariot-warriors. Different Indo-European tribes—their chariots made them supreme on land—founded the Hittite kingdom in central Anatolia, advanced to the borders of China, occupied Western Europe and Britain, invaded and conquered the Iranian plateau and India, and occupied the Greek peninsula. We have no reason to believe that the warriors in Greece differed very much in ethos from the Aryans who conquered India and sang songs in praise of their weapons—the bow, the chariot, and the horse. The Mycenaeans knew well "the triumphant shout of those killing and the screams of those being killed."

Initially, the Mycenaeans may have entered Greece overland, but by the fourteenth century they had developed a maritime presence. If they did not exactly possess the thousand ships launched by the face of Helen, contemporary records nonetheless suggest they were formidable enough to compete with the Minoans. Their ships are often portrayed with a horizontal "ladder," which indicates a gallery for oarsmen and supports the hypothesis that this design was the basis for the later biremes and penteconters.

They are much like the ships described in the *Iliad*, the "hollow" ships that were undecked and served by a fifty-man crew. The crews rowed for short distances when the wind failed, and they avoided open water, if they could, but they needed favorable winds to travel any distance—to summon a wind favorable for Troy, Agamemnon sacrificed his daughter. The Mycenaean ships' bows may have been decorated with a bird's head (like the ships of the "northerners" who later appear on Egyptian monuments and ravage the lands of the eastern Mediterranean).

The Mycenaeans were heavily influenced by the art and culture of the Minoans, who also lent them their writing system, Linear A (not yet deciphered), which the Mycenaeans adapted, as Linear B, for their own language (a dialect of Greek). They appreciated the objects imported from Crete, but however much they appreciated Minoan objects, all the more did they covet them, and, sometime in the fourteenth century, the Mycenaeans invaded and conquered Crete (as the legend of Theseus suggests), and then replaced the Minoans as the dominant maritime power in the eastern Mediterranean for two centuries. They occupied Cyprus and colonized the islands of the Aegean and the coast of Asia Minor, where they developed one of their cities, Miletus, into a significant enough power to engage the attention of the Hittite kings. The Hittites defeated the Mycenaeans in Asia Minor, seized and fortified Miletus, and attempted to cut off their trade with Syria,

By the thirteenth century, the Mycenaeans had developed a culture unified in language, religion, and art; an organized system of government centered on the fortified palace; and a chariot-warrior ethos stretching from Thessaly to the Peloponnesus and across the Aegean to Miletus and Crete (now ruled by Mycenaeans, but still clinging to remnants of the earlier Minoan culture).

Mycenaeans in Cyprus dominated sea trade throughout the eastern Mediterranean (except in Egypt), but, in addition to their peaceful trade, they also participated in raids. In 1236–1223, the Egyptians repulsed a land attack from Libya, which was supported from the sea by "northerners coming from all lands, the Akawasha, Tursha, Lukku, Shardan, and Sheklesh." The Akawasha, who are often identified with the "Achaeans," had their hands cut off as trophies, suggesting that the usual part taken as a trophy was deformed by circumcision (which would seem to rule out Greeks). The Tursha, Shardan, and Sheklesh are identified with the later occupants of western central Italy, Sardinia, Corsica, and Sicily. Over three thousand prisoners "of the sea" were taken by the pharaoh, but his victory only earned Egypt a pause in the onslaught from the north, an onslaught that was but one episode in the widespread disturbances of the northern Aegean and the massive movement of people by sea.

The Mycenaeans joined the northerners in an attack on the Hittite kingdom in central Anatolia. A series of raids became organized assaults, which wrested control of the western part of Asia Minor from the Hittites.

In this period of turmoil and destruction occurred (some modern scholars theorize) the "Trojan War."

CHAPTER THREE

The Collapse of Civilization

The Mycenaeans, in the later decades of the thirteenth century, after having attacked so many others, came under attack themselves. The local rulers strengthened the fortifications of the palaces at Mycenae, Tiryns, and Athens and secured the sources of water against siege. They built a wall across the Isthmus of Corinth and posted "watchers along the coast." Their precautions preserved Athens and transformed it into a place of refuge, but elsewhere they failed: small settlements were burned to the ground and major centers—the *Menelaion* in Laconia, *Nestor's palace* in Messenia, and sites in Boeotia, Phocis, and Thessaly—were sacked.

Some Mycenaeans escaped to the island of Euboea, some sought refuge in Attica, some sailed south to Crete and across the Aegean, and more moved, en masse, to Cyprus or to locations within Asia Minor and along the coast, where their new settlements seemed to be protected by an expanse of water. There the Mycenaeans continued to thrive and, from there, they launched their own raids. In some cases, they joined the *northerners* (or the "sea peoples," as the Egyptians knew them) in attacking Egypt, the Hittite kingdom, and other states in the Near East. Some of the invaders, including the Mycenaeans, settled in the territory of the kingdoms they had destroyed.

This period, when the "northerners" were raiding the eastern Mediterranean and attacking Egypt, is paralleled in the legendary history of the Trojan War. The *Iliad*, the *Odyssey*, and associated legends, as well as the physical remains, all tell the same story of turmoil and destruction. At the heart of the legend is a memory, transmitted through song, generation after generation, of a great naval expedition—over a thousand ships—which, ultimately, sacked the city of Troy. (Troy is mentioned, as *Ilium,* in contemporary Hittite records.)

According to the legends, some of the victors never returned to their homes, some were murdered, and some wandered the eastern Mediterranean— Cyprus, Pamphylia, Cilicia, Phoenicia, Egypt, and Libya—while others were carried by storms as far as Italy and even Spain. In Greece, itself, a Greek tribe, the Dorians, occupied the Mycenaean territories in the Argolid, Laconia, and Messenia.

The *Odyssey*'s portrayal of a time of unrest and turmoil with raiders and pirates on the loose could aptly describe both the Bronze Age and the Age of Homer. The poet drew little distinction between heroes and pirates except, perhaps, in their own minds.

"As far as any kind of work and family life and the raising of beloved children, I didn't like it; no, ever and always I preferred oared ships and wars and smooth javelins and arrows, wretched things, which fill others with dread. I loved what the gods had placed in my heart to love, as others love other employments."

Both piracy and "heroic" raids were endemic throughout ancient Mediterranean history (wherever and whenever there was something worth stealing). They appear in a contemporary Egyptian account, which suggested that some of them were sanctioned by local rulers. They launched surprise raids on shore, or they waited at choke points along the coast to intercept transports. Control of the sea, then as now, meant control of the shore and the power to destroy pirates in their lairs.

The pirates sought gold, of course, and other goods, and sheep and cattle for their own provisioning, but most profitable and most available of all were women and children for the slave trade. Pirate raids were so common that Greeks built their cities on high points some distance from the coast and set up a chain of watchtowers, from which they could spot strangers disembarking on their shore—and kill them immediately just in case they were pirates.

Everyone, even the monstrous Cyclops, hated pirates, and the Cyclops expressed his suspicions of Odysseus (who, in truth, was as ready to receive welcoming gifts as he was to raid and plunder),

"Who are you? Where are you from? Are you crossing the watery ways of the sea as merchants or are you just cruising here and there as pirates who risk their own lives to do harm to strangers?"

The "pirate" of the *Odyssey* gives an account that could apply to the northerners' raids just as well as his own pirate raid on Egypt—

I outfitted and manned nine ships. For six days, I provided the sacrificial animals to honor the gods and I laid out a feast for my shipmates. On the seventh day, we boarded the ships and sailed from wide Crete; such a strong north wind blew behind us, that it seemed as though we were being carried along by the current of a river. We lost not a single ship, and rested on the benches, while the wind and the steersmen carried us to Egypt. In five days, we had reached the broad Egyptian river and there in that great river I brought the curved ships to and I bade my shipmates to remain by the ships and stand guard while I sent out our scouts to look around, but they were so confident in their strength that they lost their heads and immediately set to looting the fertile fields of the Egyptians; they killed the men and they captured their wives and children.

The attack roused the city; the king and the townspeople filled the whole plain with infantry and horses and flashing bronze and then Zeus, the Thunderer, turned my men into cowards; not one had the courage to face the enemy. The Egyptians killed many of us with the sharp bronze, and they captured some alive (who were destined to work as slaves).

The pirate (i.e., Odysseus) threw himself on the mercy of the king, and the king saved him. Then—through a series of chances, good and bad, and culminating in Phoenician treachery—"Odysseus" wound up on a ship that was hit by a storm, a risk pirates, raiders, and merchants all ran when they took to the sea.

The wind blew us directly across the sea past Crete and beyond Crete we had no other glimpse of land, but only the sea and the sky while Zeus gathered the dark clouds above the hollow ship and stained the sea with darkness, and then he thundered and he struck the ship with his lightning bolt; the ship was hit hard, it was choked with the reek of brimstone, and it foundered. The whole crew was knocked off the ship and tossed about on the black waves like sea crows; in truth, the god stole their homecoming. I was the only one whom Zeus pitied and he brought the mast, spun free from the wreckage of the blue-prowed ship, to my hands, so that I might escape the ultimate disaster. I clung to the mast and for nine days I was borne hither and yon by the contrary winds; on the tenth in the dark of the night a great breaker cast me upon the shore. . . .

The eastern Mediterranean was an uncertain and dangerous place.

CHAPTER FOUR

The Assault on Egypt

In the year 1274 BCE, the two greatest powers in the Western world, the rival kingdoms of the Egyptians and the Hittites, fought a great battle at Qadesh; the battle, a draw, seemed at the time to establish a permanent equilibrium between these two great empires, but seventy-five years later, the Hittite kingdom was gone and the Egyptian empire was teetering on the brink of destruction. The pharaoh Ramses II had repulsed one attack by land and sea and gained a temporary respite from attack, but his successor, the pharaoh Ramses III (1198–1166), faced larger and more ferocious attacks.

Foreigners, according to the Egyptians, "conspired in their isles [Crete, Cyprus, and the Aegean islands]. Removed and scattered in the fray were the lands at that time. No land could stand before their arms, from the Hittites, Cilicia, Carchemish, Arzawa, and Cyprus on, but they were cut off at one time. A camp was set up in one place in Amurru [modern Lebanon]. They desolated its people, and its land was like that which has never come into being. They were coming, while the flame was prepared before them, forward toward Egypt."

The last king of the Hittites recorded one victory over the attackers and then fell silent. The ruler of the powerful city of Ugarit pleaded in vain for help against a fleet that was raiding the coast and sacking cities. Ugarit was destroyed. One by one the old powers of the Near East were overrun.

Ramses identified the invaders in general as the "northerners from all lands" or, simply, the "sea peoples," a combination of the "Peleset, Tjekker, Sheklesh, Denyen, and Weshesh." The Peleset, the only people positively identified, are known to us from the Old Testament as the Philistines; they came in ships and they came in chariots, accompanied by their families in oxcarts, and they settled on the borders of Egypt in the territory named after them, "Palestine." The very first Philistines may have been settled in this territory by Egyptian pharaohs as mercenaries to form a buffer state, but if so, they soon declared their independence and invited other peoples to settle around them.

The Philistines dominated the southern coast and the nearby sea with trade and piracy until their defeat by the Israelites and Tyre in the tenth century. The Philistines were noted for their ironwork—this is the beginning of the Iron Age—their feathered helmets, and their distinctive ships, powered by a sail on a central mast with a crow's nest; the prow ended in a duck's head reminiscent of the Mycenaean bird's head. The Philistines appeared to have connections with the Mycenaeans—their arms and armor, including the chariots, could have come right out of the *Iliad*—and also with Crete, Miletus, and Cyprus. Indeed, the sea peoples' intermediate stop, or staging area, appears to have been Mycenaean Cyprus. (The warriors with the feathered helmets—the Philistines—were well known to the Mycenaeans, or indeed, as some scholars believe, may actually have been Mycenaeans.)

The Egyptians fought the "sea peoples" on land and sea and stopped their land advance in 1191, perhaps as much by conceding the land already occupied as by military victories. The great battle, however, the battle to determine Egypt's fate, was fought against a sea invasion. Ramses's representation of the sea battle (in his mortuary temple Medinet Habu) is our only pictorial record of an ancient, historical sea battle.

The carvings display three phases of the battle. In the first, the sails are furled and the oars stowed on the enemy ships, which suggests that they had anchored in anticipation of a landing. The Egyptians remain out of range of the enemy's javelins and rely on their bows until they have overwhelmed the enemy with arrows. In the second phase, the Egyptians close and throw

Illustration 3. Phase One. The ship of the sea peoples is under attack by Egyptian archers. The crew members, whose armament consists of swords and spears, have little chance to respond. The enemy soldiers are distinguished by their "feathered" helmets and the enemy ship by the bird- (duck-) headed prows. (Adapted and redrawn by Alfred S. Bradford)

Illustration 4. Phase Two. Another ship of a different sea people is under attack. The mast of the ship has been grappled, and the ship is beginning to capsize. (Adapted and redrawn by Alfred S. Bradford)

Illustration 5. Phase Three. The sea people's ship has capsized. There are no survivors. (Adapted and redrawn by Alfred S. Bradford)

grapnels into the rigging of the enemy ships. Once the grapnels have caught, the Egyptian ships row away and capsize the enemy ships, throwing the survivors into the water. In the third phase, the enemy are either dead or dying; one submerged and drowning man has stretched his arms above the surface. (A survivor of the sinking of the *Lusitania* mentioned the macabre sight of hands, only hands, spread across the surface of the water.) A final scene displays numerous assorted prisoners.

Although Ramses III claimed a great and decisive victory—"I settled the captives in strongholds bound in my name. The military classes were as numerous as hundred-thousands. I assigned portions for them all with clothing and provisions from the treasuries and granaries every year"—it was a limited victory, which cut Egypt off both from Asia and from the sea; and the relocation of "captives" may be spin for the concession of Egyptian territory to foreign occupation.

In the centuries following this battle, the Greeks entered a Dark Age marked not so much by discontinuity as by devolution and, then, re-creation. The Greek tribes—collectively known as the Dorians—who had overrun and settled the fertile land in the Peloponnesus developed a new kind of society, the polis, and thrived, while outside Greece, in the Near East, kingdoms fell and were replaced by new kingdoms: Phrygia, Israel, and Assyria.

As the Mediterranean world stabilized in the beginning of the first millennium, a new seafaring, trading people, the Phoenicians, entered the vacuum left by the invasions and wars and took control of three coastal cities, Byblos, Tyre, and Sidon. They became famous for the manufacture and export of purple dye (from which they received their Greek name), but they also transported goods from India and Egypt to the west and goods from Greece and points west, including tin from Britain, back to the east. Phoenicians brought Near Eastern art to Greece and, thereby, influenced Greek art in its transition from the *geometric* to the *orientalizing* phase. And, of course, Phoenicians also introduced their simple writing system, developed to keep inventories; Greeks adapted it and transformed it into the Greek alphabet.

The Phoenicians founded trading stations and forts throughout the western Mediterranean. They reached Sardinia in the tenth century, Spain by the ninth century, and they founded Carthage, according to tradition, in 814/3 BCE. They attempted a circumnavigation of Africa from the west, but, having gotten just so far, they heard pipes and cymbals and drums in the night and turned back, "because we were afraid." The Phoenicians were the chief trading rivals of the Greeks in the eastern Mediterranean. In the western Mediterranean, the Phoenician colony, Carthage, became the most formidable opponent of the Greeks and, later, the Romans.

CHAPTER FIVE

Greek Colonization in the East

After the first wave of invaders—the "northerners"—had wreaked havoc on Asia Minor and the Near East, another wave, continuing the raids, crossed the sea from Greece in the eleventh and early tenth centuries (the Dark Age), but this time the invaders were Greek—Aeolians, Ionians, and Dorians—and they intended to stay. They had the advantage of an abundant supply of ships, young men, and aggressive leaders, who lived by the aristocratic boast: "Not without glory are the leaders who hold the land, for they have the courage of kings and they fight in the front ranks of the battle." The Greek invaders displaced, or exterminated, the local populations and occupied their lands. They campaigned systematically—first seizing a foothold, then expanding it into a stronghold, and then a settlement, from which they advanced to another foothold.

According to tradition, the first to exploit the changed situation in the eastern Aegean were the Aeolians—kin to the Boeotians in central Greece on the northern border of Attica; they invaded the island of Lesbos and founded the city of Mytilene. With the passage of time, Lesbos became famous first for its fine wine, a primary export, and then for its poets, who in wintertime were pleased to "throw a log on the fire and mix the hospitable wine with just enough water. . . ."

The Aeolians founded more cities on Lesbos and formed them into a loose confederation centered around common cults (one of which featured an annual beauty contest), and they expanded to the mainland opposite, choosing (at first) five naturally defensible areas with good harbors and a fertile hinterland. These five cities, over time, grew in prosperity and population and expanded to twelve, from which the Aeolians pushed north to the Troad and Troy (i.e., Ilium), inland along the fertile river valleys, and across the strait of the Hellespont to Europe. They also fought as mercenaries throughout the Near East—a poet of Lesbos celebrated the return of his brother: "You have returned from distant lands with a gold-and-ivory-encrusted sword you took from the nine-foot tall Babylonian you killed."

In the early tenth century, Ionians occupied Samos and Chios to the south of Aeolia and they defeated the native people, the Carians, and captured Miletus (where, by tradition, the wives would not sit down to dinner with their husbands because the Ionians, when they took Miletus, killed the Carian men and co-opted the women—the new husbands feared that their wives might use the occasion to express their poisonous resentment). According to legend, Ionia was founded (and named) by Ion, who had sought asylum in Athens during the destruction of the Mycenaean world and who launched his expedition from there. The Ionians and Athenians recognized the strong bonds of kinship between them: their common dialect, the same four tribes, and their religious calendar with the same festivals and cults.

Ion's "twelve sons" continued the assault on central Asia Minor in a coordinated movement, founded twelve cities (one son per city), and formed a twelve-city association (the *dodecapolis*) centered on the *Panionium*, a pan-Ionian shrine. The Ionians followed the rivers inland (a natural route that later, ironically enough, were the paths retraced by the kings of Lydia to conquer the Ionians). The Ionians led the first flourishing of the distinctive culture of the Greek polis, the Ionian Homer and the composition of the *Iliad* and the *Odyssey* followed by an exuberant declaration of individuality in song. Archilochus, the foremost poet of individuality as well as a mercenary soldier, described himself—"I earn my bread with my spear and with my spear the Ismarian wine and on my spear I lean to drink." Finally, Ionians were the first to attempt to explain the world without relying on myth. The Ionians spread so widely through the Near East as merchants and mercenaries that *Ionian* became the root of the word for *Greek* in Near Eastern languages: Hebrew, Assyrian, Indic, and Persian.

South of Ionia were the Dorians. They had hopped from island to island (in the tenth century) in pursuit of the Mycenaeans: Thera—Cos—Rhodes. Thera, according to Spartan legends, had been founded by a band of refugees in three triaconters fleeing from the Dorian conquest of Laconia, although one of the refugees decided to remain in Laconia despite being told that he would be a "sheep among wolves." In response, he adopted the name "Sheep-Wolf" (*Oeolycus*—it works better in Greek). Rhodes, according to the *Iliad*, was settled by Tlepolemus, who, having incurred bloodguilt, "built ships, gathered many folk and fled upon the sea. He fled from his enemies and suffered much, before he chanced upon Rhodes, and he settled Rhodes in three parts for the three [Doric] tribes and Zeus poured wealth upon them." The Dorians also occupied a portion of the mainland near Caria. Their strongest city was Cnidus, which, with Halicarnassus and the three Rhodian cities, celebrated a common festival. At the same time as these Dorians were crossing the Aegean, other Dorians, in a greater undertaking, invaded and conquered Crete. By the end of this wave of invaders, Greeks had occupied all the islands of the Aegean, Crete, the coast of Asia Minor, and Cyprus.

In the next wave, at the beginning of the Archaic Age, Greeks spread to the Black Sea, Chalcidice and the Hellespont, part of North Africa, Sicily, Southern Italy, parts of the Adriatic, the south of Gaul (modern France), and even one site in Spain. Miletus with two partners, Chalcis and Eretria (in Euboea), led the wave. In the end, colonization just about doubled the total number of Greek poleis. Greeks also founded two trading depots in the east, where, however, they ran into organized states, which reacted vigorously to the Greek modus operandi of combining trading with raiding.

First, Greeks encountered the Assyrians, who dominated the Near East for most of the ninth, eighth, and seventh centuries; and then, for the next half century, the Chaldaeans of Babylon; and, finally, the Medes and the Persians. As with the Greeks, the fortunes of their main trading rivals, the Phoenicians, waxed and waned through this period, until the Persians brought stability to the region. The Phoenicians were a formidable sea power, but they were not as interested as the Greeks in colonizing—with the exception of Cyprus—as they were in establishing trade centers.

In the last half of the seventh century, at a time when Egypt was divided between rival kings, Miletus sent an expedition of thirty ships (about fifteen hundred men) to force the foundation of a colony in the western Delta at Naucratis. By chance, an ambitious, though lesser, king, Psammetichus, had received an oracle that he would rise to power "when bronze men came from the sea." He considered the oracle fulfilled when he saw Greek and Carian soldiers in their bronze armor. He embraced them, paid them, and used them to gain control of Egypt (664–610 BCE); in return, he granted the Greeks a major trading concession in Naucratis.

Naucratis became a permanent and wealthy multiethnic (i.e., multi-Greek) trading city. Greeks found Egypt to be a thirsty market for their wine and also for olive oil and silver. Greeks were fascinated by Egypt, and they wanted Egyptian art objects as well as grain and papyrus for ropes and sails. Greek tourists visited Egypt's ancient monuments, on one of which a mercenary carved his name—"Telephos, the son of Ialysos, was here!" The Greek landed aristocracy was so eager to acquire Egyptian wares that the aristocrats exported their surplus to Egypt rather than selling it within Greece; this practice led to social dislocation and, eventually, social revolution . . . all because of one seaborne invasion.

From the late seventh century on, Egypt's kings recruited Greek and Carian mercenaries, settled them in Egypt, and, in the reign of Psammetichus II (595–589), used them to man an Egyptian fleet. Egyptian kings relied on them until the Persian king, Cambyses, invaded Egypt and the Greek mercenaries deserted to him.

At about the same time, Greeks colonized the north Aegean—led principally by Chalcis and Eretria, but Corinth (founding Potidaea), Andros, Chios, and others joined in. The island of Paros colonized Thasos (which became one of the foremost poleis in the north). Thasos was especially desirable because it had gold and access to the silver mines on the Thracian mainland, but Thracians, who had already occupied Thasos, were ferocious warriors and they did not cede the island willingly. The poet Archilochus was involved in this fighting, and he shocked the Spartans—bad enough that he threw away his shield and ran from the enemy. But then he wrote a song and boasted about it—"Let them have my shield. Who cares? I can buy another just as good."

The Propontis and the Black Sea were colonized principally by Megara and Miletus. The Megarians settled Chalcedon on the Asian shore first and, only after they had become strong enough, crossed the straits to the European side to found Byzantium. In the Black Sea region, the Greeks avoided the areas controlled by the Scythians, who were reputed, like the Cyclops, to kill Greeks and eat them.

PART 2

The Spread of Hellenism

Illustration 6. The Aristonothos vase. This painting appears to depict a pirate ship attacking an armed merchant or a foreign (possible Etruscan) warship. (Adapted and redrawn by Alfred S. Bradford)

CHAPTER SIX

How to Build a Boat in the Eighth Century BCE

"Calypso gave [Odysseus] a great ax, which fit the palm of his hand, double-headed, bronze, and sharp. The olive-wood shaft fit well and was perfectly balanced. Then she gave him a well-sharpened adze with a keen edge. She led him up the heights of the island where the tall trees grew, stretching skyward, the alder, the poplar, and the pine, straight and seasoned by age. And when she had shown him where the tall trees grew, Calypso the beautiful goddess returned home. And he cut the logs. Swiftly he finished the task and he cut down twenty in all, fashioning them with the bronze axe. He planed them cleverly and straightened them in rows [of planks].

"And then Calypso the beautiful goddess gave him a drill and he drilled them all and fit them to each other and he fastened them with pegs and made the ship's bottom as wide as a shipwright makes a well-balanced freighter, so broad did Odysseus make his boat. He set the half-deck and set ribs to the close-fitted planks and finished it with the long planks (gunnels). He set the mast and fastened to it the yardarm and he fit the rudder and he wove netting from osiers around the boat to defend it from breakers and he added a large quantity of wood as ballast. And then Calypso the beautiful goddess brought him the cloth to fashion sails and he finished these, too. And he fastened these cunningly with braces and sheets and then he drew the boat down to the sea on rollers.

"He finished the work in four days."

CHAPTER SEVEN

Greek Colonization in the West

The second wave of Greek colonization, during the Archaic Period (800–478 BCE), although military in form, sought to avoid fighting by occupying isolated and uninhabited locations, such as described in the *Odyssey*: "A wooded island—on it many wild goats played that had never been hunted. The island lies next to a people who do not have boats, a fertile land, well-watered, on which grapes could flourish and crops could be sown, with a safe harbor, where ships could be hauled up beyond wave and wind and where a stream of fresh water ran down from a cave."

This second wave was coordinated under the leadership of "Apollo of Delphi." Apollo's sacred site, Delphi, was a gathering place for Greeks—city envoys, private citizens, merchants, and even pirates—who asked questions, made offerings to ensure Apollo's favor for their journeys and to reward him for their successes, and, of course, they gossiped with the priests. Consequently, the priests knew more about the western Mediterranean than any other group of Greeks anywhere and, oracular prescience aside, could give the best advice as to where the colonists should go.

Every colony's foundation story was unique, but they all began with the reason for consulting Apollo—rival factions in the city, drought, famine, overpopulation, or, simply, a desire to expand trade—and then they quoted the response of Apollo to go out and found the colony with, often enough, a location specified by Apollo.

The colonists believed that they were being led by Apollo and that, therefore, they had a moral claim to the land of the foundation and a guarantee of success. The leadership of "Apollo" kept fledgling colonies from competing with each other, while it also secured continuity between old Greece and new Greece. Still, even though an expedition might begin as an act of a particular polis, countenanced by Apollo, each expedition was an independent military operation under the command of an aristocrat who retained his authority through the rest of his life and was enshrined as a hero after his death.

The beauty of Greek colonization was that by risking a few ships and one to two hundred men, a city could extend its reach after trade and natural resources by hundreds of miles. On the other hand, the colony, when it became self-sufficient, was an independent polis, albeit one with a moral obligation to its mother city.

The greatest target of Greek colonization after the Aegean region was southern Italy and Sicily, where Greeks were welcomed by the climate and the familiar appearance of mountain, harbor, and fertile plain, which supported the olive and the grape.

In the mid-eighth century, the Euboean cities of Chalcis and Eretria, two prosperous and (at that time) cooperating allies—which had a modest sea empire in the Cyclades and dominated trade in central, coastal Greece and the Near East—sent an expedition that founded Pithecusa on the island of Ischia off the coast of Italy. The founders were attracted by the natural resources, fertile land and minerals, and accommodating neighbors, the Etruscans, who had an appetite for Greek culture, wine, and decorated cups.

Nonetheless, the colonists had to leave their families at home, nor could they transport sufficient supplies to support themselves indefinitely, so that they had to feed themselves off the local resources, partly by hunting, partly by fishing, but mostly by trading with the inhabitants of the mainland, until their crops—grains and grapes—fruited. (The olive takes years to mature.) They were as far from home in travel time as we are from the moon, but in their case a "moon" with aliens, who might prove as inimical as the Cyclops or Charybdis and Scylla. Still, these first colonists persevered and prospered enough both to send for their families and to found a second city—Cyme—on an easily fortified, and defended, acropolis on the mainland opposite.

After their success in Italy, the Chalcidians in 734 sent an expedition, including a contingent from the island of Naxos, to Sicily under the command of the aristocrat Theocles ("Godly"). He founded a second "Naxos" and dedicated a shrine to Apollo Archegetes ("the Leader") to express his thanks and to establish the moral claim that the god had given the land to them. As Greeks settled Italy and Sicily, they discovered—we would say invented—a rich mythical history linking the new land to their gods and heroes.

The god Apollo had led them there. The god Dionysus was present among the grapes. Persephone, the daughter of the goddess Demeter, gathered blooms in the Sicilian fields, which abounded in flowers of such intense scent that they overpowered the noses of hounds and prevented them from tracking their quarry. Persephone had been gathering flowers there when she was kidnapped by Hades, who issued from one of the underworld's gates in Sicily. Demeter's search for her blighted the earth. Heracles, too, traveled through Sicily and

Southern Italy and left his mark in just about every polis there. (In similar fashion, as the Romans grew in power, Greek academics in Alexandria found them a place in the Greek world—the Romans were Trojans.)

Unlike Ischia, however, the land on which Naxos was situated was already occupied by a native people, the Sicels. This people, who, at the very beginning, could have wiped out the initial Greek expedition, instead welcomed it; they appreciated the trade goods the Greeks brought, they expected that the settlement would remain small, and they put their faith in an oath those Greeks swore that they would never make war on the Sicels. Within five years, the first colony had expanded so much that the original founder, Theokles, founded a second city, Leontini, inland among the Sicels. As a harbinger of their future relations, Theocles protected his new city with heavy fortifications.

Then the Chalcidians sent another expedition under the command of the aristocrat Euarchos ("Good Leader") to found Catana on the north edge of the plain (of Catania). They intended that these three foundations would dominate the whole of this fertile plain. (The fields were so rich that sheep had to be restrained from "eating themselves to death.") The Sicels, no more than other native peoples, did not understand the power Greeks derived from their superiority at sea—each colonizing power had fleets of ships and could transport hundreds of people to these new sites—nor did the Sicels grasp how hungry Greeks were for land.

The Greeks wanted the whole plain for themselves, and, since they had only sworn an oath that *they* would not make war on the Sicels, they were free to hire Greeks from outside Sicily, who were not bound by the oath, to expel the Sicels. (Greeks did not practice a morality-based religion. They believed that their gods only punished mortals who violated the letter of an oath and, specifically, an oath sworn in a particular god's name.)

In 733, the Corinthians founded what was to become the greatest city in Sicily, Syracuse. Corinth (according to Thucydides) was the first major Greek mainland trading city—it exploited its central location to trade both in the Aegean and points east and also through the Gulf of Corinth to the west. As increased trade encouraged increased piracy, they developed a navy to suppress the pirates. (Part of the naval development was the introduction of the trireme). Corinth became the wealthiest city in Greece.

They sent an expedition, under the command of an aristocrat, Archias ("Leader"), to Sicily. On the way, he seized the island of Corcyra in the Adriatic as a way station to Italy and Sicily. (Corcyra became the most important way station to the west, but, over time, the relationship between Corinth and Corcyra deteriorated—the low point was probably reached when the tyrant of Corinth had three hundred Corcyraean aristocratic youths sent to the Lydians to be castrated. The two fought a sea battle in 664.)

Archias landed on the peninsula of Ortygia (just off the coast from the future site of Syracuse), expelled the native people, and built a fort on top of the native settlement. As his colony grew quickly beyond the agricultural resources of the immediate area, Archias expanded to the mainland and founded the city of Syracuse.

After these successful foundations, word of the fertile lands in the west spread and more cities participated. Achaeans founded Sybaris (later famed for its luxurious and dissolute way of life) and Croton on the Gulf of Tarentum in the last decades of the eighth century; Megara founded another city in Sicel territory; Cyme (the one in Asia Minor) in cooperation with Chalcis (and Eretria) founded Rhegium and across the strait from it, Messana—which was settled (so tradition relates) by Messenian refugees from the First Messenian War (ca. 740–720).

The Spartans founded Taras (Tarentum, traditional date 706), also as a result of the First Messenian War. The Spartan aristocrats involved in the conquest of Messenia had sworn an oath that they would not return home until they had conquered Messenia, but, in their absence, their wives continued to produce babies. Since these babies could neither be the result of forsworn liaisons nor liaisons between their wives and the base born, they had to be virgin births, that is, *Partheniai*, and these *Partheniai* were shuffled off to Italy to found Taras.

In the space of a generation, Greeks had opened the coasts of Sicily and Italy to settlement. Then, throughout the seventh and sixth centuries, they expanded into the interior to open up that fertile land for more settlers. These Greek settlers supported themselves by farming, pasturage, fishing, and, occasionally, piracy, and they prospered through their control of the sea and their trade with neighboring people.

For the most part, the Greeks had colonized Sicily without any opposition from Carthage. The Carthaginians had three unfortified settlements on the westernmost coast of Sicily, but as the Greeks advanced toward them in the mid- to later seventh century and laid claim to the western lands through stories of the travels of Heracles—wherever he had traveled, that land, they insisted, was Greek—the Carthaginians fortified their principal stronghold, Motya.

Greeks attempted, with a surprise landing from the sea, to establish a colony, Lilybaeum, to cut Motya off from the mainland, but the Carthaginians, who had a formidable navy of their own, drove them off. The Greeks then massacred the natives of the Lipari Islands and established a colony (ca. 580) on a readily defensible hill with two harbors but so little fertile land that the colonists had to farm the mainland, where they were vulnerable to attack. And, indeed, they *were* attacked so constantly by Tyrrhenian pirates that, just to survive, they had to become as proficient at sea as the Tyrrhenians; and then, having learned how to defend themselves from pirates, they themselves became pirates. They organized their state to support their pirate life. They parceled out the land (and redistributed it every twenty years) and divided the men into two groups by lot, one-half to farm while the other half roamed the sea as pirates. They were careful always to dedicate a portion of their loot to Apollo in Delphi to curry his (and Greek) favor.

By the end of the sixth century, the Greeks had colonized all the readily available places in the Mediterranean, and their further attempts ran into stiff resistance. In 510 BCE, the Spartan prince, Dorieus, who refused to live in Sparta so long as his half-brother, Cleomenes, was king, gathered comrades and sailed away without consulting Delphi. After two years in north Africa, he was driven out by the Carthaginians; he returned to Greece; and he consulted Delphi about settling Eryx, a site in Sicily associated with Heracles, whose descendants, the *Heraclids*, could rightfully claim it. Dorieus, by the way, considered himself a Heraclid.

Delphi assured him that he would "possess" the land, an ambiguous word always open to interpretation in an oracle. Indeed, Dorieus and his men sailed to Eryx and fought the Carthaginians and their allies for the possession of that land. He was defeated and killed with many of his men. As the victors surveyed the battlefield, they noticed among the enemy dead a man (an exile from Croton) so handsome that they gave him special burial, erected a shrine on his grave, and made offerings to him as a hero, while Dorieus was left to "possess" an unmarked grave.

With this episode, Greeks had reached the limits of their expansion; they had founded some 140 colonies and now could continue only at the expense of fellow Greeks or the Carthaginians or some of the fierce tribes in the Italian interior, all of whom were well able to defend themselves.

Greek colonization shows the advantage of sea power. When, to cite just one contrary instance, the Helvetians wanted to move to more fertile lands, they had to fight their way through other Gauls and the Romans and, in the end, were defeated. On the other hand, the Greeks did not need to form massive fleets in order to succeed. They met no resistance on the way and were able to pick and choose their landing places. Greek colonization was the greatest and most successful military operation in the history of the ancient Mediterranean.

A Typical Foundation Story

In 632 BCE, an expedition from the small island of Thera founded Cyrene in Africa. The story of the founding of Cyrene is typical: the choosing of the founder, the founding document, and the successful conclusion of the expedition (narrated by Herodotus and augmented by an inscription).

The island of Thera (writes Herodotus) was suffering from a drought, and its king and a small party consulted Delphi, but the Delphic priestess gave the king an unexpected response that he should found a state in Libya. He replied,

"Lord, I am too old and weary to send on such a trip. Name one of the young men here to undertake the affair."

As he spoke, he gestured at a young man named Battos, but after the king returned home, he forgot all about the oracle. Seven years of drought ensued, a second embassy visited Delphi, Delphi reminded them of the earlier oracle, and they returned home. On their advice, the assembly passed this decree:

> Since Apollo gave a spontaneous oracle to Battos and the Theraeans to colonize Cyrene, it was thought best for the Theraeans to send Battos as founder and king to Libya and that the Theraeans accompany him on ships and that they sail with him on equal terms, household by household, one son to be chosen [from each] . . . and that anyone else who is free and in the prime of life may also sail. And if the colonists establish the colony, others from their households may sail later to Libya and be admitted to political rights and honors and be allotted unoccupied land. If the Theraeans are unable to establish a colony in five years, they may return from that land without fear to Thera to their own possessions and to be citizens.
>
> Whoever refuses to sail in the expedition from the city, shall suffer death and his possessions shall be confiscated. Whosoever shall conceal him, whether the father a son or brother a brother, shall be punished equally

with the one who refused to sail. These oaths shall apply both to those remaining and those who are sailing as colonists and they shall have the same force regarding those remaining and those sailing as colonists to Libya. May those who violate these oaths, men, women, children . . .

The Theraeans molded a large wax statue.

. . . melt and burn like the wax effigy both himself and his family and his possessions, but may those remaining faithful to the oaths, both those sailing to Libya and those remaining in Thera have good fortune.

Battos was the commander and founder. His first duties—the same duties as every founder had—after selecting a site, were to "build a city wall, see to the construction of houses, establish shrines, and divide the farmland into lots." Battos set out in two penteconters, but failed to establish a colony on his first attempt, so he returned home . . . only the Theraeans would not let him land. Therefore, he sailed back, could still not find a suitable location, tried to return home again and again was repulsed, consulted Delphi again, and finally founded Cyrene in Libya—it became one of the great grain exporters of antiquity and was the major source of Silphium, a plant that was a reputed cure-all much sought after in Greece.

CHAPTER NINE

Ramming

Every Greek polis with access to the sea had ships, both to carry merchandise and also to protect the ships that carried the merchandise; the more powerful cities had more powerful fleets and used them to extend their own power at the expense of the less powerful. Even the Spartans, who had conquered their western neighbors and gained possession of the largest amount of fertile land south of Thessaly, these Spartans, who had created a sort of system of serfs—the helots—and who lived off their labor without the necessity of import or export, had a substantial fleet.

The Athenians—if we can trust that their vase painting reflects a measure of reality—had a significant navy at the end of the eighth and beginning of the seventh century. They needed one, because they were struggling with the island of Aegina for control of the Saronic Gulf and, hence, the free flow of trade. The two fought an indecisive war in the early seventh century, and Aegina remained prosperous and powerful enough to continue to challenge Athens for control of the gulf.

The origin of the hostility, the Aeginetans claimed, involved two Aeginetan sacred statues, which the Athenians declared were theirs. The Athenians invaded, surprised, and routed the Aeginetans, and then tried, and tried again, to pull the sacred statues from their bases, until the statues dropped to their knees in supplication (and "remain so to this day," Herodotus writes, "although, personally, I don't believe it."). An Argive fleet, allied with Aegina, landed its crews and cut the Athenians off from their ships; a providential storm of thunder and lightning deprived the Athenians of their wits, and only one Athenian survived to bring the disastrous news to Athens. When he told the new widows what had happened, they mobbed him and stabbed him to death with the straight pins fastening their dresses. And this twofold disaster was why the Athenians and the Aeginetans hated each other. (And also why Athenian men insisted that, henceforth, their wives would fasten their dresses with safety pins.)

Athens also fought for control of the city of Sigeum in the Troad toward the end of the seventh century in order to secure its trading routes to the north. (During the fighting, the poet Alcaeus threw away his shield and thus survived, like Archilochus, to compose a song about it—"Alcaeus lives! Although the Athenians have dedicated his armor in the temple of Athena.") In the first half of the sixth century, while Solon was reforming Athens's political structure and Pisistratus was conspiring to become its tyrant, Athens fought a war with Megara for possession of the island of Salamis. The situation was finally resolved by arbitration in the mid-sixth century, when the arbiters (five Spartans) on the basis of a line in the *Iliad*—"Ajax led twelve ships from Salamis and stationed them among the ranks of the Athenians"—awarded the island to the Athenians.

The Athenian aristocrat Miltiades the Elder, in the 550s, accepted a commission offered by the Dolonki Thracians in the Chersonese to help them defend themselves. They had sent a delegation to Delphi to ask the oracle for advice and it had replied, "Choose as your founder the man who—after you have departed this holy place and gone on your way—first offers you hospitality." And they had walked through Phocis and Boeotia and into Attica before someone—Miltiades—invited them into his house. Miltiades took with him whoever of the Athenians wanted to get away from Athens and its tyrant Pisistratus. Once he had arrived there and he was proclaimed king, he built a wall across the neck of the peninsula to protect the Chersonese from raids and established a colony. Although he was independent, nonetheless he, and, later, his nephew and heir of the same name, maintained a friendly connection with Athens.

Pisistratus established his tyranny on his third attempt (546 BCE) by landing at Marathon and scattering his political opponents. While tyrant, he dispatched an Athenian fleet to install Lygdamis as tyrant of Naxos—this was no small undertaking (with estimates of a required force of up to one hundred warships)—and later Lygdamis returned the favor by helping install the tyrant Polycrates in Samos. Pisistratus established a claim, by purifying Delos, that (in his person) Athens was the leader of the Ionians. He fought Mitylene (on Lesbos) to keep control of Sigeum (in the Troad), which, subsequently, remained in the Pisistratid family for half a century.

Athens, despite its increasing influence in the Aegean, was not the equal in power or prestige to the Greeks of the Aegean islands and Asia Minor. In the course of two centuries, the Ionians had developed and then enjoyed a vibrant, rich culture, based on trade, a life of symposia—wine, conversation, and song—the gymnasium, and outdoor life, from which arose the epic (Homer), the songs of individuality (Archilochus, Sappho, Alcaeus), and philosophy and science. Ionian trade, carried on between the newly prosperous colonies and old Greece and with new markets among native peoples (an ever-expanding market), brought the Greeks enormous wealth. A ship from Samos on its way to Egypt was blown so completely off course that it was driven through the Pillars of Heracles to Tartessos, where the crew collected such riches that a tithe paid on their return amounted to six talents. No crew member ever had to work again. Greek life was so intertwined with the sea that the poet Alcaeus, when he wanted to describe his polis, riven with stasis, compared it to a ship in a storm—the "ship of state."

However, the Ionians lost their independence in the sixth century when the Lydian kings forced the coastal cities into dependency—though the Lydians ruled with a light hand because they loved Greek wine, olive oil, and the vases containing them, not to mention the drinking cups and the symposia. As the Lydians had no navy to speak of, perforce, they accepted the independence of the island city-states; and when the king was seeking allies against the burgeoning power of the new Persian empire, he consulted Delphi and followed the oracle's advice to seek an alliance with Sparta.

The Lydian king, however, relied too much on his own interpretation of a Delphic oracle that if he crossed the boundary river into Persian territory, "a great kingdom would fall," and it did fall. In 546, he was defeated by the new Persian king, Cyrus; by 540, the Persians had attacked and subjugated all the coastal Greeks excepting only Miletus. Cyrus occupied Babylon by 539 and extended the eastern border of his empire to India (where he was killed). The Greeks considered that their subjugation by the Persians was the greatest tragedy they had ever suffered. Afterwards, when they asked visiting strangers the usual questions—what is your name, your family, your native city—they added, and where were you when the Persians came? For the time being, however, Miletus and the islanders remained independent (except insofar as they depended for their food on mainland farms). The strongest of these, besides Miletus, were Samos, Rhodes, Chios, and Lesbos.

One of the first victims of the Persians had been Phocaea. Phocaea had dominated trade in the far west, a dangerous enough region that they traveled there in warships, the penteconter. At the mouth of the Rhone River they founded Massilia (tr. 600), which was expected to support itself through trade up the Rhone into the hinterland, where the founder had ties of friendship with the Gauls. They traded with "Tartessos," that is, southwest Spain, a voyage requiring a three-month round trip of over thirteen hundred miles. A local king loved them so much that he offered them land and a share in his kingdom if they would settle there, but they declined, although they did establish a trading depot—Emporia—in Spain, and they founded Alalia in Corsica (about 565 BCE).

They were a leading naval power through the mid-sixth century, and they had protected their mother city, located on a peninsula, with a high, thick wall paid for by the Tartessan king. They needed that wall because they had turned to piracy in the Aegean, though who is to condemn them when any penteconter might take to the sea with the intention of trading but, instead, encounter an unexpected opportunity for a quick profit, like a rich and slow merchantman. Later, they needed the wall to defend against the Persians, for all the good it did them.

Not long after Lydia fell, the Persians began their assault on the Greek cities. The commander of the Persians, Harpagos, launched his first assault in Ionia on Phocaea. (He had been one of the first Medes to support the rebellion of Cyrus—after the Median king had fed him the flesh of Harpagos's own son.) His method of attack was to construct a ramp to the top of the enemy wall and, if the city did not surrender before the ramp was completed, cross the wall and sack the city. At first, the Phocaeans were confident in the strength of their fortifications, but as the ramp increased in size, they asked Harpagos to withdraw for one day while they debated whether to surrender or not. Harpagos told them he knew what they intended, but that he would give them a day.

"While Harpagos held the army back, the Phocaeans launched their fleet of penteconters, and embarked women, children, and all their household goods, even the images of the gods from the temples and, in addition, the dedications of clay, marble, and the painted images, and then the men boarded and they all sailed to Chios. The Persians took the empty city."

The Phocaeans tried to buy an island from the Chians, but the Chians refused—they hardly wanted to help establish a trade rival.

"The Phocaeans then decided that they would travel to Corsica where, twenty years earlier, they had founded Alalia. Before they sailed, they returned to Phocaea and massacred the Persian garrison that Harpagos had installed. They required every citizen who had agreed on the voyage to Corsica to swear an oath. They threw a lump of iron into the sea, and they all swore that they would not return to Phocaea before the iron floated, but, when they actually began the voyage, about half of the citizens broke their oath and turned back, because they were so homesick."

The Phocaeans were welcomed at Alalia (about 545 BCE), but the expanded colony could not support itself through agriculture, fishing, or trade, and so it turned to piratical raids along the Italian and Sardinian coasts. The Carthaginians and the Etruscans formed an alliance to stop them and in about 540 BCE fought a sea battle, the battle of Alalia.

The Phocaeans had a fleet of sixty penteconters, probably the modern bireme with two tiers of oarsmen. The Carthaginians may also have had biremes, while the Etruscans probably did not, as they were relatively new to naval warfare. The bireme had the advantage in speed and maneuverability.

"The Carthaginians and Etruscans each had sixty ships, and they campaigned under one command. The Phocaeans themselves manned their fleet, in number sixty ships. They met in the so-called Sardinian Sea. The Phocaeans won the sea battle in a *Cadmeian* victory [i.e., a *Pyrrhic* victory before Pyrrhus], for they had forty ships put out of action and the other twenty were rendered useless, as their rams were knocked askew."

The Phocaeans and their enemies employed different tactics, which is why the Phocaeans, outnumbered two to one, could win. The Carthaginians and Etruscans tried to close and board, while the Phocaeans employed maneuver and the ram. The rams were most likely no more than the wooden projections in the bows, sheathed in bronze. (Sculptors had recently perfected hollow casting.) As the enemy tried to close (and, in some cases, did close), the Phocaeans maneuvered to avoid being boarded and to strike the enemy ships at an angle, puncturing the side and knocking them out of action.

The battle of Alalia is the first in which one side employed rams exclusively and, hence, the first battle in which the ships themselves were weapons. The Phocaeans could not have had much experience in ramming, nor could they have understood the risks to their own ships. Ramming requires a precise speed (a modern estimate is eight knots) and the proper angle: the attacking ships ran the risk that if they rammed a moving ship, the momentum of the target would wrench the ram to one side or even break it off. Their second problem was the construction of their penteconters. Early ships were more likely to have been constructed with the "lash" method—lashing the planks together rather than pinning them—which, although quicker and less expensive, produced a ship wholly inadequate for ramming.

The Phocaeans won the battle, but they lost the war. They returned to Alalia, embarked their families and property and sailed away, later to settle in a new foundation, Elea, in southern Italy. (Perhaps they had learned their lesson, because they prospered there without resorting to piracy.) The Carthaginians and Etruscans divided up the prisoners, and the Etruscans brought theirs home and stoned them to death, as was the normal fate of captured pirates.

CHAPTER TEN

The Trireme

The trireme was the premier fighting vessel of the Greeks from its invention at the end of the eighth century down into the fourth century. "Trireme" (*triremis*) is the Roman word for the Greek *trieres*. The first to design and build triremes, according to Thucydides, was Ameinocles the Corinthian (their most prominent shipwright) about 700 BCE; he built four triremes for the Samians. (Some ancient sources credit the Phoenicians with the invention.) The earliest extant literary mention of a trireme dates to about 550—the author, Hipponax of Ephesus, reviled an artist for painting a serpent slithering along the side of a trireme from bow to stern, a dreadful omen—what if the snake struck the helmsman (*kubernetes*) in the heel?

Few physical representations of a trireme are extant, and no wreck has ever been found, because the trireme had positive buoyancy, being constructed with the lightest wood possible and no ballast. Much of what we know about the trireme derives from the eccentric project of an English historian, an English naval architect, and the Greek navy to actually build one. It—the *Olympias*—was launched on August 26, 1987. The *Olympias* was constructed to be about thirty-seven meters (i.e., 120 feet) long, and a little less than six meters (19–20 feet) wide, built to dimensions based on the Athenian ship sheds (where the triremes were stored).

The trireme had 170 rowers arranged in three files. The individual rower's equipment was basic: an oar, a circular strip of leather to fasten the oar to the thole pin (a single pin for each oar), a leather square on which to sit (to avoid blisters and splinters), and some fat to grease the leather. The oars were of two lengths: those used at the narrower end of the ship were fourteen feet, five inches long, the rest were fifteen feet. The space between rowers was about three feet, and the longest file of rowers, the topmost, comprised thirty-one men, the other two twenty-seven. The ship had two sails, which were stowed or left on shore when the trireme was expected to fight.

The trireme was built shell first, after which the keel and ribs were laid. (The modern trireme required forty thousand mortises and pegs.) The construction of a trireme required a minimum of thirty days. The ship was not decked and needed to be strengthened with *hypozomata*, thick ropes stretched between bow and stern, mechanically tightened and, after some time at sea, retightened. A single hypozoma weighed 250 pounds and was 280–340 feet long. Spares were carried, because the trireme could not survive without its hypozoma. (It functioned something like "a bowstring on a bow.")

The triremes were constructed mostly of fir (or pine, if fir was not available), a light wood, easy to work, which also lessened the weight of the trireme and made it easier to pull up on a beach, shift into a ship shed, or launch—all stressful activities that required an oak keel. The cutwater, which supported the ram, was fashioned from the toughest woods: ash, mulberry, or elm. Fir and pine, while light, also tended to soak up water, which was tolerable only if the ships could be pulled up out of the water; if not, if they had to stay at sea for long, uninterrupted periods, they would become waterlogged. They also were susceptible to wood borers (*teredo navalis*). The ships were waterproofed and partially protected from the teredos with a coat of pitch. The ships had eyes of painted marble. And the sole purpose of all this sophisticated engineering and expert construction was to deliver a blow with a bronze ram fixed in the prow.

The issue of engineering a weapon of war is the same whether the weapon is a chariot, a trireme, or a fighter plane. The machine needs to be as light as possible to enable it to go as fast as possible and to be quick to maneuver, but it also needs to be as tough as possible to withstand the rigors of combat. The trireme existed at the very edge of the practicable. The ratio of waterline length to breadth was 9:1 and the ratio of the length to depth-below-water was 10:1. For the sake of the stability of the ship, the lowest file of oarsmen had to sit at the waterline—but that arrangement allowed water to rush on board, so the oar-ports had to be covered with leather. Even so, the trireme had such a high center of gravity that if it had been produced in the modern age of sail, Lloyd's of London would have declared it unseaworthy and would not have insured it.

One of the issues for the Athenians, or any naval power, was the supply of shipbuilding timber. The Athenians procured theirs in the north and, at times, for the sake of efficiency, established shipyards there, where they could build the ships at the source of the timber. The fleet put a heavy strain on the Athenians' resources, first to purchase the timber, and then to build the ships, to repair and refit them, to stock them with the necessary equipment, to recruit and pay the crews, to pay the dockyard workers, and, as Pericles said, to practice continually to maintain the requisite skills. He kept a fleet of sixty triremes at sea for the eight-month sailing season every year (more, his aristocratic opponents complained, to funnel money from the wealthy to the poor than to train the crews).

The lowest file of oarsmen was the file of twenty-seven *thalamioi*. Above them were twenty-seven *zugioi* (thwart rowers). Above them, on an outrigger, so that they were about half a man's height above the *zugioi*, were thirty-one *thranitai*. The *thranitai* were the leaders of their three-man tier. Their position was the most demanding for three reasons: first, because of the steep angle at which they had to row; second, because only they could see where the oars struck the water and so had to use their skill to ensure that the lower tiers' oars did not jam together; and, third, because they were the most vulnerable to enemy arrows and javelins. For these reasons they were paid a bonus.

It is hard to think of the lowest tier, where the *thalamiai* rowed, as anything other than hell. Imagine the odor of 170 hardworking oarsmen (who knew neither soap nor deodorant), crammed together, three feet of space between them, with no respite through a long day, sweat dripping down, various effluvia from a diet of beans, onions, and garlic—Aristophanes even gives expression to the sounds of escaping gas, like frogs croaking: *brekekekexkoaxkoax*. And yes, if they had to relieve themselves, they might have used the oar-ports or they might have let it fall where it would—particularly at the moment of battle when stress can clear the bowels.

The interior of the ship was noisy with men chattering, or chanting, or singing, and the chunk of oars against the thole pins and the blades' splashing in the water, not to mention bodily sounds. (The first order given before action was always to be quiet, so everyone could hear the commands of the *keleustes*. In short, it was smelly, dark, crowded, noisy, dangerous, and particularly frightening, because, in addition to everything else, the lower tiers of oarsmen could not see what was happening outside the ship and they had to hope that their officers knew what they were doing. In the case of the lowest tier, if their ship was holed by an enemy ram, they were dead. Thus crews had to be tolerant, willing to work together, and willing to risk their lives. That is why the crews could not be slaves.

The citizen who had paid the liturgy (tax) to build the trireme had the right to assume command, that is, to be the *trierarch*. He might be someone with quite a bit of experience or he might not, in which case he could appoint another, more experienced man to command the ship, or he could still decide to take command and run the risks of battle or, if he mismanaged his duties, the risks of the wrath of the Athenian assembly. Pericles once chided Sophocles, who was then a trierarch, for telling him that there was a very good-looking young man in his crew. "Yes," Pericles said, "that may be true, but when you are an officer of the Athenian people, you must not only not have hands, you must not have eyes either."

Other than the trierarch, the two most important officers on an Athenian ship were the *kubernetes* (helmsman) and the *keleustes* (usually translated inadequately as "boatswain"). The *kubernetes* was the most important single individual on the ship in battle—he maneuvered the ship to ram and to avoid being rammed. He had to know exactly what performance he could expect from his ship, which would vary as the conditions on the sea varied, or as the ship's hull took on more water, or as his crew grew tired, or as inexperienced oarsmen replaced the experienced. He had to know the reaction time of the ship and the crew, and he had to make split-second decisions when and how to maneuver.

Almost as important was the *keleustes*. He controlled the oarsmen, called the time, understood the state of the crew and exactly what he could get out of them. He controlled the speed, which was crucial to an efficient ramming—fast enough to puncture the enemy's hull without getting stuck, not so fast as to damage his own ship.

In addition to the *trierarch*, the *kubernetes*, and the *keleustes*, each trireme had ten hoplites, twenty to thirty years of age, and four archers (though sometimes there were more archers and fewer hoplites), an officer on the bow, a shipwright, and a flute player who signaled the tempo—the notes of a flute carry better than the beating of a drum.

How fast a trireme could go is suggested by a few bits of ancient evidence. A trireme, rowing continually, went from Athens to Mitylene (184.5 sea miles) in twenty-four hours; another went 124 sea miles between dawn and dark with a stop for lunch and a crew that had been rowing in the days before; 129 miles was considered a possible, but a long day's, voyage under optimal conditions.

Based on the performance of the *Olympias* (which had a crew of experienced rowers, but *not* experienced in a trireme!), a trireme, starting from a dead stop, could reach six knots in thirty seconds; it could turn 90° and bring the ship back to six knots in thirty seconds; it could traverse a length of five

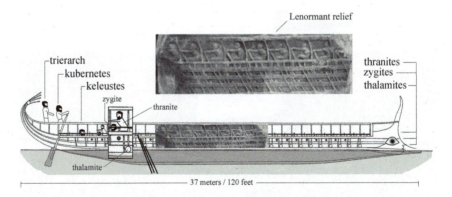

Illustration 7. A schematic of a trireme with the Lenormant relief superimposed. (Adapted and redrawn by Alfred S. Bradford)

hundred meters in two and a half minutes (six and a half knots), a length of two kilometers in thirteen minutes with a maximum speed of seven knots. It is estimated that a good crew, well practiced, could reach a sprinting speed of eleven and a half knots.

The trireme was a formidable weapon.

CHAPTER ELEVEN

Polycrates: King, Tyrant, Pirate

Sixth-century Greece was in turmoil. The king of Argos had developed a battle system, the hoplite phalanx, which drew upon a newly prosperous, non-aristocratic class, who could afford to buy the sixty pounds of hoplite equipment (shield, helmet, breastplate, and greaves), could afford the time required to train, and could afford the time to march out—in the heat of the summer—to fight their neighbors. Adding to the turmoil was the introduction of coinage; men could now measure their wealth, not in land or produce, but in cash.

The Athenian tyrant Pisistratus came to power with the support of the new hoplite class. While he was not responsible for the original introduction of coinage into Athens, he established a new issue, the tetradrachma, featuring Athena, her owl, a sprig of olive, and the prominent letters AΘE. This tetradrachma became the beloved coin of Athenians and the premier coin of Greece, trustworthy for more than a century and a half and a symbol of Athenian power.

Both coinage and hoplite warfare led to social dislocation, as the hoplites of each city sought rights rejected by an aristocracy that had devolved into a greedy, narrow class (in one city called "the Fat"). The hoplites supported tyrants who promised to give them their due.

Greeks had been free to work out the consequences of this social and political upheaval until the middle of the sixth century, when they collided with a power that, on the face of it, appeared to be many times greater than their own—Cyrus and the Persians. Cyrus had conquered Lydia, and he expected that the Greeks, who had been subservient to the Lydian kings, should be subservient to him. When they resisted, he delegated the reduction of Ionia to his subordinates (Harpagos among them).

The times seemed to demand of the Greeks a unified command under one individual—a fruitful time for tyrants. On the island of Samos an ambitious man named Polycrates took advantage of a religious festival during which the men of Samos left their weapons at home. Polycrates was supported by Lygdamis, the tyrant of Naxos (who in turn had been established by the tyrant of Athens, Pisistratus). Polycrates was lent fifteen hoplites by Lygdamis, and with their help and the help of his two brothers, Syloson and Pantagnostos, Polycrates seized control of Samos sometime around 540. (Their father seems to have chosen names with a definite purpose—Polycrates ["very powerful"], Syloson ["loot-taker"], and Pantagnostos ["know-it-all"], or, in other words, the *leader*, the *looter*, and the *bookkeeper.*)

When the brothers first seized power in Samos, Polycrates divided the city into three parts, each brother to rule one part while they cooperated in ruling the whole. But once Polycrates was firmly established, he murdered his brother Pantagnostos (whose name could also be interpreted "know-nothing") and forced Syloson to go to Italy to found a colony (Dicaearchia, the modern Puteoli).

Polycrates appealed to the Ionians as their protector against the Persians; and, when Pisistratus, the tyrant of Athens, tried to assume that role by purifying the tiny island of Delos (a central religious site for Ionians), Polycrates purified another important Ionian site, Rheneia, and dedicated it to Delian Apollo. He attacked the mainland city, Miletus, ostensibly because it had gone over to the Persians, and, when the Lesbians came to their help, he defeated them, captured a large number of prisoners, and set them to hard labor, digging a defensive trench around the city of Samos.

Polycrates used his position to gain control of the Samian privateers operating in the Aegean and forced them to disgorge all their loot, which he redistributed in part back to them, thus earning their gratitude. As he said, "You get more thanks from your friends by returning some of what you stole, than if you had never taken anything in the first place." Once he had control of the privateers, he organized a fleet of one hundred penteconters and one thousand archers; he plundered the Aegean at will, not only the islands but also cities on the mainland; and he defeated anyone who tried to stop him. The ancient chroniclers named Polycrates the first lord of the seas after Minos (mythical king of the Cretan people).

Polycrates created a luxurious court, as many tyrants did, in an attempt to transform Samos into a center of culture and also, of course, to promote himself. With his newly acquired wealth, he collected a large library, bred pedigreed dogs, and undertook massive building projects—"the mightiest construction in the whole of Greece"—that redounded to his glory, improved Samos, and kept the poor citizens employed, occupied, and content. He also invented a new ship, the *samaina*, by modifying, widening, and pooching out the hull of the bireme to increase its sailing quality and seaworthiness, its capacity to stow plunder . . . and to provide a steady platform for archers. Its prow curved up like a boar's snout. The ship became so much the symbol of Samos that the Athenians, when they branded some Samian prisoners, burned its image into their foreheads. (Aristophanes jested that the Samians were "deep-lettered.")

His first work was a mountain tunnel, forty-two hundred feet long and eight feet high-and-broad with a channel running through it, to bring water from a spring into the city. The second work was a mole, 120 feet deep and twelve hundred feet long, that improved the harbor. The third work was a temple that, Herodotus wrote, was the biggest he knew. Polycrates abolished the gymnasia, which he perceived as a threat to his power (as a meeting place of aristocrats). One of the most prominent aristocrats to seek a more congenial place in Greater Greece was Pythagoras.

Polycrates attracted the most famous poet of his age, Anacreon (who composed a long ode of praise for his mighty patron), although, as court poet, he wrote mostly about the pleasures of being drunk and, thereby, gave his name to a corpus of drinking songs—"Come, boy, and bring me a bowl of five parts wine to ten parts water so that I may drink without pause" and "after a breakfast of a little honey cake, I drained a pint of wine"—and about love affairs, including the tyrant's, who shaved the head of a favorite boy he suspected had developed rival interests.

Polycrates was tyrant in the interlude between Cyrus's conquest of Lydia (and Ionia) and Cambyses's invasion of Egypt in 526. At the beginning of his tyranny, Polycrates had the support of the tyrants of Athens and Naxos and an alliance and friendship with the king of Egypt, Amasis. Amasis had taken a Greek wife and he conciliated and depended upon Greek mercenaries and allies to protect his kingdom on land and sea.

He sought out Polycrates as an ally against the Persians and offered him his friendship, which Polycrates accepted but later regretted, as he saw the Persians advance on Egypt. Polycrates pursued his own advantage and, to cover his betrayal of Amasis, concocted the following fable of luck, fate, a precious ring, and a fortuitous fish.

Amasis, the story goes, had heard of the tyrant's continuing good fortune, and he advised Polycrates to throw away his most precious possession—a selfmade bit of bad luck to balance all the good luck and avoid the envy of the gods—so Polycrates threw a cherished ring into the sea. A few days later, a humble fisherman brought him a gift.

"O king," the fisherman said, "I caught this fish and rather than selling it in the market—even though I earn my living as a fisherman—I thought, this is a fish fit only for you. So I brought it to you as a gift."

The tyrant thanked him and invited him to dinner to share the fish with him, but, lo and behold, when the cooks filleted the fish, they found the ring. Polycrates imparted this bit of news to Amasis and Amasis broke off the friendship, because he knew that the story of Polycrates could only end badly and "he did not want to weep for a friend pulled down by a tragic fate."

In any case, Polycrates reached an accommodation with Cambyses. and Amasis died and bequeathed the defense of Egypt to his son, Psammetichus III. Unfortunately, Polycrates's previous anti-Persian policy had left him with one big problem: he had received many Ionian refugees, they had brought a fleet of forty triremes with them, and they in no way wanted to help Persians. Polycrates also faced opposition from some of his own Samians, so he tried to kill two birds with one stone. He manned the trireme fleet with the exiles and with the disaffected Samians (a combined force of some eight thousand men) and sent the fleet to Cambyses with the suggestion that he, Polycrates, would not be sorry if he never saw it again.

The Persians and Psammetichus III fought a decisive battle at Pelusium with Greek and Carian mercenaries on both sides. Neither the Egyptian navy nor the Samian triremes seem to have played any part in the war. Cambyses's invasion succeeded, and he dismissed the triremes. The fleet returned to Samos and tried to overthrow Polycrates, the triremes defeated the tyrant's pente-conters, the crews landed, and were defeated themselves and forced to withdraw, so they appealed to the Spartans to come to their aid. (They spoke at such length that the Spartans said they had forgotten the beginning and so could not understand the end, whereupon the Samians returned with a flour sack and said only, "The bag is empty.")

The Spartans had promoted themselves as defenders of the Ionians, and they had suffered from Polycrates's piracy, so in 525 BCE, the Spartans, with their allies the Corinthians, set out on an expedition against Polycrates. On the way, they overthrew Polycrates's ally, Lygdamis, the tyrant of Naxos, and then they landed on Samos, defeated Polycrates's forces, and drove them back into the city. Two Spartans got caught up in the pursuit, entered the city with the fugitives, but were cut off and killed. (They fought so bravely that the Samians put up memorials to them.) The Spartans abandoned the siege after forty days and returned home, leaving the exiles to fend for themselves.

The exiles put back to sea. They still had a formidable fleet in an Aegean with no organized, central power to stop them from plundering the weak. Their first victims were the Syphnians, the richest, most vulnerable place they knew. The Syphnians had discovered silver and gold, and with a tenth of it they built one of the most extraordinary treasure houses in Delphi. (The reliefs can still be seen today.) The Syphnians also, while they were at Delphi, used the opportunity to ask the oracle how long their good luck would last. The oracle responded,

"When first the council house in Syphnos and the market around turn white, then it is time for the sensible to be wary of the wooden enemy and the red herald."

The first part was clear—the Syphnians had used their new fortune to redo the council house and the marketplace in white Parian marble, but what was meant by the "wooden enemy" and the "red herald"? Alas, when the Syphnians were visited by one of the exiles, an envoy from a single ship who asked for a "loan" of ten talents, they did not recognize that the ship was both the "wooden enemy" and the "red herald"—its upper works were painted red—and they refused to pay.

The Samian exiles ravaged the land, routed the Syphnians, and captured so many prisoners that their ransom reached one hundred talents. With that money they bought an island, Hydrea, that lies off the Peloponnesian coast, and, after entrusting it for safekeeping to the city of Troezen, sailed to Crete and founded the city of Kydonia. There, for five years, they prospered as pirates, but in the sixth year, they were driven out by the Cretans and Aeginetans (who at that time were a formidable sea power and had an old grudge against Samos); they were defeated in a sea battle and sold into slavery. Such was the fate of those pirates who weren't executed on the spot. The story of the exiles illustrates the power, but also the limits, of a modest fleet.

So far, Polycrates had adjusted to the changing situation, had survived several attacks, and, by his accommodation with the Persians, seemed to have secured his power, but to the Persians, since he was not a tribute-paying member of their empire, he was a potential enemy. His very existence interfered with their plan to expand to the islands (with the help of their new subjects, the Phoenicians). Consequently, a satrap pandered to his ambition, held out the hopes of fabulous wealth—*he, the satrap, had had a falling out with the king and wanted to entrust his treasury to Polycrates's safekeeping*—and he persuaded Polycrates to come in person to seal the arrangement. Polycrates's daughter had a horrible, prophetic dream that he was suspended in the air and Zeus was washing him and the sun god was rubbing him down and she begged him not to go, but he, who had fooled so many others, was fooled himself. He went and, at the satrap's orders, was nailed to a cross and left to disintegrate under the sun—"the sun god rubbing him down"—and the rain—"Zeus washing him."

The Persians seized Samos and massacred the population.

PART 3

The Persian Wars

Trireme Tactics

The "old-fashioned" way—bow to bow. Sometimes both ships are put out of action.

Maneuvering and ramming from the side. The ram can stick or be twisted askew if the angle and speed are not exactly correct.

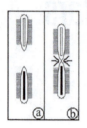

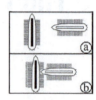

"Modern" tactics—a) pretend to ram bow-to-bow, b) sheer off at the last minute, c) pull in oars, and d) shatter enemy oars and batter the oarsmen.

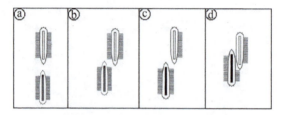

The battle line and the *diekplous.* a) Row through, smashing enemy oars, b) turn, and attack the enemy ships before they can recover. Strike them amid-ships with just enough force to roll them over.

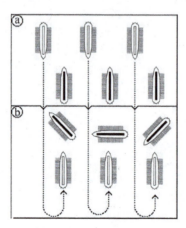

The trireme required three talents to commission and one talent/month to keep at sea. Athenian policy was to have sixty triremes constantly at sea during the 8-month sailing season (480 talents). Athens' annual income (including its tribute from its subjects) was 800 talents/year. (One siege cost 2000 talents.)

Illustration 8. Trireme tactics. (Drawn by Alfred S. Bradford)

CHAPTER TWELVE

Darius and the Greeks

In the same year that Polycrates was crucified, 522 BCE, the Persian king, Cambyses, died of a "self-inflicted wound," and Darius, a collateral relative and an adherent of the god Ahura Mazda, seized the throne. He spent a year putting down rivals (*devotees of the lie,* he said) and rebellions, and then, as was the duty of the king, he initiated campaigns to extend the borders of his empire. By 517, he had accepted the submission of Lesbos and Chios and had captured Samos (and massacred the population, although later the island was resettled).

Darius's first major campaign (in 513) had a threefold purpose: first, to extend the Persian empire into Europe; second, to punish, if not subdue, the nomadic Scythians, who lived on the steppes north of the borders of the Persian empire and for years had been raiding the empire; and, third, to compel the Greeks of the northern Aegean to submit to him. One of the independent Greeks whom he intended to bring to heel was the Athenian hegemon of the Chersonese, Miltiades the Younger.

Three years earlier in 516, Miltiades the Younger had been sent by the Athenian tyrants—the sons of Pisistratus—to replace his relative, the elder Miltiades, who had been killed. The younger Miltiades sailed to the Chersonese on a trireme, the first Athenian to be associated in extant literature with this type of ship. (Later he acquired a modest fleet of five triremes.) Miltiades, when he assumed control of the Chersonese, avowed a personal hostility to the Persians, although, in reality, he could not have ruled there without Persian acquiescence.

When Darius marched west with his army in 513 to initiate his campaign across the Danube against the Scythians, he summoned his Greek subjects and fleet, including Miltiades, for a massive naval undertaking. He commissioned Mandrocles of Samos to build a bridge of boats across the Bosporos. (The bridge had to span a distance of over a kilometer of swiftly—four-knot—flowing water and strong winds. Mandrocles's feat of engineering was not duplicated until 1973.) Darius advanced through Thrace, organized it into a satrapy, conquered the contiguous regions, and paused at the Danube long enough to give Mandrocles time to construct another bridge. Here Darius was joined by the Greek fleet under the command of the tyrants, whom he ordered to guard the bridge, while he crossed the Danube and commenced his operation against the Scythians.

Darius's strategy turned out to have a fatal flaw—it assumed that the Scythians would stand and fight. Instead, the Scythians retreated, burned everything behind them, and harassed the Persians continually. Darius had never considered this possibility, and he sent a message to the Scythian king asking him why he did not stand and fight like a man, to which the Scythian king replied, "We Scythians have neither cities nor cultivated land to protect from devastation and, therefore, feel no compulsion to rush to battle with you." Darius's strategy, and the strategy of the Persian kings before him (and also the kings after him), was to apply overwhelming force systematically, advancing from objective to objective. Darius not only failed to subdue the Scythians, but he was gone longer than he had anticipated, and rumors flew back to the Greeks that he had suffered a catastrophe.

Miltiades suggested to the tyrants guarding the Danube bridge that they destroy it and maroon Darius on the farther shore. At first, he seemed to them to make sense, but then they reconsidered—without Persian support, they would be overthrown by their own people and lynched, so they continued to guard the bridge until Darius returned. When he learned of Miltiades's suggestion, he expelled him from the Chersonese.

Although Darius could not conceal the failure of his campaign against the Scythians, he was consoled by one major success—he had subdued most of Thrace. To subjugate the rest, and the contiguous regions, he detailed his general Megabazus. Megabazus forced the king of Macedonia, Amyntas, to submit, that is, to give the Persians "earth and water." His successor brought over the remainder of the north Aegean.

Darius suspected the loyalty of the tyrants, because they had listened to Miltiades and were initially swayed by his arguments. Darius and the Persians supported the tyrants in Asia Minor and the Aegean, only because tyranny seemed to be the normal government of the Greek polis (as it had been in the reign of Cyrus). He cultivated Apollo as the principal god of the Greeks; advised a Persian official who had cut trees in Apollo's sacred grove to beware lest he learn what the "wrath of a king is"; and respected his most holy site, Delphi, in the expectation that he would win the support of Apollo and, thereby, the Greeks. He did not understand Greek aspirations for self-rule in both their politics and their religion—Greeks acknowledged no central, religious authority—and, while Persian control, at first, gave the Ionians peace and prosperity, they discovered that the expansion of Persia and its incorporation in the empire of the four cities of Phoenicia—Tyre, Sidon, Byblos, and Arados—hurt Ionian trade and furnished the Persians with a competent and dependable fleet.

While the Ionians seemed content, circumstances on mainland Greece were changing. The Spartans had cleared the Peloponnesus of tyrants, and in 510, led by their king, Cleomenes, expelled the Athenian tyrant, Hippias, the son of Pisistratus. Freed by Cleomenes, the Athenians instituted a reformulation of the social and political structure of their state, which resulted in a gradual increase of power in the citizen assembly and loss of power in the magistracies.

The Athenians created ten new tribes out of the traditional four, and they instituted the tribal election of generals: each of the ten tribes had its own general. The generals served for one year but were eligible for reelection, so that the Athenians could retain generals who had proved themselves competent. (Later, Philip mocked the "good fortune" of the Athenians, that every year they could find ten generals when in his whole life he had only been able to find one—Parmenion.)

They also instituted ostracism as a way for the Athenian assembly to rid the city of a potential tyrant. (Once a year they called a special assembly, the people voted, the ballots—the *ostraka* [potsherds]—were counted, and, if there was a quorum, the man who had received the most votes was required on pain of death to leave Athens for ten years.) The reforms created a cohesive body of citizens, proud of what they had accomplished and confident that they could govern themselves.

The Spartans had not foreseen, and they abhorred, the democratic reforms; they tried to subvert them; and, when they failed, they tried to restore the tyranny. Consequently, the Athenians sent an embassy to the Persian satrap Artaphernes to seek an accommodation of some sort. When the ambassadors returned to Athens with a treaty (in which they submitted to the Persians), the Athenians repudiated it. But then they learned that their former tyrant, Hippias, was attempting to convince Artaphernes to reinstate him in Athens, and so they sent a second embassy. Artaphernes rejected the second embassy, because as far as he was concerned, the Athenians had already submitted to the Persians.

Meanwhile, in 500 BCE, a group of exiled Naxian aristocrats appealed to the tyrant of Miletus, Aristagoras, and through him to the Persians, to help reinstate them. The Persians agreed, because they thought they could use Naxos, if it submitted, as a staging area in the Cyclades, but the attack fell apart and the Persians blamed Aristagoras. Aristagoras feared they might execute him, so he returned to Miletus, laid down his tyranny, and proclaimed a new age of freedom and equality. He appealed to the sailors in the Ionian fleet, which had not disbanded after the expedition to Naxos, and they responded enthusiastically to the promise of political freedom by arresting the tyrants present in the fleet, overthrowing their tyrannies, and declaring themselves free of Persian rule.

The Persians were taken completely by surprise and spent some time in responding, which gave the Ionians a chance to prepare their resistance, to select leaders—they could not agree on a commander-in-chief—and to seek allies. They organized a confederation of Ionians and sent their representatives to meet at the Panionium, the religious center of Ionia. They agreed to cooperate at sea but not so much on land, where they knew they were no match for the Persian army.

In the winter of 499/8, Aristagoras traveled to Greece to enlist the Spartans in the Ionian cause, but when his first attempt to convince the king failed, he tried to bribe him, and had almost succeeded when the king's ten-year-old daughter said, "Daddy, get away from this bad man!" The Spartan king ordered Aristagoras expelled from Sparta, from Laconia, and from the whole Peloponnesus. Aristagoras continued on to Athens, where he appealed to their common heritage and love of freedom and persuaded the Athenians to help—as Herodotus writes, "thus proving it is easier to persuade 30,000 men than one."

The Athenians sent twenty ships—with four ships from the Eretrians (on the island of Euboea)—to join with Miletus in an expedition against Sardis. The allies took the lower town of Sardis but failed to dislodge the Persians from the citadel; the Athenians accidentally set the town on fire; and, upon hearing news that a Persian force was closing on the city, they retreated to their ships, sailed home, and did not venture out again.

The Ionians had better luck with the Greeks on the Hellespont and Cyprus. They persuaded the Cypriots to revolt from Persia, but the Persians reacted quickly and vigorously. In the early summer of 497, a Phoenician fleet landed a Persian army on Cyprus, where an army of Greeks defeated them, killed their commander, and then, in an all too common Greek reaction to victory, split into factions, one faction betrayed another, and their rebellion collapsed.

At sea, however, the Ionian fleet was more fortunate. It destroyed the Phoenician fleet and gained complete, albeit temporary, control of the Aegean. In response, Darius dispatched three armies under the command of three sons-in-law, two of them to concentrate in the north against the cities of the Hellespontine region including Miltiades, who had returned to the Chersonese; but as the armies were advancing, the king learned that the Carians had joined the revolt, and he shifted two of his armies south. The Persians defeated the Carians in two big battles; after the second victory, they believed that they had destroyed all resistance, they grew careless, fell into a Carian ambush, and were massacred.

Greeks everywhere were amazed at the rebels' victories—they had characterized the Ionians as "sheep attacking wolves"—but the Ionians now squandered their advantage in the interlude (496–495), which their victory had given them to unite and prepare a common strategy to meet the inevitable Persian onslaught. Instead, they fell apart. They lost their leader, Aristagoras, in the fighting; they refused to do the hard work of training for the coming sea battle; they split into factions; and some, for fear or profit, accepted a secret deal from the Persians.

In 494, the Persians resumed the offensive. They concentrated on Miletus, the city they blamed for the revolt, and attacked it by land and sea. Their combined fleet from Phoenicia, Egypt, Cilicia, and Cyprus, was reputed to number six hundred triremes. The Ionians abandoned the Milesians to their fate and in the autumn of 494 concentrated their naval forces at Lade. When the Persian fleet initiated its attack, the Samians deserted and the other city contingents fled with them, except for the Chians, who fought to the end.

The Persians now had a free hand at Miletus; they broke through its walls, killed the men and enslaved the women and children, sacked the city, and razed it as an object lesson. They rewarded Samos by sparing it, except that they reinstated its tyrant, and then they advanced, rebel city by rebel city, killing the men, enslaving the women and children, and burning everything. When they approached the Chersonese, Miltiades withdrew to Athens, where he used his wealth and prestige—he had won a chariot victory at the Olympic games—to advocate for resistance to Persia. In 493, he was cleared of a charge of tyranny in the Chersonese brought by his political enemies, and, as a result, he became an even more prominent political figure.

After the Persians had thoroughly suppressed the Ionian rebellion and punished the participants, the king appointed a central council to settle disputes. It surveyed the territories of the individual states to establish fair borders, and, in 492, under the newly appointed leader, Mardonius (the son-in-law of Darius), it dismissed the tyrants and organized the cities into "democracies." (The Persians were satisfied with any form of government, or religion, so long as the governed accepted Persia as overlord and paid their tribute.) Ionia lost its mercantile prominence in the Greek world and became a backwater, which caused Herodotus to reflect that "the great places of old have now become small and those once small have become great."

Once Mardonius had completed the reorganization of Ionia, Darius sent him to Europe to prepare for the invasion of Greece and the punishment of Athens and Eretria. Mardonius and his army rode to Thrace on Ionian ships; he built depots and roads to facilitate his advance through Thrace, but bad luck dogged the operation—lions gathered by the hundreds to feast on the laborers, his fleet was destroyed trying to sail around Mt. Athos, and Mardonius, himself, was badly wounded in a Thracian raid. Nonetheless, and despite these setbacks, the Persians by 491 had regained control of the northern Aegean, Thrace, and Macedonia down to Mt. Olympus, and they had rebuilt their fleet, which now included ships designed for landing troops.

In this period of impending doom, an Athenian tragedian named Phrynichus produced a tragedy, *The Fall of Miletus.* The Athenian audience wept and then fined him one thousand drachmas for reminding them of the disaster.

The First Naval Assault on Athens

In 491 BCE, Darius sent Persian envoys throughout Greece to demand "earth and water." The envoys who came to Athens were executed on the advice of Miltiades; the envoys who went to Sparta were thrown down a well "to get their own earth and water," but in many places the envoys' demands were met, and one of those places, which seemed all too ready to accede to the Persian demands, was Aegina. Aegina was in a position to do real harm to the allied cause. It had a substantial fleet and was a rival to Athens in the Saronic Gulf, where for years it had been fighting an undeclared war with the Athenians. The Aeginetans might well have considered that immediate Persian help against Athens outweighed any potential harm to some nebulous idea of Greek freedom.

The Athenians asked the Spartan king, Cleomenes, to intervene. Cleomenes had little reason to love the Athenians, who had humiliated him after he had expelled their tyrant, Hippias, but nonetheless, the king was determined to prepare the Spartan alliance, including Aegina, to meet the Persian threat. He seized and transferred ten hostages from Aegina to Athens as a surety for Aegina's good behavior and to conciliate the Athenians.

With the potential threat of Aegina removed, Cleomenes directed his attention to Sparta's one rival within the Peloponnesus, Argos. In 494, Cleomenes led an invasion force to the boundary river between Laconia and the Argolid; there, however, when he performed a sacrifice, the river god rejected it—that is, prohibited Cleomenes from crossing his stream. The king commented, "Very patriotic of you, but you will not save the Argives," and he collected ships, some from Aegina, and ferried his army by sea into the Argolid near the town of Sepeia. There he routed the Argive army, trapped it in a sacred grove, set the trees on fire, and incinerated six thousand Argive soldiers. So complete was his victory that slaves had to rule Argos on behalf of the sons of the slaughtered men. Cleomenes knocked Argos completely out of the Persian wars.

Cleomenes, and his anti-Persian policy, had been opposed within Sparta by his fellow king, Demaratus. Cleomenes charged Demaratus with being a bastard and, therefore, not royal, not a descendant of Heracles, and not eligible to be king. Delphi (where Spartan kings were tried) agreed, and Demaratus was deposed. In the end, Demaratus fled to Persia and became an adviser to the king, but then it came out that Cleomenes had bribed the high priest at Delphi to ensure the verdict he wanted and he was forced into temporary exile in Arcadia—the exile was temporary because he so frightened the Spartans with his plans of revenge against them that they reinstated him. In the end, however, his relatives judged him insane—he wandered around Sparta and rapped his fellow citizens on the head with his staff—and confined him in stocks; while confined, he acquired a small knife, sliced himself from his ankles to his waist, and bled to death. He was succeeded by his half-brother Leonidas.

The messy end of Cleomenes created turmoil and crisis in Sparta (and Greece). The Spartans debated whether they should continue to pursue the active anti-Persian policy of Cleomenes (and live up to the terms of their alliance with the Athenians) or maintain a defensive posture in the Peloponnesus and refrain from any action that would provoke the Persians. In response, many Athenians, not convinced that they could depend upon the Spartans, advocated for another attempt to reach some accommodation with the Persians, while their opponents, concerned that the Persians wanted to reinstate Hippias, elected Athens's foremost anti-Persian advocate, Miltiades, general for 490/489.

Meanwhile, as the Persians' preparation for an assault from the north through Thrace and Macedonia stalled, a Mede named Datis and a Persian, Artaphernes (the nephew of Darius), formulated a plan to attack Athens and Eretria directly across the Aegean. Fundamental to the plan was their conversion of ships into horse transports to carry their cavalry, the main arm of the Persian military and absolutely essential in defeating a hoplite phalanx.

The Athenians knew full well that a Persian expedition was coming and that the Persians intended to reinstate Hippias as tyrant of Athens. But, with the assurances of Miltiades that they could defeat the Persians and with the reassurance of Leonidas, the new Spartan king, about the Spartan alliance, they prepared to resist, although not at sea—the Persian (Phoenician) fleet was reputed to have three hundred triremes and enough transports to carry twelve hundred horses (mounts for eight hundred cavalrymen) and thirty thousand infantry plus ample supplies.

The Persian expedition took its time, subduing Rhodes and then sailing up to Miletus and Samos, perhaps in the hope that the Athenians would believe the fleet was headed to the Hellespont, but in midsummer it crossed the central Aegean directly, rather than skirting the coast, and so caught the people of Naxos completely by surprise. The Naxians had successfully withstood the Persians earlier, but now they fled for the hills. The Persians caught some, whom they enslaved, and they incinerated the city including the temples (which the Persians, as good Zoroastrians, believed were the domiciles of demons).

Next the fleet stopped at Delos, from which the Delians had fled, but when the Persian commander announced that he certainly would not dishonor the birthplace of Apollo and Artemis and invited the Delians back, they returned. He made an offering to the gods before he resumed his voyage. The Persians forced other islanders to furnish troops and to give them children as hostages. So far, the expedition had been a success, even before it arrived at the main objectives, Athens and Eretria.

The Persians reached the island of Euboea in August, seized Carystus at the southern tip of the island, and established it as their main base. The Persian fleet, by its presence at Carystus, threatened both Eretria and Athens equally and prevented the Athenians from bringing aid to the Eretrians, whom the Persians soon attacked. They laid siege to it and pressed the operation for six days before a pair of traitors let them into the city. The Persians sacked the city, temples and all, and eventually resettled the whole population in the heart of the Persian empire.

Now the former Athenian tyrant, Hippias, advised the Persians to land at Marathon. Hippias chose Marathon primarily because there was a good beach, a road to Athens—once off the beach and through the hills—and suitable terrain for cavalry, but also because his father had landed there on his way to establishing his tyranny. Hippias believed that the Athenians would welcome him back and, as clinching and incontrovertible evidence, he reported a dream in which he had had intercourse with his mother, a good sign, because the dream, according to the soothsayers, predicted that he would have communion with the mother of us all, the earth, his homeland. (Alas, when his ship beached—sometime around September 8, 490—he leaped to the shore, coughed out a tooth, lost the tooth in the sand, and thus fulfilled the dream—a one-tooth reunion with his motherland.)

The Persians landed without opposition, did some minor ravaging of farms, and waited to advance until the following day (because their horses were seasick). But in the meantime, the Athenians sent an urgent message to Sparta for help, while the Athenian army (nine thousand hoplites) marched the twenty-six miles to Marathon (followed soon after by one thousand Plataean hoplites) and blocked the routes into the interior. The Athenians' quick action neutralized all the advantages the Persians had gained by their surprise landing, confined the Persian foot and horse to the small plain by the sea, and disappointed Hippias's expectations that he would be welcomed. On the next day, the Athenian runner arrived in Sparta with the news and found that the Spartans were celebrating a festival, which prevented their troops from leaving Laconia until the end of the lunar cycle. Consequently, the Athenians were told not to expect them before the 18th of September.

Nonetheless, the Athenians had placed the Persians in an untenable situation, growing worse day by day because the season of storms was approaching and soon the Spartans would be on the march. The Persians could not break through the prepared position of the Athenian army, their advantage in cavalry was neutralized, they had to resupply by sea, and any attempt to withdraw—loading the horses on the transports and isolating their infantry—would make them vulnerable to an Athenian assault. On the Athenian side, five of the Athenian generals wanted to avoid battle—eventually, they believed, the Persians would have to withdraw and go home—but five, including Miltiades, wanted to fight, and the Polemarch (i.e., the commander-in-chief) cast the deciding vote in favor of fighting and gave Miltiades the authority to say *when*.

After five days, the Persians were uncertain whether the Athenians were afraid to attack them or were waiting for the Spartans (who were expected to arrive now within a few days), and they concluded that they had to recover the initiative immediately by re-embarking that night, transporting their army around Sunion, and landing closer to Athens.

As soon as Miltiades learned from scouts that the Persians were loading their cavalry, he gave the signal to attack. The Athenian phalanx rushed down into the plain and charged the Persian infantry on the run. The Athenians in their armor completely outmatched the Persians (although part of the Persian infantry broke through the Athenian center). The Athenians rushed the ships and tried to prevent their departure—one Athenian grabbed the stern of a ship and had his hands chopped off—but the fleet pushed out to sea and left their infantry to die. The Athenians pursued the panic-stricken Persians into the marshes, hunted them down, and killed them, sixty-four hundred men.

We know the exact number because the Polemarch had vowed to dedicate for every Persian killed one kid—so many the supply of baby goats ran out—and the Athenians made an exact accounting. (One hundred ninety-two Athenians were killed.) As the Persian fleet sailed for the unprotected Athenian harbor of Phalerum, the Athenian army re-formed, marched at the double, and arrived in time to prevent a Persian landing. Their swift reaction left the Persian fleet no option except to withdraw back across the Aegean. On the next day, the Spartans arrived, visited the battlefield, congratulated the Athenians on their victory, and marched back to Sparta.

Miltiades, the hero of the hour, proposed that the Athenians send a naval expedition (seventy triremes, fourteen thousand men, and funds to support a campaign) under his sole command to attack those islands that had gone over to the Persians. He had some early successes, but on the island of Paros he suffered a debilitating wound, and, mistakenly believing that a Persian relief force was close, he lifted his month-long siege and withdrew. He returned to Athens, where he was charged with lying to the Athenian people—he had promised them success and riches, but he hadn't delivered. The people out of gratitude for Marathon voted not to execute him, but did fine him fifty talents. (The annual income of the whole city of Athens was about four hundred talents.) Miltiades died of his wounds. His son, Cimon, paid the fine.

For the Persians, the battle of Marathon was a significant setback in an otherwise successful campaign. They still had the preponderance of power at sea, and Darius was even more determined to force Greece into the Persian empire, although he was convinced by the failure at Athens that his original strategy was the best—to advance by land and sea with overwhelming force. For the Athenians, however, the battle of Marathon was the greatest victory ever won—veterans of Marathon were still regaling their fellow citizens with stories of their derring-do sixty years later. And more significantly, the majority of Athenians now believed that they could defeat the Persians and, no less importantly, that they could depend upon the Spartans, dilatory though they had been.

CHAPTER FOURTEEN

"Flee to the Ends of the Earth"

The Athenians knew that Marathon was not the end of the war. The Persians still controlled all the lands and people from the Danube to the Aegean and from the Bosporus to Macedonia including the Greek cities and Macedonia itself, which extended Persian control to the northern border of Thessaly, the northernmost region of Greece. Darius was still determined to conquer Greece, this time with a massive and coordinated attack by land and sea. Fortunately for the Greeks, Darius died in 486 before his preparations were complete; his son and successor, Xerxes, was delayed first by an Egyptian rebellion and then by a rebellion in Babylon.

In Athens, the anti-Persia faction had lost its most effective advocate, Miltiades; his replacement was a newcomer (named Themistocles); and his political opponents were seizing the opportunity to take control of Athenian politics by promoting a policy of peace and accommodation with Persia. They claimed that the advocate of war, Themistocles, was mostly a Thracian, hardly an Athenian at all; that his mother had committed suicide from shame that she had such a son; and that he was an uneducated boor, to the last of which charges he replied, "True, I have never learned how to tune a lyre, but I do know how to transform a small and insignificant city into a world power."

To settle this issue, which could be peacefully settled in no other way, the Athenian assembly voted an ostracism each year during the 480s; each year Themistocles received the second-most votes, but one of his opponents received the most and was ostracized. In 488/7, the Athenians ostracized a leader of the tyrant Hippias's family, in the next year they ostracized one of the prosecutors of Miltiades, and in the following years, they ostracized other advocates of accommodation, until they had made it crystal clear that advocating accommodation was political suicide. (Feelings ran high. On one ballot a neat hexameter couplet called Xanthippus—the father of Pericles—"the worst criminal of all the politicians.")

During those same years, year after year, Themistocles proposed measures to upgrade the Piraeus and to increase Athenian naval power for the anticipated war. In 483, when the Athenians discovered a rich new vein of silver in the mines at Laurion, Themistocles's opponents attempted to ingratiate themselves with the assembly by proposing that the silver be coined and distributed to every Athenian, but Themistocles proposed instead to use it to construct a modern fleet of triremes.

This new fleet, he promised, would overwhelm their rival and enemy in the Saronic Gulf, Aegina, with whom they had resumed the undeclared war, were doing rather poorly, and certainly could use a new, enlarged fleet. But the longer-term necessity for the fleet, to resist Persia, was not lost on either himself or the people, nor was the fact that they would still receive the silver in wages for building and manning the fleet. They approved Themistocles's proposal and used the silver to pay for the construction of two hundred modern triremes. By 481 BCE, the Athenians had compelled the Aeginetans to accept terms and, in the process, had been transformed by Themistocles from steady hoplites to "sea-tossed sailors." The aristocrats hated him.

Meanwhile, in 481, after two years of labor, Persian engineers completed a canal through the promontory of Mt. Athos. (The canal was twenty-two-hundred meters long and twenty meters wide.) The Persians also built a series of roads, paved where necessary, capable of handling carts, and punctuated with guard posts, inns, and courier stations. They bridged rivers or established a ferry service, and they organized supply depots. They also bridged the Hellespont with a structure that was a combination of a boat- and suspension bridge about fifteen hundred meters long. It was designed by a Greek engineer and mathematician named Harpalus, who was so far ahead of his time that Greek writers were unable to describe just how the bridge worked.

This bridge and the Mt. Athos canal were the first undeniable proofs that the Persians really were coming, they revealed the Persians' strategy, and they demonstrated their material advantage—674 warships were used in the construction of the bridge; approximately twice that number comprised the Persians' active fleet with six times that number of supporting vessels, all requiring in total more than two hundred thousand naval personnel. Their land army—which Herodotus put at one million men—was huge. (One modern estimate puts it at three hundred thousand men.)

In the autumn of 481, while the Athenians were still building triremes, Xerxes sent envoys throughout Greece to demand "earth and water," though expressly not to Sparta and Athens, since they had murdered the Persian envoys sent a decade earlier. (The Spartans tried to expiate the sacrilege of the murder of the envoys by sending two Spartan volunteers to Xerxes, to be executed by the king if he wished, but Xerxes, who particularly admired brave men, declined to take their lives.)

Xerxes, in the initial stage of his march to Greece, stopped at Troy and sacrificed to Athena. He, the ruler of Asia, would avenge the European sack of Troy (and write the conclusion to the legendary history of Asian-Greek enmity). Xerxes, as an adherent of Ahura-Mazda, believed that Ahura-Mazda was the one, true god and the so-called "gods" worshipped by the Greeks, including Athena, were demons, but as far as he was concerned, *his* Greeks, so long as they remained loyal subjects, were welcome to worship whatever demons they wished. And if his sacrifice encouraged them and maybe even won over their demons, so much the better.

While Xerxes was making his leisurely way through Asia Minor—he planned to enter Greece during the summer (of 480), when his preparations were complete and crops would be available to feed his army—the Spartans convened an international (Greek) assembly to discuss preparations for the war. The representatives agreed to end their internal wars and to swear an oath of loyalty to each other. They called themselves the "Greeks" with the implication that any Greek who did not join them was a traitor. They conferred the leadership of the war on the Spartan kings after rejecting an Athenian demand to command the naval forces. The "Greeks" vowed to confiscate the property of those who had "medized," except under compulsion—the Greeks called the Persians "Medes" and those who favored them "medizers." Some Greeks, who had already medized, recanted, but in the end, "the Greeks" comprised only the members of the Peloponnesian League and the Athenians and their several allies; all the Greek states in the path of the Persian advance medized.

Greeks everywhere turned to Apollo at Delphi for advice, and in general, Apollo advised them not to get involved. He delivered an oracle to the Spartans that either one of their kings would die or the city of Sparta would fall. He told the Athenians,

"Pitiable men, are you still sitting here? Flee from your homes to the ends of the earth, yes, abandon the city of heights! For neither the head nor the body will escape terrible destruction. Nor the hands nor the feet nor even the midsection, nothing will remain unsacked, for all will fall to the destructive fire or the rage of the war god who is coming in a Persian chariot. Athens, he will not destroy only you but other cities, too. He will raze many temples of the gods with his flames. Now they stand there, sweat pouring over them, trembling and shaking through fear and from the rooftree of the temple runs black blood and knowledge of the coming disaster. Go from this shrine. Bow your hearts in despair."

Well! Apollo seemed to believe that the Persians were going to win (and after the war, Greeks concluded that Apollo had medized), but the oracle did no more than reflect public opinion. Most Greeks believed that the Persians were certain to win. Nonetheless, the Athenians were so horrified by this prophecy that they came back to the god as suppliants to beg for some reassurance. Apollo's response was hardly supportive, but, in a marvel of obfuscation, told them to trust only in their "wooden wall" and to "flee! . . . Salamis, divine island, you will kill the sons of mothers, when Demeter sows the grain or gathers it in."

Although the Athenians were shaken, Themistocles convinced them that the second response with its admonition to trust in the "wooden wall" and its prediction that "divine" Salamis would witness the death of many a mother's son was a favorable omen. Indeed, the "wooden wall" was not a fence on the Acropolis, as Athenian priests claimed, but the fleet, while the epithet "divine," linked with Salamis, instead of such terms as "fatal" or "disastrous," indicated that the "wooden wall," in which they should trust, would fight and win at Salamis. Still, the bad news was that they would have to abandon Athens and station their fleet at Salamis. At this critical juncture, Themistocles's last, and most vigorous, political opponent, Aristides—he had opposed every measure supported by Themistocles—was ostracized. One voter called him "Aristides the brother of Datis."

In the spring of 480, the representatives of the states in the alliance met in the temple of Poseidon on the Isthmus of Corinth and planned to oppose the advance of the Persians as far north as they could. In June, after one false start, they decided to draw up their line of defense at the narrow pass at Thermopylae and the promontory of Artemisium. Meanwhile, Xerxes entered Macedonia, waited while his army constructed a road for his supply train, and then advanced in three columns into Thessaly, where the Thessalians welcomed him and supplied him with cavalry. Xerxes now proceeded south with his army and navy until he encountered the Spartans at Thermopylae.

CHAPTER FIFTEEN

"Pray to the Winds"

The news of the Persian advance arrived in Sparta, during the festival cele-brating Apollo Carneia, when the Spartan army was barred from leaving Laco-nia. Spartans, like other Greeks, had not believed that the call for troops would come before the day of the full moon (September 18, 480), when the Carneian and Olympic festivals concluded. Nonetheless, as soon as Leonidas received the news, he organized a force comprising helots, a limited number of Peloponnesian hoplites, and his personal guard of three hundred, and he set out for Thermopylae. (The fact that he chose only married men with sons suggests his expectations.) Leonidas had about five thousand infantry in all, a small force made smaller, when he reached Thermopylae and learned of a way around the pass. He had to detach a part of his force, one thousand Pho-cians, to block the path.

Greek strategy was simple and straightforward: Leonidas would block the narrow pass at Thermopylae and stop the Persian advance on land; the Spar-tan naval commander, Eurybiades, would occupy an advanced position near Artemisium (named for the local shrine of Artemis), but, if necessary, would withdraw to the Oreus Channel (between the mainland and the north coast of Euboea), relying on its narrow passage to thwart the Persian advance by sea. To aid in the defense of the approaches around Artemisium, Athens sent two hundred triremes, a majority of its fleet, commanded by Themistocles, who had been appointed second-in-command to Eurybiades. Eurybiades, thus, had in total 324 triremes and nine penteconters with crews approximat-ing sixty-five thousand men. (Corinth contributed forty ships.)

Artemisium offered a firm and level beach with deep water and no obstruc-tions offshore, so that ships could easily be beached and launched. The posi-tion also provided the Greeks with double lines of retreat (if necessary), ready communications with Leonidas at Thermopylae (sixty-five kilometers by sea), and an advantageous point from which to observe the Persians' maneuvers.

For his part, Leonidas was supposed to have a sizable army, drawn from all of the members of the League of the Greeks, to balance the fleet, but the Persian king and his army arrived sooner than expected and Leonidas's runners, carrying his urgent messages, found allies who dragged their feet and offered a plentitude of excuses. His reinforcements never arrived.

Meanwhile, the Persian fleet, which had gathered at Therma (west of Chalcidice at the head of the Thermaic Gulf), sent a contingent, ten ships strong, to sail south, down the coast; it surprised a trio of Greek ships, which were posted as lookouts at Sciathos Island, attacked them, and boarded two. The hand-to-hand engagement was fierce—an Aeginetan marine fought until he fainted from loss of blood. (The Persians admired his courage so much that they did everything they could to preserve his life.) They weren't so generous toward the rest of the captives, but chose the handsomest man and slit his throat above the open sea as a sacrifice to victory—the victim's name was Leon ("Lion"), which enhanced the potency of the gesture. They sold the rest of the captives into slavery. While they were so occupied, the third ship got away, beached, and sent a fire signal to the allied fleet at Artemisium.

Once the captains of the Persian ships had had sufficient time to mark the reef in the Sciathos Channel (because, Herodotus suggests, some Persian ships had once been wrecked there), the bulk of the Persian fleet at Therma set out. The leading ships arrived at the Sciathos Channel that evening, but the rest of the fleet was still stretched out along the inhospitable, rock-strewn coast and, hence, was completely vulnerable to the violent storm (the *Hellespontias*), which struck the following day, continued to rage for four more days, and hurled a mass of ships upon the rocks—Herodotus gives the number of wrecks at four hundred warships and many transports. (Delphi later took credit for its divine advice "to pray to the winds.")

When the storm at last abated—after the magi had cast their magic spells upon the winds and prayed to Thetis and all her Nereids—only then could their fleet continue past Cape Sepias (about September 15, 480), while the Greeks were sending thank-prayers to Poseidon the Savior. (One land-bound Greek, who lived along that shore and was renowned for his misfortunes, scavenged the gold and silver cups and other valuable goods cast up on the shore and thus became a wealthy man.)

So soon as Eurybiades, the Spartan commander, had been told of the signal lit by the one surviving ship and, in addition, had heard an estimate of just how many Persian ships there were, he had retreated through the Oreus Channel into the Euripus to avoid, as he feared, his ships being overwhelmed by the magnitude of the Persian fleet in the waters off Artemisium. But then he heard the welcome news of the wreck of the Persian fleet and resumed his position at Artemisium, with the erroneous expectation, perhaps, that only remnants from a shattered fleet remained. Instead, upon his return, he witnessed a sizable enemy fleet go cruising past him to Aphetae, where the Persians' warships anchored. (The transports stopped in the Gulf of Pagasae.)

Fifteen Persian captains misunderstood exactly where they were to anchor; they thought that the ships of the Greeks were theirs, and there they sailed. When the Greeks observed the detachment of Persian ships approaching them, they attacked, captured them all, and sent the captives south to raise the morale of the council of Greeks at the Isthmus of Corinth. The Persian command, despite the wreckage caused by the storm and the modest enemy victory, still expected the Greeks to sail away—and some of the allied leaders, in truth, did recommend retreat—but Themistocles, the Athenian leader, and Eurybiades, the Spartan commander, prevailed. Of course, the rumors flew— these *were* Greeks—that Themistocles had accepted a bribe from the men of Euboea to remain and he had shared a part of it with Eurybiades, but, bribe or not, Eurybiades could hardly abandon his king, Leonidas, to be flanked, surrounded, annihilated. And where would the fleet be better off or more able to fight?

Xerxes ordered two hundred ships to slip through the Sciathos Channel, proceed along the eastern shore of Euboea, round the southern end of the island past Carystus, then continue up the Euripus strait, and trap not only Eurybiades at Artemisium, but also Leonidas at Thermopylae. The Persian detachment set out early on the 17th, intending to reach its objective at the end of the 18th. Xerxes delayed an attack by his fleet until the trap had closed. In the meantime, he ordered his troops to assault the Spartan army.

A famous swimmer and diver in Xerxes's fleet—a Greek, that is—deserted the fleet and dove in the water at Aphetai, so the story goes, and only surfaced again when he reached the Greek position a mile away. (Since the modern underwater record is 380 feet, one may have one's doubts—Herodotus, rather, believed that his dive was made from a boat come close to the Greeks at Artemisium.) Still, he brought the message to the Greeks that a Persian fleet was sailing around Euboea, and this news convinced the Greeks to engage the Persians, even though the day was passing into evening, and, primarily, to test the Persians' understanding of modern naval tactics. Were the enemy crews familiar with the *diekplous*—the tactic in which the attacking ships, precisely at the critical moment of a bow-to-bow collision, veered slightly, pulled in their oars, and ran down the side of the enemy ship, close enough to shatter its oars and throw about the oarsmen before turning and ramming whichever enemy ship was hopelessly damaged or had not been able to turn in time to meet the new attack?

When the Persians saw the (relatively) tiny number of triremes approaching their lines, they mocked the crazy Greeks, lifted anchor, and rowed out to meet them. They expected to win by employing their usual tactics, to ram them, bow to bow, and board them—they carried thirty Persian marines on every ship—and, after boarding, to butcher the crews and capture the ships. Their expectation appeared sound, given their advantage in numbers of ships, the ships' solid construction and their superior handling. About one-half of the Persian ships were crewed by Phoenicians and half by Ionian Greeks, who, mostly, were quite loyal to the Persian king. Some Ionians sympathized with Athens—they all accepted the truth that their principal foe was Athens—and some did sympathize with the Greek ideals of freedom, but others were eager to win a reward from the king for being the first to seize an Athenian ship.

As the Persians began to encircle the Greeks, the Greeks maneuvered to form what appeared to the Persians to be a defensive half-circle, to keep the Persian fleet from outflanking them, while, in fact, they wanted to give the Persians time to disperse; and then, when the moment was right, they issued the signal, charged through the gaps between the enemy triremes, smashed their oars and crushed the oarsmen, cleared the line, and turned to ram the targets of opportunity. First to capture an enemy ship (and receive the prize of valor) was an Athenian. All in all, the allies captured thirty Persian ships before the fall of night brought an end to the battle. The Greeks returned to Artemisium and the Persians to Aphetae, there to muse upon a battle quite unlike the battle they had planned. Nonetheless, Persian losses had not been insupportable, nor did any suspicion linger that their subjects, the Ionians, were disloyal: only a single Ionian ship had deserted.

That night, although it wasn't yet winter, the fleets were struck by a storm with heavy, continuous rain and blasts of thunder and lightning. The winds whipped up the waves and carried the corpses and wreckage from the site of the battle to Aphetae, where they became entangled on the beaks and the steering oars of the ships. The Persians were terrified. They believed that some demon had directed the storm at them, one more calamity in a series of calamities—the storm off Pelion, the naval battle, and now this thunderstorm, the heavy rain, and the turbulent sea. (This storm, like all such storms, according to Greeks, had come from Zeus, because Zeus was the god of thunder and lightning, and Greeks said not "*it* is raining," but "*Zeus* is raining." If Zeus opposed them, what chance did they have?) Still, however frightful the storm had been at Aphetae, there the ships had been at anchor. The storm, which struck Euboea, was catastrophic—the whole of the Persian fleet, as it rounded the island, was dashed upon the rocky shore and destroyed.

The weather on the next day dawned fair, and both Persians and Greeks were relieved. The Greeks received a reinforcement of fifty-three Athenian triremes, and with the triremes came the welcome news that the Persian detachment rounding Euboea had been annihilated. Later that day the Greeks attacked, destroyed a contingent of ships from Cilicia, returned to Artemisium, and beached. The Persian commanders were furious that a much smaller fleet had defeated them. Xerxes, they knew, would be furious, unless they could, somehow, retrieve the disaster. So, about midday—while Greeks and

Persians were engaged at Thermopylae—the Persians took their fleet to sea to force a battle.

As the enemy ships came on in battle formation, the Greeks lay quiet at Artemisium, until the Persian fleet had extended its line to form a crescent, once again to attempt to encircle the Greeks. As before, the allies waited, and when they thought the moment was right, they launched their ships. The fleets were approximately equal in fighting ability, because, while the Persian fleet was larger, it lost this advantage through a lack of coordination, due to the Persian commanders' inexperience. Individual ships advanced at different speeds and on different courses and ran afoul of each other. Nonetheless, both sides were eager to fight, and the battle was fierce and hotly contested. By the end of the battle, each fleet had heavily damaged the other—Egyptian ships had captured five of the allied ships and their crews—but the Greeks had inflicted slightly greater damage on the Persians. One Athenian stood out above the rest for his zeal, because he himself had paid the construction costs of his trireme and the salaries of his two hundred-man crew.

Due to favorable currents, the Greeks recovered their own wreckage, and some of the enemy's. (Centuries later, a man could dig in the sand and find a layer of ash where the unsalvageable ships and the dead had been burned.) The Greeks had gained an edge, but when they beached and examined their ships and assessed their situation, they reached the conclusion, despite their narrow victory and a reason for optimism about engagements to come, they would have to repair and refit their ships before they could fight another battle. For the moment, they rounded up the famous Euboean cattle ("Euboea" means "Good-Cattle Country"), relaxed, and threw a party on the beach, but the party ended when a triaconter arrived from Thermopylae with the dismal news that Leonidas had fallen and the pass to Greece was open.

The allies boarded their ships and, with heavy hearts, sailed south.

CHAPTER SIXTEEN

"Brave Sons of Greece, Advance!"

Themistocles led the fastest ships on ahead through the Oreus Channel and the Euripus; he stopped at every watering place and cut a message into the stone, "Ionians! Do not fight against your forefathers to enslave Greece. Come over to us! . . ."

The Athenians had already planned to send the fighting men, the elderly, and their treasury to Salamis and the women and children into the Peloponnesus; now they carried out their plans. They called upon the gods to protect the city and land, while the treasurers themselves and the priests decided to remain on the Acropolis and, as literalists, depend upon the protection of an actual wooden wall. "All the other Athenians and the resident-foreigners who are in the prime of life will embark on the two hundred ships ready to defend against the barbarian on behalf of the freedom of themselves and all other Greeks including the Spartans, the Corinthians, and the Aeginetans and any others willing to run the risk."

Each ship was to be commanded by a trierarch, crewed by men under fifty years of age with a complement of ten marines between twenty and thirty years of age and four archers. The names of the crew members allotted to each ship were posted on white boards under the name of the trierarch and the trireme. (Three triremes were *Phosphoros*, *Parthenos*, and *Tritogenes*.) The generals were directed to make sacrifices to "Zeus the All-Powerful, Athena, Nike, and Poseidon the Protector."

The advancing Persians punished the Greeks who had resisted and welcomed those who had medized. They occupied Athens, looted and destroyed the temples, and murdered the Athenians who had remained behind. The Persian fleet drew up on the beach in the harbor at Phalerum (while the Greek allies were at Salamis). Xerxes might well have rejoiced that his objectives were now half accomplished.

The Greeks met in council at Salamis and supported Eurybiades's initial decision to pull the fleet back from Salamis to defend the Isthmus (where the Spartans supervised the construction of a wall), but Themistocles, in private, threatened to withdraw the whole Athenian fleet and sail off to the west to found a new city. His was not an idle threat—the Delphic oracle had advised the Athenians to do exactly that and it was practicable, because the hardest step had already been completed, the packing up and removal of the people from Attica. The threat worked. Without the Athenian ships, the remaining fleet had no chance, and Eurybiades agreed to remain at Salamis, but the other Greek commanders demanded another council, and the arguments continued far into the night, until the council received some shocking news, verified by two separate informants: the Persians had sent ships to the west of Salamis and the Greek fleet was trapped.

What the council did not know was that Themistocles had sent one of his slaves to deliver a message to Xerxes, a message that was a mixture of truth, half-truth, and outright lie . . . that the council was divided (true), that they were hesitant to fight (half-true), that they wanted to withdraw (half-true), and that they would withdraw that very night (the lie). Xerxes's commanders had been advising him to fight, except for Artemisia, the tyrant of Halicarnassus, who was advising him to wait, because the Greeks would not be able to sustain their position at Salamis and would soon withdraw to defend the Peloponnesus and their separate cities. At that point in the discussion, Themistocles's messenger arrived and his message convinced Xerxes, because the king, from his experience with Greeks so far, expected that some Greeks would betray the rest and the Greek alliance would collapse.

He acted immediately, sent a third of his fleet behind Salamis to prevent the Greeks' escape, and ordered the rest of the fleet to block the main entrance that night. At first light, Xerxes took a seat on a throne where he had a clear view of the action—he rather thought that his fleet at Artemisium had not performed well because he had not kept his eye on them. And he had four hundred hand-picked Persians stationed on the island of Psyttalia ("Parrot") to assist the fleet by rescuing any Persian cast ashore or by killing any Greek.

An eyewitness account (of a sort) exists—Aeschylus, the great tragic writer, was there and he wrote a tragedy, *Persians,* told from the Persians' point of view. (Aeschylus is hard to translate, partly because of his archaic language, but more because he could put into a couple of words an experience most Athenians understood, but which is completely unfamiliar to us—for instance, the "dissonant consonance" of the advancing fleet's oars, that is, the rhythmic striking of the oars of each single ship on the water and the dissonant sound of the oars of different ships striking the water at different times.) What follows—unless otherwise noted—are the accounts of Aeschylus amplified by the *Histories* of Herodotus (who was able to interview veterans of Salamis). A Persian speaks,

"Our [Ionian and Phoenician] crews ate their dinner and got themselves in order; the rowers bound a thong around each oar, and, when the sunlight faded, every man was at his oar, every man at arms, and man encouraged man and rowed the triremes to their appointed stations. All night the captains kept their crews awake, but the Greeks did not set sail secretly, and, when the dazzling chariot of the sun began to cross the sky, a songlike, happy tumult sounded from the Greeks, and echoed from the island rocks. We were afraid, for we had not expected this, and they, as though they never intended to flee, chanted a solemn paean, and rushed to battle. At once we heard the dissonant consonance of oars striking the water and soon we saw them all. First the right wing and next the whole fleet advancing and we heard a great concerted cry,

"'Greek sons, advance. Free your fathers' land, free your children, your wives, the sanctuaries of your paternal gods, the grave sites of your ancestors. Now the struggle is joined. All is at stake.'

"The Greeks backed water until it appeared that they might run aground. The Phoenicians were drawn up opposite the Athenians, on the western wing, the Spartans and the Ionians on the eastern wing toward the Piraeus. A few of the Ionians followed the advice of Themistocles (and held themselves back), but most did not. Some say that a figure of a woman appeared and with a voice heard by all shouted, 'Cowards, how far do you want to retreat?'

"A Greek ship charged and sheared off the entire stern of a Phoenician vessel. Each captain drove his ship straight against some other ship. Triremes struck their bronze beaks together. At first the stream of Persian arms held its own, but when the mass of our ships had been crowded in the narrows and none could render another aid and each smashed its bronze beak against another of its own line and shattered their whole array of oars, then the Greek triremes recognized their chance, hemmed us in and battered us on every side.

"The hulls of our vessels rolled over and the sea was hidden from our sight, so thick were the wrecks and slaughtered men. The shores and reefs were covered with our dead and the foe kept striking and hacking our men in the water with broken oars and fragments of wrecked ships."

"Most of the enemy ships [writes Herodotus] destroyed at Salamis were destroyed by the Athenians and the Aeginetans, because they were more skillful in naval warfare and they held themselves in line and at the proper interval. The barbarians did not keep any order and fought as individual ships. Therefore, the outcome of the battle could not have been in any doubt, but, nonetheless, the barbarians proved themselves far abler than they had at Artemisium. Everyone did his utmost out of fear of Xerxes, since every one of them believed that Xerxes was watching him personally.

"As for the others, no one can give much of a description of what they did, but Artemisia conducted herself very well and her reputation with the king rose even more. As the king's fleet began to fall into difficulties, Artemisia's ship was pursued by an Athenian ship. She couldn't escape, because other, friendly ships, were in her way and her ship was the Athenian's nearest target. She saved herself from the pursuing Athenian ship by ramming a barbarian ship. It was a Calyndian ship and the king of Calynda was on board. She rammed it and put it out of action and she profited from this trick doubly. The ship pursuing her, seeing her ram an enemy ship, believed she was an ally or, perhaps, a former enemy who had turned to help the Greeks and he broke off pursuit and attacked another ship. [The Greeks had put a bounty on Artemisia of ten thousand drachmas.]

"So Artemisia escaped, but her trick had another consequence, that Xerxes held her in even more esteem, because he believed that she had rammed an enemy Greek ship, when one of his staff pointed her ship out to him and said, 'Lord, look how cleverly Artemisia fights. She has rammed an enemy ship and put it out of action.' Artemisia's ship was easily recognized and she was lucky that there were no survivors from the ship she had rammed to denounce her.

"Xerxes declared, 'My men have become women and my women men!'

"Xerxes's brother was killed in this battle and many other Persian nobles. The brother, Ariamnes, commanded a particularly large ship from which his marines threw javelins and shot arrows down on the Greeks (as though he were in a fort on land), but an Athenian ship rammed his ship head on, the two ships were stuck fast, Ariamnes led a boarding party, and the Athenians ran him through with spears and tossed his body overboard. Artemisia recognized the body as it was drifting in the water, picked it up, and brought it to Xerxes.

"Very few Greeks, except for those who had been killed in the hand-to-hand combat, died, because they knew how to swim, and, when their ships went under, they swam to Salamis. Most of the barbarians drowned, because they did not know how to swim. As soon as the front line of the enemy turned to flight, the second line was put out of commission, because they pressed forward and crashed into those who were retreating."

As the battle was proceeding some Phoenicians appeared before the king and accused the Ionians of cowardice—or treason—and blamed them for the loss of the battle.

"As they were speaking, a Samothracian ship rammed an Athenian. The Athenian foundered, but an Aeginetan ship, fighting nearby, rammed the Samothracian ship and put it out of action, except that the two ships were stuck together and the Samothracians boarded the Aeginetan ship and took it and manned the very ship that had destroyed theirs."

When Xerxes witnessed this, he had the Phoenicians' heads cut off, as "cowards slandering brave men."

During the course of the battle, Aristides on Salamis—he had had his ostracism suspended—noticed the Persians on Psyttalia and used auxiliary ships to transport hoplites to the island where they slaughtered the Persians, as Xerxes, helpless, watched. The Persian fleet broke and fled. The Greeks recovered their damaged ships and the Persian wreckage. Perhaps two hundred Persian ships had been lost, the best built of the Persian fleet with the most aggressive captains, and also with them six thousand elite Persian marines. So much of the wreckage of the battle washed up on one part of the Attic shore (called Colias) that the women there used oars as firewood.

And then, as Aeschylus writes, "Groans and shrieks together filled the open sea until night hid the scene."

The Greeks had won a great victory, an absolutely indispensable victory, and yet to them, at that moment, the victory did not seem so decisive. The Persian army was constructing a mole from the mainland to Salamis and the Persian fleet was being refitted, as though to renew the battle. The Greeks got themselves ready to fight again, and then, to their surprise, the Persian fleet was gone. The Spartan commander, Eurybiades, followed slowly, suspecting a trap, but he soon learned that the Persians really had withdrawn. Nonetheless, Eurybiades rejected Themistocles's risky suggestion that the fleet sail to the Hellespont and destroy the Persian bridges; instead, he led it back into winter quarters. (Themistocles, according to one version, never intended to destroy the bridge, but only proposed it to frighten Xerxes and convince him to beat a hasty retreat.)

Eurybiades invited Themistocles to accompany him to Sparta to be honored there, and, when Themistocles, after his visit, was ready to depart, the Spartans gave him a carriage and an escort by the royal bodyguard to the Laconian border. The Spartans thought more highly of Themistocles than of any other Greek, because he had been the architect of the victory that had saved Sparta. Other Greeks were less enthusiastic. Timocreon, a poet from Rhodes, wrote some verses about Themistocles, which included the words *liar, cheat,* and *traitor.*

The Athenians, too, had become less enthused with him—they did not even elect him one of the ten generals for the following year. He reacted to that by saying he was like the plane tree: during a storm Athenians took shelter under it, but when the weather was fine, they plucked its leaves and cut off its branches. (Nor was Athenian history kind to him. The place where he dedicated a statue to commemorate his victories became the place where the Athenian executioners cast out the bodies of the executed.) Rightly or wrongly, the Athenians blamed him for the destruction of Athens, and they thought that his stratagem to draw the Persians into battle was a bit too clever—yes, he was the hero of the day, but if the Greeks had lost, their whole fleet would have been destroyed, and Themistocles would still have been the hero of the day . . . to Xerxes.

CHAPTER SEVENTEEN

"Lead the Army"

Xerxes, at the head of his army and accompanied by his fleet, retreated north through Thessaly. There he left Mardonius with a sizable army, and continued on, escorted by Artabazus with "sixty thousand" cavalry, through Macedonia and Thrace to the Hellespont in forty-five days. A storm had destroyed the bridges—he ordered them rebuilt—and the fleet ferried the army across. He assigned Artabazus to put down a rebellion by the cities of Chalcidice, but the cities managed to hold out through the winter, until Artabazus had to abandon the operations and join Mardonius for the spring campaign.

In the Spring of 479, the Spartan king, Leotychidas, assumed command of a fleet of 110 Peloponnesian and Aeginetan ships and took up station at Delos. The Persian fleet, comprising about three hundred Ionian and Phoenician ships, took up station at Samos, and the two sides waited to see what the other would do. Leotychidas was all too aware how heavily outnumbered he was, but the three new Persian fleet commanders were just as aware that their fleet had been defeated in a major sea battle; now they had to wonder how well their ships would fight and whether they could trust their Greek crews.

The Athenians held their fleet at Salamis, protecting themselves and waiting to see what the Spartan army would do. The Persians had withdrawn from Attica, and some Athenians visited their land and even began cultivation. The Greek League had reached a critical moment—how would the Athenians react if the "Greeks" chose to remain behind the Isthmus fortification. Mardonius sent the king of Macedonia, Alexandros, a friend of the Athenians, to present an offer: if the Athenians accepted Persian suzerainty, the Persians would not only allow the Athenians to recover their land and rebuild with Persian help, they could also live under whatever political system they wanted, and the Persians would appoint them, as a city, to become the satrap of a new satrapy of Greece. However, Mardonius also added threats to his offer, "Your seaborne chunks of wood have defeated men who know nothing about rowing, but now you will be fighting on a broad plain against the world's bravest infantry and cavalry."

When the Athenian envoys visited Sparta one last time and bluntly told the Spartan magistrates (the ephors) that if the Spartans did not go north and fight Mardonius, the Athenians would have to do what was in their own best interests, the ephors replied, "Well, you had better hurry on your way then, if you want to catch up with our army." The Spartans were on the march north to confront the Persians with an army of five thousand Spartiates, five thousand free Laconians, thirty-five thousand helots, and their Peloponnesian allies.

Mardonius, who had advanced into Attica, now withdrew to the Asopus River in Boeotia near Plataea. The Greek army was commanded by Pausanias, the nephew of Leonidas and regent for his infant son. He advanced to the Asopus River, and there the two armies occupied positions with the river between them, while their soothsayers predicted that the first side to attack would lose.

Meanwhile, the Athenian fleet under the command of Xanthippus joined Leotychidas at Delos. (The two men became close friends, a friendship they passed on to their descendants, Pericles, the democratic leader of Athens, and Archidamus, the king of Sparta.) Leotychidas received envoys from Samos, who assured him that the Samians were ready to rise against Persia and so were most Ionians, but the passage to Samos—forty kilometers of open water— was not without risk. Leotychidas hesitated until the envoy, when asked, said that his name was Hegestratos ("Lead the Army"). Leotychidas declared, "I accept the omen," and agreed to the expedition. The fleet arrived safely at the west end of Samos, formed a line, and offered battle to the Persians. The Persians emerged, sure enough, but then, to the surprise of the Greek commanders, they sailed away into the gulf by Mt. Mycale.

The Persian commanders had lost all confidence in their Ionian crews, and they no longer had any Phoenician ships, because, at some point, Xerxes had ordered the Phoenician division of the fleet to return home. We cannot blame the crews for their low morale. What can possibly be more terrifying than rowing on the lowest tiers, unable to see outside, with noise and confusion all around—will a ram suddenly smash into the side of your ship, water rush in, everyone, trapped in the ship, fighting to get out, and those who do escape to the open sea, run down, speared, or drowned? They had not won a single battle. They had heard the screams of the dying. Their morale was abysmal

The Persian commanders decided to beach their ships, build a stockade around them, and retreat into a fortification, defended by a contingent of troops sent south from Sardis as a reinforcement. Leotychidas skirted the shore while heralds shouted out instructions to the Ionian Greeks to rise and fight for their freedom.

The Persian commanders were convinced, even if the Ionians weren't, and they disarmed some of the Ionians and dismissed others. They strengthened their fortifications, but the Greeks landed anyway. At first, the Greeks on the beach hesitated, but then they found a herald's staff and a rumor—true enough, as it turned out—spread that the Greeks at Plataea had won a great victory.

(At Plataea, in a series of misunderstandings and blunders on both sides, the Greek force had split and retreated and was attacked separately by the medizing Thebans and the Persian infantry and cavalry, but the Athenians defeated the Thebans and the Spartans defeated the Persians and killed Mardonius. The Persian survivors were exterminated on their retreat north.)

The Athenians and allies, fired up by the rumor, made a frontal assault on the fortifications, while the Spartans took a flanking route to attack the Persians from the rear. When it was obvious that the Persians were losing, their Greek allies rose against them. Then the Spartan force arrived and cut off their retreat. Persian soldiers scattered into the mountains, where they were hunted down and killed. The victorious Greeks burned the Persian ships—perhaps they did not entirely trust the Ionians to crew them—and Leotychidas returned to Samos.

Leotychidas accepted Samos, Chios, Lesbos, and lesser islands into the Greek alliance; drove out the tyrant of Miletus; and then brought the fleet to the Hellespont, intending to break down the newly rebuilt bridge, but storms had already broken it. The victors now deliberated on their future course of action. Unwilling to spend a winter in the north, Leotychidas led the Peloponnesians home, but Xanthippus kept the Athenian contingent there and lay siege to the satrap, Artaÿctes, in his headquarters at Cardia. Xanthippus pushed the siege on and on until he had starved the Persians to the point that they abandoned Cardia and retreated. He pursued them, cornered them, and defeated them near Aegospotami. Xanthippus then took Cardia and found therein cables of linen and papyrus (for the Hellespontine bridges), which he transported back to Athens as a prize.

In the next year, after victories at Byzantium and Sestos, which netted a large number of Persian prisoners, the new Athenian leader Cimon offered the Greek allies the choice of the material possessions of the Persian prisoners or their (naked) persons. The Greeks chose the material and thought that Cimon was a fool, but in the end, at a time when the Athenians were struggling to pay the expenses of their naval operations, his prisoners fetched a ransom large enough to maintain the Athenian fleet for four months and still have something left over.

The great battles had been fought and won, and the Greeks erected monuments to commemorate the victors. Each city commissioned memorials, the Spartans for Thermopylae and Plataea, the Athenians for Salamis and Plataea;

and the Athenians also created three annual occasions when they would celebrate Marathon, Salamis, and Plataea. They commemorated both the exploits of Athenians fighting for themselves and, in a larger sense, as Greeks, fighting for Greek freedom.

In 472, Aeschylus produced his play *Persians* for an audience who, from their seats, could look beyond the stage to the waters where the battle of Salamis had been fought. The great memorial poet Simonides summed up the Athenian achievement best in one line: "In their ships they saved all Greece from slavery."

The war continued, but in 467 BCE, Cimon led an Athenian fleet to the Eurymedon River, the Persians rowed upriver to escape him, but he caught them and forced them to turn and fight. He routed the Persian fleet, captured two hundred ships, and then he landed his hoplites and attacked and routed the Persian army. Cimon had initiated the battle, because he knew a reinforcement of eighty Phoenician ships was on the way; after the victory of the Eurymedon, he intercepted the Phoenicians and destroyed their fleet. His victory was so complete that the Persians, either by royal fiat or the caution of experience, never entered the Aegean again.

Xerxes remained in Persia, until he was assassinated in 465. He should have been succeeded by the crown prince, his son Darius, but Darius was assassinated by his brother, Artaxerxes, and Artaxerxes became king.

PART 4

The Peloponnesian Wars

Illustration 9. The Kerameikos vase. An amphibious assault. (Adapted and redrawn by Alfred S. Bradford)

CHAPTER EIGHTEEN

Yoke Mates

Sparta and Athens, working together "like a pair of oxen under one yoke," had defeated Persia and kept Greece free. Fifty years later they fought a war with such catastrophic consequences that a Greek writer called the leaders of this period "the murderers of Greece." How had things gone so wrong? The root cause of the war, the great Athenian historian Thucydides wrote, was the growth of Athenian power and the fear it engendered in the Spartans.

It all began so innocuously. In 478, the Athenians were asked by the islanders, as "fellow Ionians," to assume the leadership of the sea alliance, and the Athenians agreed. They established the Delian League—based on Delos, the most sacred island of the Ionians—as an equal partnership between Athens as one partner and all the league members combined as the other. The Athenians determined how much each member had to contribute in ships and men or, if a state preferred not to supply ships or men, how much money they would need to pay to build the required ships and pay their (Athenian) crews. Athens's proposal to assume the risks of service at sea tempted many Aegean states, as they failed to understand that they were paying for their own eventual subjugation. In addition, the Athenians required that every Aegean state without exception had to join and contribute and that none, once in, could leave. Athens received a first payment of 460 talents, which was sufficient to put forty-six fully-equipped and crewed triremes to sea for the eight-month sailing season.

By the year 465, the Delian League had become, for all intents and purposes, the Athenian empire. In the same year, Sparta suffered a devastating earthquake. The Spartans sent an appeal to the Athenians to help them, the Athenians came immediately to their assistance, and then were dismissed so abruptly that they considered their dismissal a hostile act. They ostracized the man (Cimon, the son of Miltiades) who had persuaded them to help, and they concluded that the Spartans had become as dangerous to them as the

Persians, or rather, more so, because the Spartans could march an army to the walls of Athens and put Athens under siege. Therefore, Pericles, the new democratic leader in Athens, transformed Athens into an island by building the "Long Walls"—the Athenians called them "The Legs"—that connected Athens with its port, the Piraeus, and rendered Athens invulnerable to a siege, so long as it held command of the sea.

Pericles defined the primary objective of the Athenians (as it had been of the Minoans and is of all naval powers) to maintain their own superiority at sea and to eliminate potential rivals. (Supposedly, after Salamis, Themistocles had told the Athenians that he had a plan to ensure their own supremacy, but that it had to be kept secret and they might not approve. The Athenians told him to discuss it with Aristides (nicknamed "the Just"), and if Aristides agreed, they would do it. Aristides said that nothing could be more profitable for Athens and nothing more outrageous—Themistocles had proposed that the Athenians burn the allied Greek fleet.)

To further their control of the sea, the Athenians occupied Naupactus in the Corinthian Gulf, where they could interdict Corinthian trade with the west. They fought and defeated a Peloponnesian fleet (which made the Peloponnesians wary of challenging the Athenians at sea), captured seventy ships in a battle with the Aeginetans, and thus, once and for all, secured control of the Saronic Gulf.

Pericles also understood a basic reality of the power struggle in Greece; if the Athenians could defeat the Spartans in just one land battle, the Spartans would be finished. Pericles brought Sparta's enemies together into an alliance, but it fell apart the moment it faced the Spartan army, and Pericles abandoned any further attempts to confront Sparta on land.

At the same time, the Athenians were still at war with Persia. While they were campaigning in Cyprus with two hundred ships, they heard that Egypt had rebelled. They immediately quit Cyprus, sailed to Egypt, and up the Nile to Memphis to support the Egyptian rebels.

The Athenians were paying a high price for this double war. A stele in Athens lists the casualties of one tribe, the Erechtheids, at the end of the first year of the campaign in Egypt (460 or 459 BCE).

"These died in the war in Cyprus, in Egypt, in Phoenicia, in Haliae, Aegina, Megara *in the same year.*"

The list of names includes two generals, a seer, four citizen archers, and 170 others, all from a tribe that had three to four thousand men of military age. This number—and particularly the number of citizen archers—might suggest the loss of a single trireme.

The Athenian campaign in Egypt was disastrous—the whole Athenian (and allied) fleet was captured, and then a reinforcement of fifty more ships was also captured. In the face of such losses, Pericles was forced to reassess his strategy and to limit his objectives. The Athenians reached a peace agreement with Persia in 448 and two years later concluded a thirty-year truce with the Spartans. Both sides, the Athenians and the Spartans, agreed to respect the independence of Delphi, and each side agreed not to attack the other's allies. Neutrals, except for Argos, were free to join either side, and both sides agreed, in principle, to respect the freedom of the seas and to submit all disputes to arbitration.

Pericles and the Athenians, however, remained active and aggressive, although, personally, Pericles was careful of his men's lives. On one expedition he told his crews, "As far as I am concerned, you can live forever." When the peace encouraged the island of Samos to try to leave the league, Pericles, at the head of an expeditionary force of forty-four ships, caught a Samian fleet of seventy ships by surprise and defeated it. With reinforcements from Athens, Chios, and Lesbos, Pericles forced Samos to surrender, confiscated its fleet, and levied a fine sufficient to pay for the cost of the expedition. The Athenians also founded the city of Amphipolis (437/6) on the northern coast of the Aegean, a joint foundation in which the Athenians were a minority, but which, nonetheless, guaranteed their access to the timber and the gold of that region.

The Thirty-Year Truce, which lasted hardly fifteen years, was broken by a combination of three events: first, the Athenians passed the Megarian decree, which barred all traffic between Megara (a Spartan ally) and any port in the Athenian Empire and was a virtual blockade; second, the Athenians lay siege to the city of Potidaea, which was a colony of Corinth, but also a member of the Athenian Empire—the Potidaeans had refused an Athenian order to tear down their seaward wall and allow the Athenian fleet free access to the city; third, the Athenians helped Corcyra, a neutral, in its war against Corinth, an ally of Sparta.

The comic poet Aristophanes had a simpler and more direct explanation of the cause of the war, which may better reflect the opinion of the man on the street: "Some Athenian individuals—not the city, but some lecherous lowlife sots—went to Megara and kidnapped the whore Simaetha, so a few Megarians, all garlicked up, stole two whores from the brothel of Aspasia, and, consequently, her lover, Olympian Pericles, thundered and lightninged and scattered war all over Greece."

There does appear to be some truth to the story that Pericles had a personal grievance toward Megara; and the Spartans, too, seemed to think that the Megarian Decree was the crux of the matter. A Spartan envoy had asked Pericles if he could not disregard the decree, and Pericles had pointed to the bronze plaque inscribed with the decree and had said that it was impossible to rescind it (because *there it is fixed to the wall*). The Spartan, then, had asked him, "Might not the decree be turned with its face to the wall?"

The Athenians had agreed to help Corcyra, even though the decision risked war with Sparta, because they feared that Corinth might win and add the

Corcyraean fleet to its own. (Corinth had a combined fleet of 150 ships, Corcyra a fleet of 110 ships.) The Athenians, also, considered the opportunity to degrade a potential adversary's fleet just too tempting to resist. They sent ten ships with ambiguous orders not to allow Corcyra to lose, but not to provoke a war with Corinth. The battle (an "old-fashioned" battle, Thucydides writes) is described in detail by him as the largest naval battle—almost three hundred ships—up to this time between Greek poleis. (As a rule, Thucydides describes naval tactics in detail, because he knows that his non-Athenian audience would be unfamiliar with complex and sophisticated "modern" maneuvers.)

> They met, when the signals were given to both sides, and fought a sea battle—both sides had many hoplites on their superstructures, many archers, and many javelin-throwers, for they had a certain lack of expertise and they were arranged in the old-fashioned way. The sea battle was hard fought, indeed, but in skill not equal to the effort, because it was rather a land battle fought on water. Once they engaged with each other, they could not easily break free from the ill-disciplined mob of ships, so they fought on ships that were immobile, and they depended rather on the hoplites for victory. They did not maneuver; instead, they relied on heart and muscle. Everywhere in the battle were shouts, noise, and confusion. Whenever the Athenian ships observed the Corcyraeans in trouble, they advanced and threatened the enemy, but they did not engage, for they kept in mind the instructions they had received in Athens.
>
> The right wing of the Corinthians was in the most trouble; the Corcyraeans with twenty ships turned them and pursued them, scattered as they were, to the mainland and rowed right up to their camp, disembarked, and burned the abandoned hulls. Here the Corinthians were defeated and the Corcyraeans were victorious, but, on the left wing, the Corinthians were completely successful. The Athenians hesitated and held back at first, but then, seeing that the Corcyraeans were being defeated, they engaged directly with the Corinthians and fought them.

The Corinthians rowed through the wreckage and killed the enemy in the water—and some of their own, because they did not realize that their right wing had been defeated—and then, toward evening, they withdrew to re-form and renew the attack. They were advancing again into battle, when they noticed twenty ships approaching from their rear. They suspected, and they were right, that the ships were Athenian. (The Athenians had sent out twenty more ships, because they feared that the original ten might not be enough to save the Corcyraeans.) The Corinthians backed water and returned to their base. The Athenians rowed through the wreckage and floating bodies to join their fellow citizens and the Corcyraeans.

The next day the Corcyraeans and the thirty Athenian ships advanced on the Corinthians. The Corinthians formed a battle line but did not initiate combat. Instead they sent a ship to ask the Athenians what their intentions were. The Athenians told them the Corinthians were free to sail wherever they wished, except against the Corcyraeans, and the Corinthians withdrew.

The Athenians had gained their objective—the Corcyraeans lost seventy ships and the Corinthians thirty ships. The Athenians had also learned that neither Corcyra nor Corinth understood modern naval warfare. On the other hand, they had provoked the Corinthians, and the Corinthians sent envoys to their ally, Sparta, to ask the Spartans to declare war on the Athenians.

CHAPTER NINETEEN

"A Bad Day for Greece"

In 432, the Spartan assembly, at the urging of their allies, agreed that the Athenians had broken the treaty and it voted for war, but Archidamus, their king, posed a question: how would Sparta, a land power without monetary resources, fight against a sea power and the wealthiest state in Greece? The Spartan ephors, who had pressed for the war, had their answer—Archidamus would collect all of their allies, march into Attica, ravage the land until the Athenians gave battle, then defeat them, and dictate peace terms. And so the ephors ordered. But just before actually entering Attica, Archidamus sent one last envoy to Athens. Pericles refused to negotiate and allowed the envoy only one day to leave Attica. As the Spartan departed, he said, "This will be a bad day for Greece."

Unfortunately for the ephors, when the Spartans and their allies invaded Attica in May 431, the Athenians did not come out from behind their walls; and so, after doing some damage to the Attic countryside, the Spartans withdrew. On the Athenian side, Pericles also had a clear strategy, if not a clear objective: the Athenians would stay secure within their walls, relying upon their command of the sea to supply themselves, while their fleet would attack the Peloponnesians wherever they could, until the enemy was so sick of the war that they would agree to terms dictated by the Athenians.

Pericles relied upon a huge reserve of money, over six thousand available talents with a further one thousand talents set aside in an untouchable fund; an annual income of approximately eight hundred talents; a large fleet and, for the security of Athens, a defensive force of one hundred of the very best triremes to be kept always near Athens. However, Pericles's plan had a number of flaws. The first flaw was his failure to understand just how expensive the war would be—one siege (the siege of Potidaea) cost two thousand talents (i.e., two and a half years' income)—and the second flaw was his failure to understand just how tenacious the Peloponnesians would be.

To wage the war the way he wanted required patience and absolute adherence to the principle of the security of Athens, the fleet, and Athenian citizens. He himself, when in command, had always been cautious of Athenian lives. He believed that so long as the Athenians did not undertake overly ambitious campaigns or try to expand their empire or commit some catastrophic error, they could not lose the war. On the other hand, could they win it? What, exactly, did victory mean: . . . breaking up the Peloponnesian League? . . . forcing Sparta to allow Athens a free hand at sea? . . . isolating Sparta? The failure to define the ultimate objective was a third flaw (although Pericles himself may have known exactly what he wanted).

And then, too—the fourth flaw—Pericles could hardly have foretold that a devastating plague would hit Athens in the year 430 and in the next year kill him and leave Athens leaderless. And besides him, by a conservative estimate, it would kill at least a quarter of the population; the plague affected the Athenian troops at Potidaea, men in the prime of life, and killed 25 percent of them. Despite the plague, the Athenians persevered in the siege, and the Potidaeans eventually—after resorting to cannibalism—accepted the surrender terms: to leave their city with the clothes on their backs. Meanwhile, the Spartans, unable to get at the Athenians, lay siege to Plataea and, in the end, in a victory that had absolutely no effect upon the war, accepted the surrender of the defenders and then executed them.

The Athenians sent a fleet of 150 ships to sail around the Peloponnesus and do whatever damage they could. They made a surprise attack upon Methone, a city in Laconia that had not kept its walls in repair, because they never expected to be attacked. Only the quick thinking of a Spartan commander named Brasidas—he just happened to be in the area—saved the city. The Athenians then continued on their way, raiding as they went and retreating when they met a superior force. They expelled the Aeginetans from their island and resettled it with Athenians. (Pericles had called Aegina the "eyesore of the Piraeus.") They raided the territory of Megara in the Isthmus. They improved their defenses, demonstrated to their enemies how much harm they could do, and made a show of force to confirm the loyalty of their subjects.

The Athenians sent their general Phormio with twenty ships into the Gulf of Corinth to support operations there, where an ally was under attack. Phormio encountered a Corinthian fleet of forty-seven ships, which had been trying to cross the Gulf before first light, and he prepared to attack them. The Corinthians were nonplused, because they just did not think that the Athenians would dare to attack a fleet more than twice their size. Phormio, however, estimated that the Corinthians' fear of the Athenians, their inexperience, and their ignorance of the dawn winds and currents, would work to the Athenians' favor.

The Corinthians circled their ships, with the prows outward, and stationed their five swiftest ships in the middle to go to the help of any ship in trouble.

By forming a circle, they expected that they could prevent the Athenians from using their favorite tactic, the *diekplous*—that is, rowing through an enemy line, turning back on them (before the enemy could turn), and ramming them in the rear or flank.

Phormio ordered his ships to circle (*periplous*—another favorite tactic) the enemy, feigning attacks here and there, but holding off until he gave the signal. As he expected, the enemy backed water away from the feigned attacks; the currents and the winds drove them together; and in the confusion, while they pulled their oars in and tried to fend each other off, all the while yelling and cursing at each other, Phormio attacked. The Athenians sank every ship they encountered, pursued the rest, and captured twelve.

(Thucydides's term for "sink" is *kataduo*, which means something like "dunk with extreme prejudice." Triremes didn't sink to the bottom—they were constructed of the lightest wood available—but sank just far enough to drown the two lower tiers of oarsmen; since we don't use triremes, English does not have a congenial term for "sink to the waterline.")

When the Spartans heard about this defeat, they were convinced that the Corinthian commanders were either incompetent fools or cowards; they replaced them and increased the size of the fleet to seventy-six ships, so many ships, they thought, that the Athenians' twenty ships would be overwhelmed by sheer numbers. The new commanders tried to raise morale by telling their troops that Peloponnesians were by nature braver than Athenians, and, yes, the Athenians might have better technique, but that was not going to help them in the next battle. On the other side, Phormio pointed out how far superior in skill the Athenians were to their enemies at sea and how much their enemies feared the Athenians' "reckless audacity"—to attack at any time, under any circumstances, against any number.

The Peloponnesian fleet set out from its base at Rhion and rowed, four abreast, up the Gulf of Corinth in a feint at Naupactus to force the Athenians to respond. The Athenians rowed along in single file, close to the shore, parallel to the head of the enemy fleet. Suddenly the Peloponnesian ships turned and charged the Athenians. The first eleven Athenian ships rowed fast enough to escape, with the Peloponnesians in hot pursuit. The other nine ships were cut off and fled toward the shore. Some of the crews dove off the ships and swam for it, some were captured (and subsequently executed), some beached their ships near a unit of allied hoplites, who beat off the attackers.

The eleven Athenian ships that had escaped rowed into the harbor of Naupactus; ten of them drew up by the shore, prows outward, ready to fight, but the last of the ships, pursued closely by one of the enemy, entered the harbor, executed a 360° swing around a merchantman anchored in the middle, rammed the enemy in the side, and put it out of action. The rest of the Peloponnesian ships, which had entered the harbor in no particular formation, were thrown into confusion by the Athenians' unexpected maneuver. The ships in front tried to use their oars to brake, so they could wait for the rest of their detachment to catch up; but when they lost way, the Athenian ships attacked, sank some, captured others, routed them all, pursued them, and then attacked the main fleet (still sixty-some ships!), routed it, and recaptured those of their own ships that were being towed off. The battle of Rhion, its outcome so totally unexpected, convinced the Peloponnesians that no matter how the odds were stacked, they could not beat the Athenians at sea, and from then on, they did not try.

The Spartans' response to Athenian naval operations was to invade Attica and do as much damage as they could, but they suspended these operations while the plague was raging, so they sought some other way to hurt the Athenians. They came up with an imaginative plan—to make a surprise attack on the Piraeus, the main port of Athens. They slipped oarsmen, each carrying his oar and thong across the Isthmus of Corinth to Megara and there manned forty ships—which, admittedly were in poor condition because they had been kept in dry dock—and set out to raid the Piraeus.

At this point, the raiding party was overcome with second thoughts; they lost all confidence in the enterprise; and so, instead of the planned coup, they landed on Salamis, assaulted a fort, and ravaged the land. As soon as the Athenians heard about the attack, they put together a force, crossed to Salamis, and drove the Peloponnesians back to Megara. Afterwards, having been heartily scared by what might have happened, they fortified the Piraeus against future attacks. They were lucky—the Peloponnesians could have done a lot of damage in the Piraeus, although probably not enough to affect the outcome of the war—for that they would have had to have brought an army—but certainly enough to seriously embarrass the Athenians.

No incident illustrates the difference between the Athenians and their enemies better. The Athenians never missed an opportunity to be aggressive and were willing to take huge chances in naval engagements—Phormio attacked and defeated a fleet twice his size and then engaged (and defeated) a fleet almost four times his size. Every raid they carried out was chancy. Just being at sea was chancy. On the other hand, when the Peloponnesians put to sea, these ordinarily brave men lost their nerve. The Athenians had become as formidable on water as the Spartans were on land.

About this time, an Athenian known as the "Old Oligarch" composed an essay on the Athenian political system and the nature of sea power. The Old Oligarch despised the democracy and the common people, but he wrote, "Let me say first, that the poor and the mass of people justly have more power than the well-born and the rich, because the people propel the ships and make the city powerful—the *kubernetai* (helmsmen), *keleustai* (boatswains), *pentekont-archoi* (commanders of fifty), *proratai* (lookouts), *naupegoi* (ship-wrights)—these, more than the hoplites and the well-born have brought power to the city."

The Athenians row and steer and learn all sorts of nautical terms, because the empire necessitates their going to sea.

For land powers it is possible for small cities to band together and fight. For sea powers, being islanders they are unable to band together, for the sea intercedes and the Athenians rule the sea. And, even if they could gather together on one island, they would die of starvation. As for the many mainland cities, which are allies of the Athenians, the largest are ruled by fear, the small entirely by necessity, for there is no city anywhere that does not rely on imports and exports. And they cannot import or export, unless the rulers of the sea permit them to.

The rulers of the sea can ravage the territory of the powerful; they can sail to a point where there are no defenders or very few, and, if the enemy arrive, they re-embark and sail away. Moreover, those who rule the sea can sail wherever they please; those on land, when they leave their home country, require a multi-day march. Progress is slow and rations insufficient for a long march. And they must either march through friendly territory or fight to secure their way. Those who control the seas may go wherever they are stronger or continue sailing until they come to a friendly state or an inferior one. And when crops fail, as Zeus wills, those on land are in trouble, but sea powers bear that easily for not every place has disease and sea powers can import from the healthy places.

At sea the Athenians were having things their own way, but at home the death of Pericles had thrown their internal affairs into turmoil. One faction leader, Nicias, represented the landowners, most of whom wanted peace, while the faction that had been led by Pericles was leaderless. Into that void stepped Cleon; he was, according to his enemies, a "Paphlagonian" (i.e., someone who spits while he talks); a walking cesspit of body odor; and, worst of all, a demagogue, trotting back and forth on the rostrum, waving his arms in the air, slapping his leg, and ranting about the necessity of waging war, all for his own political advantage—the Athenian assembly loved it. Cleon first appears when he proposed that the survivors of a failed rebellion in Mitylene (on the island of Lesbos) all be killed or sold into slavery. The assembly had approved and dispatched a trireme to give the order, but then the Athenians went home, slept on it, and changed their minds.

Cleon spoke against the new measure—it was, he said, more merciful for the Athenians to kill them all now. Why? Because if they did not, other subject states, thinking that nothing bad would happen to them if they rebelled, would rebel, and then the Athenians would have to kill many more. The Athenians, however, voted, not to kill all the men, but *only* to kill one thousand, confiscate all property, and force the survivors to pay rent on what once had been their own land. They dispatched a trireme, which rowed continually, the men eating at their oars, and arrived just as the original order was being read.

As the war went on, each side desperately sought a winning strategy. The Athenians, when they discovered just how expensive the war was, doubled the amount of tribute their subjects had to pay; and in 425, they sent a fleet to seek allies and, more importantly, to raise money in Sicily—where, they believed, everyone ate every meal off solid gold plates. At the last moment, they decided to include their best general, Demosthenes (with a small force); they ordered him, if he saw a chance to hurt the Spartans, to take it.

The fleet put in near Pylos on the west coast of Messenia; and there, suddenly, Demosthenes realized if the Athenians built and manned a fort, it would open a way for the Messenian helots to escape from their masters and drain the power of the Spartans like a festering wound. The generals, however, were impatient to be on their way, and they did not want to commit the time and manpower to constructing a fort. Then, fortuitously, a storm blew up and kept them there; the Athenian crew members were bored; they knew what Demosthenes had proposed; they thought it was a good idea, and on their own, and with great effort, they set about building the fort. (The great advantage of the Athenian democracy was that the soldiers and sailors knew what the orders were, they felt a part of the operation, and they were willing to express an opinion and act on it.)

When the fort—and the storm—was finished, the fleet continued on its way, leaving Demosthenes with five ships and his small detachment. The Spartans, foolishly unconcerned—the "very best enemies the Athenians could have had"—took their time in mustering a force and attacking Demosthenes by land and sea. The assault failed—Brasidas, who commanded the assault from the sea, was badly wounded as he jumped from his ship, and lost his shield—and so, for ill-considered reasons and no discernible objective, the Spartans landed a unit of 440 Lacedaemonians (part elite, full citizens—the Spartiates—and part not) on the island of Sphacteria, and Demosthenes quickly realized that the Athenians had an opportunity for a coup that could change the course of the war.

He sent a ship to recall the fleet, the fleet commanders recognized the opportunity to strike a substantial blow at Sparta, and they returned. They drove the Spartan fleet into the harbor and up on shore, took stations around the island, and marooned the Spartans. The Spartans on the mainland were caught completely by surprise and were so shocked that they proposed a truce to begin negotiations for peace terms. As a condition of the truce, they were required to hand their ships over to the Athenians (until the truce was concluded) and not to remove their unit from Sphacteria nor to supply it with more than one-day's rations.

The Spartans were willing to concede almost anything, even a separate peace without the consent of their allies—which would have fractured the Peloponnesian League—but Cleon killed any possibility of an accord by saying, "If they are so eager to make peace now, how much more eager will they be when we capture their soldiers?" (Cleon did not specify exactly what further conditions the Athenians wanted.) The Athenians declared that the truce was over and (of course) kept the Spartan ships.

Nicias was chosen to take out reinforcements—the season for sailing was almost past—and Cleon announced in the assembly that if he had been chosen commander, he could guarantee that he would capture the Spartans within a month. Nicias offered to withdraw from the command, Cleon said *no, the people have spoken,* but the people spoke again . . . loudly, "Sail! Sail!" He did sail, and everyone was delighted, Thucydides tells us, because something good was bound to happen: either Cleon would fail and the Athenians would be rid of him or he would succeed and the Athenians would win a significant victory.

After Cleon had arrived at Sphacteria, an accidental fire cleared the island of its concealing brush, Demosthenes could see where the Spartans were, and he made a surprise landing that resulted in the Spartans, after taking heavy casualties, surrendering—292 Lacedaemonians surrendered, of whom 120 were Spartiates. Greeks were shocked by the Spartan surrender—they thought Spartans were incapable of surrender—and confidence in Sparta was shaken. The Athenians' fort at Pylos attracted thousands of helots. The Athenians trained and armed some of them as hoplites and had them man the fort and conduct raids into Messenia. The Athenians also threatened to execute their Spartan prisoners if the Spartans invaded Attica.

The Athenians had won this victory, and they were victorious everywhere, because of their total command of the sea. Nicias with a force of sixty ships and two thousand hoplites (and some cavalry) seized the island of Cythera off the southern coast of Laconia and from there raided up and down Laconia. The Spartans were helpless against these sudden raids; their morale plummeted, for obvious reasons but also because they believed that they were suffering divine retribution for unjustly beginning the war—they had refused arbitration—and they had no idea what to do.

One extraordinary Spartan leader, however, Brasidas, understood the reality that underlay the Athenian empire: Athens held its subjects by force. The Spartans did not have much of a navy, but they did have magnificent infantry, and Brasidas, who had led two notable actions so far in the war, now proposed that the Spartans send him with a small army to march the length of Greece (700 kilometers), up to the Athenians' northernmost subjects and free them. The Spartans so obviously believed that such an expedition had little chance that they hardly supported him at all—they allowed him to recruit helots to train as hoplites and gave him enough money to hire a couple of thousand mercenaries from the Peloponnesus.

Notwithstanding this slender support and the distance he had to march, Brasidas reached Chalcidice and detached some subject cities, the most important of which was Amphipolis. His dash and his personality (he spoke "pretty well for a Spartan," Thucydides writes), as well as his persuasive claim that the Spartans only wanted all Greeks to be free, won over the northern Greeks. The Athenian general charged with defending Amphipolis failed to act quickly enough and was condemned to death by the Athenian assembly guided by Cleon. The general was Thucydides.

The Athenians immediately sent Cleon in command of a sizable force to retake the rebellious cities and, in particular, to retake Amphipolis. Cleon had every advantage—he had total control of the sea, he was fully supplied, and he also had an important ally, the king of Macedonia. Cleon decided to wait for the king before he undertook any operations, but as the time stretched on, the disadvantages of commanding a democratic army were revealed.

The Athenian troops grumbled about hanging around with no action, and they grumbled about the dilatory and perhaps even cowardly Cleon compared to the decisive and heroic Brasidas, until Cleon, fearing for his political future, decided to make a show of force by marching up to Amphipolis and then marching back down again. His show of force, however, disintegrated under a surprise attack by Brasidas. The Athenians broke and ran and Cleon was killed, as was Brasidas. Both sides had their vulnerabilities revealed, both had suffered, and under the guidance of the Athenian Nicias and the Spartan king Agis, both were ready to consider peace.

CHAPTER TWENTY

The Strong Do What They Want

The resulting peace (in 421 BCE)—the "peace of Nicias"—was, to say the least, uneasy. The Athenians believed that the Spartans, who, according to the Athenians, "thought one thing and said another," had no intention of living up to the terms of the peace, while the new leader of Cleon's faction, Alcibiades, the nephew of Pericles, played upon Athenian suspicions and adopted active hostility to Sparta as a campaign platform. Alcibiades was the aristocrats' aristocrat. On one side of his family he traced his ancestry back to Ajax and on the other to the founder of the most prestigious—and most suspect—clan in Athens, Alcmaeon. His father had fought well at Artemisium in a ship paid for by himself. And Alcibiades was handsome, healthy, and wealthy, if not quite wise, although he mixed in the intellectual circles of Socrates. He had been a young man during the plague, and he had learned the lesson of the plague, as Thucydides characterized it, to satisfy all his desires without fear of consequences—his chief desire was political power.

During the peace, the Athenians retook most of the places that had gone over to Brasidas, they executed the adult males, and sold the rest of the populations into slavery, but, try as they might, they could not recover Amphipolis. (Recovering Amphipolis became a central tenet of their foreign policy for the next century.) In accordance with the treaty, they returned their Spartan prisoners and withdrew from Cythera and from Pylos, all while Alcibiades sought to win over Sparta's dissatisfied allies within the Peloponnesus. Particularly dissatisfied were the Corinthians, because they had suffered considerably in the war and had got nothing for it—the Athenians still controlled Naupactus (and, therefore, the Gulf of Corinth), and they still controlled the Saronic Gulf (and, therefore, access to the Aegean). The Spartans' allies had lost confidence in Sparta, because of their uninspired leadership in the war and the debacle at Pylos, and some defected from its system of alliances and joined an alliance headed by Athens and a newly assertive Argos.

The Spartans were forced to fight a battle in 418 at Mantinea against Alcibiades's Peloponnesian allies. If the Spartans had lost, that would have been the end for them, but even though their king, Agis, mismanaged the battle, they routed Alcibiades's coalition and completely restored their reputation. Their victory, however, did not discourage Alcibiades; he developed another scheme to fire the imagination of the Athenians.

In the meantime, the Athenians in 416 sent an expedition of some forty ships with about three thousand heavy infantry to force the tiny, insignificant, and neutral island of Melos to join the Athenian empire as a "tribute-paying ally." In the course of a pseudo-tragic dialogue (written by Thucydides) between the Athenians and the Melians, the Athenians lay bare their philosophy of empire, justice, the gods, and the kind of power derived from their command of the sea.

"Justice in this world," the envoys said, "only exists between equals—otherwise the strong do what they want and the weak suffer." The Athenians have more to fear, they said, from their subjects than they do from the Spartans. The moment the Athenians show weakness, their subjects will revolt—and Athens would certainly appear weak if it allowed Melos to remain neutral. The Athenians derided the Melians' faith in "prophecies and oracles, which destroy people." In the end, the Melians refused the Athenian demand, the Athenians took Melos, and, by Alcibiades's decree, executed the men and sold the women and children into slavery. Thucydides concludes his account of Melos and then immediately begins his account of the Sicilian expedition (which, likewise, would end in vain hope and misplaced faith in prophecies).

The Athenians had been asked by envoys from the Sicilian city of Egesta to help them against their rival Selinus, an ally of Syracuse. The Athenians were warned by the envoys that without Athenian intervention, Syracuse would gain control of the whole island and then help its mother city, Corinth, against Athens. Furthermore, the Athenians would not have to pay a single drachma, because the envoys would provide sixty talents of silver now, that is, one month's pay for sixty ships, with the promise to pay for the whole cost of the expedition. Alcibiades proposed that the Athenians accept and use this request as a pretext to attack and conquer Syracuse. He, and the Athenians, had an exaggerated estimate of their own power and a very poor idea of how large Sicily was and how great a war it would be. They had also forgotten Pericles's warning, not to engage in adventures until the Spartans had been defeated. Thereupon, the Athenians voted to send an expedition of sixty ships under the command of Alcibiades, Nicias, and Lamachus (a competent nonpolitical general).

Nicias spoke against the expedition. He warned the Athenian assembly that they were not only leaving enemies behind them, but they were going out and creating new enemies, who previously had had no intention of coming to Greece to fight them. Moreover, Sparta was still a formidable enemy and was just waiting for them to make a mistake. They should hang on to, and secure, the empire they had before trying to add to it. Sicily was both too far away to be governed and too far away to be a threat. Lastly, the Athenians should not form alliances with those who "seek our help but would never help us."

Alcibiades, for his part, had to address the Athenians' perception of his spendthrift and licentious character, and while his activities for the state were good and he was a capable leader, he aroused a suspicion that he wanted to be tyrant. So, first, he spoke about himself, that he had, it is true, used his wealth for himself, but he had also spent it for Athens to increase Athens's reputation abroad. As for Sicily, the Athenians could afford to send a large expedition, because they would still have a powerful fleet at home. Moreover, they needed to remain aggressive, and that meant expanding their empire.

Nicias now realized that the assembly agreed with Alcibiades and that he would not be able to convince his fellow citizens that the expedition was ill-advised and risky. So he tried to scare them by asserting that the expedition would need to be much larger, as they would be fighting against great and powerful cities, far from home, with the consequent supply problems, the inability to communicate for four months of the year, and the necessity of a large infantry force. But rather than discouraging the assembly, his speech increased its enthusiasm for the expedition—a larger force would certainly be secure, see new sights, make new conquests, earn pay, and gain booty. The assembly approved a force of one hundred triremes, five thousand hoplites, and the necessary transport and anything else "the commanders thought necessary."

The preparations went forward, but on the eve of the expedition the Athenians awoke to find that their beloved *herms*, little pillars with a bust of Hermes and a phallus, had been mutilated. What could it mean? Was it a stupid, drunken prank, or was it an aristocratic plot against the democracy? Was it the first step to a coup? Was Alcibiades involved? The Athenians arrested everyone on whom any suspicion fell, threw them all into prison, and were prepared to torture them, until an informer accepted immunity and denounced a specific number, whom the Athenians executed. He did not implicate Alcibiades, but Alcibiades was still suspected, and his political opponents planned to indict him. He asked to be tried before the fleet sailed, so he could be cleared, but his opponents saw a political advantage in letting him go and then recalling him, after the fleet had sailed and carried many of his supporters away.

And so the fleet was prepared, and it was magnificent. Every ship's trierarch competed with the others to make his ship the most beautiful and the fastest. They used high pay and bonuses to attract the best oarsmen. The hop-lites were men in their prime, decked out in their finest equipment. Excitement was in the air.

"The city is filled with the uproar of soldiers, shouting around the trier-arch, distributions of pay, Athena gilded, echoes from the crowded stoas, rations measured out, purchases of wine skins, oar loops, pots, garlic, olives, onions in a bag, wreaths, anchovies, flute girls, fist fights, oars planed in dockyards, oar pins banged out, oar ports drilled, flutes, bosuns, tootlings, and whistlings."

On the day of departure, the whole city saw the fleet off. The trumpet blew, prayers were chanted, hymns sung by all the crews together, libations poured, and then the fleet set out; the triremes raced under oars to be the first to reach the island of Aegina. (Meanwhile the Syracusans, debating whether the Athenians were coming at all, concluded that the rumors of an expedition were false.)

In the summer of 415, the Athenian expedition mustered at Corcyra. The total fleet comprised 134 triremes (and two Rhodian penteconters), of which 100 were Athenian—sixty men-of-war and forty converted troopships—and the remainder from Chios and the other allies; 5,100 hoplites of whom 1,500 were citizens; 700 thete-marines and the rest allied troops, some of them Athenian subjects; plus 500 Argives and 250 Mantineans serving as mercenaries; 480 archers in all, 80 of whom were Cretans; 700 slingers from Rhodes; 120 peltasts from Megara; and one horse transport carrying thirty horses. There were thirty grain ships, which transported the bakers, stonemasons and carpenters, and the tools for making fortifications, accompanied by one hundred boats, and, besides, many other private boats and merchant ships, expecting to profit from the expedition.

The commanders mustered again at Rhegium (on the eastern side of the strait between Italy and Sicily), where they learned a sober truth—no Greek city would receive them nor join their expedition; and, worst of all, Egesta did not have the promised funds. (The Athenians, on their earlier visit, had been totally duped.)

The three commanders now faced a critical decision. Nicias proposed that they settle the war between Egesta and Selinus and then sail home. Alcibiades said that it would be a disgrace, for such a large expedition to return home without doing anything worthwhile, and he proposed that they ask Messana to take them in and that they operate from there to form alliances against Syracuse and Selinus. Lamachus proposed that they attack Syracuse immediately while the Syracusans were most afraid and the Athenian fleet was at its most powerful.

In the end, they compromised, which meant they rejected three plausible courses of action and settled on a fourth that did more harm than good. They seized Catana as a base, made a show of force against Syracuse, and returned to Catana, where they went into winter quarters. About the only notable result of their operation so far was the capture and sale into slavery of a young girl named Lais, who became one of the most famous courtesans in the Greek world.

Upon their return to Catana they found the dispatch boat *Salaminia* waiting to take Alcibiades back to Athens for trial on a charge of sacrilege: thus Athenian politics removed the one general who truly believed in the expedition. Alcibiades jumped ship en route and escaped to Sparta, whereupon he was sentenced to death in absentia. (When he was asked if he did not trust an Athenian jury, he replied that if it was for his life, he would not trust his own mother to distinguish between a black [guilty] and a white [innocent] token.)

During the winter, the Syracusans extended their wall into the plain of Epipolae to improve their defense against a siege, and they sent envoys to Corinth and to Sparta to ask them either to send help or to invade Attica. The Spartans were charmed by Alcibiades, who ingratiated himself by being more Spartan than the Spartans themselves, and they were convinced by his insights into Athenian objectives that the Athenians intended to force the Greeks of Sicily and Italy to join their empire, to make an alliance with Carthage—or conquer it—and to lead the whole in an offensive against the Peloponnesus and Sparta; therefore, if the Spartans did not help the Syracusans, they might soon find themselves overwhelmed. He also advised them to build a fort in Attica at Decelea, occupy it year-round, and keep the Athenians permanently cooped up in their city. He seemed to make sense. and the Spartans appointed a Spartiate—one lone Spartiate—to go to Syracuse and organize its defense.

In the Summer of 414, the Athenians landed suddenly and occupied the plain of Epipolae outside Syracuse. The Syracusan army was slow to react and disorganized; the Athenians defeated it and built a fort in the middle of the plain, the "Circle Fort," from which they extended two walls south toward the harbor and one wall north to close off Epipolae.

Success or failure now depended upon whether the Syracusans could extend counter-walls to prevent the Athenians from completing the circumvallation of the city. The Syracusans' first attempt, a counter-wall below the Circle Fort, failed, and so did their second, in Epipolae. But while they and the Athenians were engaged in that battle, another Syracusan force launched a surprise attack on the Circle Fort. Nicias was still in the fort, because he was ill, and only his quick—and desperate—action, setting fire to the outworks, forced the Syracusans to back away from the blaze and saved the fort. The Syracusan army retreated into the city.

On balance, the Athenian situation was encouraging. On the one hand, they had built and defended the Circle Fort, completed the double walls down to the Great Harbor, brought their fleet into the harbor and within the safety of the walls, and laid out the stones to complete the northern wall and close the siege works around Syracuse. On the other hand, their third general,

Lamachus, had been killed in the fighting, and his death left in sole command the one general who had expressed profound reservations about the campaign and, moreover, was ill.

And then, at this moment when the Syracusans, utterly discouraged, were debating whether to seek terms from the Athenians, their salvation arrived, slipping past the Athenians into the city—the Spartan named Gylippus.

"Thrice Nine Days"

Gylippus infused the Syracusans with hope, drilled the Syracusan army, and led it out to fight the Athenians, who were trying to complete their northern siege wall. The Syracusans were defeated in the first skirmish, but Gylippus immediately assumed the blame: he was at fault, he said, because he had not brought them out into the open, where their cavalry could operate.

"Courage! You are Dorians. You are fighting Ionians and islanders and such riffraff and you are going to defeat them and drive them from your land."

In a second engagement, he maneuvered his forces into the open and his cavalry routed the left wing of the Athenians, the Athenian army abandoned their wall and retreated, and the Syracusans finished their northern counter wall, which precluded the Athenians putting Syracuse under siege and meant, in essence, that the Athenian expedition had failed. By this victory Gylippus convinced the Syracusans that they were superior to the Athenians on land and that they should now man their fleet and challenge the Athenians on the water.

Nicias responded to the defeat at the northern wall by seizing and fortifying the Plemmyrium, a headland at the entrance of the Great Harbor opposite the city. By controlling the Plemmyrium, he could see what the Syracusans were doing, station part of the Athenian fleet there, and more easily intercept the Syracusan fleet at sea. Here, in this secure—or so it seemed—location, he could store Athenian supplies. From here he could put pressure on Syracuse. Nonetheless, Nicias refused to accept that he was in an impossible situation, that he could not attain his objective, and that his first priority should be the safety of the fleet and its citizen crews. Instead, he wrote a letter to the Athenians asking for reinforcements and more money, and, he added, until he received a reply, he would go on the defensive and limit himself to holding his position.

The Athenians, themselves, [Nicias explained] were now more the besieged than the besiegers, their fleet was deteriorating—the ships had to remain in the water all the time—the crews were not what they had been, because they lacked those individuals who inspired the others, morale was low, and . . .

"God knows, you Athenians are not easy to command."

As Aeschylus says (in Aristophanes's *Frogs*), "Once upon a time, oarsmen only knew two words, *barley-bread* and *heave-ho,* but now they talk back to their officers."

In response to the letter, the Athenian assembly voted to send their general, Eurymedon, with ten ships, 150 talents, and the message that more reinforcements were coming under the command of Demosthenes. Eurymedon left immediately, and, after a brief delay, Demosthenes followed, sailing from Athens with sixty-five ships, twelve hundred hoplites, and as much support as he could gather from the subjects and allies. On the other side, the Spartans reinforced Gylippus with one thousand allied and six hundred Lacedaemonian (but not Spartiate) hoplites.

Gylippus already recognized that success at Syracuse would change the whole course of the war, and he launched a coordinated attack upon the Athenians. He landed his full infantry force in secret at night in a position from which they could assault the Athenian forts on the Plemmyrium, and he instructed the two wings of the Syracusan fleet, thirty-five Syracusan triremes on station within the Great Harbor and forty-five in the lesser harbor, to attack the Athenians. The Athenians responded immediately and sent twenty-five ships to fight the Syracusans within the harbor and thirty-five ships to fight the remaining force outside the harbor. The fleets met at the mouth of the Great Harbor and fought an extended battle, half outside the harbor and half within.

Many of the Athenian troops on the Plemmyrium descended to the shore to support their men on the water or simply to watch the action. At that moment Gylippus launched his attack and overran the larger fort without much resistance—the remaining Athenians fled down to the water, boarded a merchant ship, and barely escaped a Syracusan trireme. At this point, the Syracusan fleet out at sea drove the Athenian ships before it and forced its way into the Great Harbor, but then lost its discipline, ship collided with ship, and that fleet was routed by the Athenians. The victorious Athenians turned on the Syracusan ships fighting within the harbor, sank eleven ships, killed the crews of eight, captured the crews of the other three, and towed the damaged ships into their lines. The Athenians lost three ships.

The Athenians were exultant at their naval victory, but then reality sank in. They had won a decisive victory on the water, but they had suffered a much greater defeat in the loss of the Plemmyrium: the enemy had killed or captured many Athenians; they had seized the Athenians' grain supply, and masts and rigging for forty triremes, as well as three beached triremes; they cut off the Athenians' main supply line; and they made the task of securing the harbor much more difficult for the Athenians. The Athenian soldiers and sailors could not quite grasp what had happened—they had won a victory and now they were much worse off than before; this revelation of the ineptitude of their leaders demoralized them, especially when they compared their own leaders to the active and crafty Gylippus. On the other side, the elated Syracusans dispatched ships to the Peloponnesus to carry word of their victory.

During this time, Demosthenes was on his way down the coast of Laconia attacking targets of opportunity; Agis, the Spartan king, had established and manned the Decelean fort for year-round occupancy—twenty thousand Athenian slaves deserted; the Athenians imposed a tax on imports and exports in their empire, to increase their revenues, as they fought two wars, one at home and one in Sicily; and in Sicily most Sicilians joined the fight against the Athenians.

In the Corinthian Gulf, the Corinthians engaged the Athenians at the entrance of the harbor of Naupactus. They figured that their best chance to defeat the Athenians was to deny them the opportunity to maneuver, and, if they strengthened the bows of their ships, they could attack bow-to-bow and win. Even so, the Corinthians lost three ships, the Athenians none (although seven were put out of action). The Corinthians erected a trophy, because (as Thucydides wrote) "any battle that wasn't a defeat they considered a victory."

In Sicily, the Syracusans decided to attack the Athenians by land and sea before Demosthenes could arrive. They lowered their ships' prows and reinforced them with timbers, as the Corinthians had done, to give them an advantage in the confined space of the harbor, where ships, denied the ability to maneuver, would ram each other head-on. In addition, they deployed troops along the shore, so that the Athenians, if they were forced to retreat, would have only the space between their two walls in which to beach their ships.

Again Gylippus employed a stratagem—the Syracusan army advanced on the Circle Fort from two sides. While the Athenians' full attention was on the defense of their fortifications, eighty Syracusan ships entered the harbor. Only at the last moment did the Athenians notice the approach of the Syracusan fleet. Nonetheless, they managed to man seventy-five ships. Both sides advanced and retreated throughout the day, as neither side was willing to commit entirely—the Athenians because they knew that one defeat could finish them; the Syracusans because they suspected that the Athenians were their superiors. Toward evening, the Syracusans withdrew.

The Syracusans remained quiet the next day, but Nicias expected them to renew the battle. He recognized that one of the greatest disadvantages of the Athenian position was that their ships had only a narrow zone of safe retreat within the harbor, so he anchored merchant ships about two hundred feet apart, put hoplites and archers and slingers and other marines on board, and armed the ships with "dolphins." These dolphins were, in effect, heavy weights (originally shaped like a dolphin) suspended from cranes. When an enemy ship came within range, a crane was swung out over the enemy, a dolphin was released, and it plunged straight through the enemy ship. Nicias intended that any Athenian in trouble could back water between the merchant ships—where the Syracusan ships would not dare pursue—recover, and return to the fight.

The Syracusans again initiated battle, and the two sides fought for much of the day, before the Syracusans broke off. The Athenians believed that the Syracusans had had enough, but Gylippus was employing another stratagem. While the Athenians beached their ships and scattered to prepare their meals, the Syracusans had food brought to the shore, so that they could take a quick break, eat, and resume the attack. The Athenians had to rush to man their own ships and put to sea; there the two sides remained, the Syracusans well-fed and content to wait, while the Athenians felt the pinch of hunger. At last, the Athenians decided that they had to attack before they were incapacitated by hunger and exhaustion.

In the ensuing battle, the Syracusans' reinforced bows did considerable damage to the Athenian ships, but another Syracusan innovation did even more damage—small boats sailed between the triremes and attacked the Athenian oarsmen. In the end, the Athenians retreated, safely, because of Nicias's merchant ships and the dolphins, which destroyed a pair of Syracusan ships, that had pursued too closely. And one was captured. Nonetheless, the Athenians lost seven ships.

The Syracusans were jubilant, and then, as they were celebrating, just when victory seemed to be in their grasp, Demosthenes arrived with seventy-three ships, five thousand hoplites, and a considerable force of peltasts, archers, and slingers. His arrival plunged the Syracusans from jubilation to dismay—they had defeated an Athenian army and now another Athenian army just as big had arrived. On the other side, however, Demosthenes was appalled by the number of sick and demoralized soldiers and oarsmen; he believed that they should withdraw immediately.

No, no, Nicias argued: *the Syracusans were close to capitulation—Syracusan informants had told him so—and now, with the reinforcement, victory was within their grasp.* So Demosthenes proposed that that very night they attack the Syracusan counter-wall; and if they took it, and could extend their own wall to complete the encirclement of the city, then they would stay, because they could still succeed. Otherwise they would withdraw. The attack failed.

Demosthenes now argued that the Athenians should withdraw while they still could. Nicias, however, clung to the hope—encouraged by his informants—that, somehow, everything would work out. ("Ah, hope, that deceiver of men," Thucydides had written.) In truth, Nicias knew full well, and admitted, that if he returned to Athens,

"Those who are now complaining the most about being in terrible danger here, when they arrive there, will complain about the opposite, that the generals betrayed them through bribery and they withdrew for that reason."

He would be tried, condemned, and executed. (Perhaps not unjustly—he was, after all, responsible for an extensive string of bad decisions.) Then, Demosthenes argued, if he insisted on staying, the Athenians should withdraw to a secure place in Sicily from which they could continue to put pressure on Syracuse and fight the Syracusans in the open sea, where the Athenians would have room to maneuver.

As Nicias dithered—and he was famous for his dithering—the Syracusans gathered allies and prepared for another attack by land and sea. At that point, finally, when Nicias was prepared to withdraw, a peculiar catastrophe struck—there was an eclipse of the moon (August 27, 413). The soothsayers advised that they take no action for thrice nine days (a lunar month), and Nicias agreed. (By contrast, once, when an eclipse had unsettled the crews of Pericles's ships, he held his cloak up before the eyes of his helmsman and asked him, "Does that frighten you?" The helmsman said, "No," and Pericles then asked him, "Why, then, are you afraid of an eclipse which is just the same, only farther away and involving larger objects?") Nicias, by clinging to superstition and rejecting the science of his day, destroyed Athens's magnificent fleet and its chances in the war.

Nicias was not solely to blame. Everything wrong with the Athenian system and its commander came together in that one unfortunate set of circumstances. Nicias had never favored the expedition and yet had become its sole commander, because Lamachus had been killed in battle and Alcibiades had been recalled to Athens by his political rivals, who put their own political interests ahead of the best interests of Athens. Nicias fell ill, but was not replaced, and he was constrained in his decisions by the knowledge that the Athenian assembly would second-guess him and could very possibly vote to execute him.

The Syracusans advanced into the Great Harbor with seventy-six ships, while their infantry attacked the Athenians' walls. The Athenians rowed out with eighty-six ships. The Athenian commander Eurymedon tried to maneuver within the harbor and was cut off, killed, and his ships were wrecked. The whole fleet fled to shore and only through heroic action by their ground forces were the ships saved. Nonetheless, they lost eighteen ships and barely fended off an attack by a fire ship.

"The Athenians were as low in spirits [Thucydides wrote] as they could be, because the result was totally unexpected, and they all the more repented the expedition. For they had come upon single cities much like themselves, democracies like their own, which had ships and cavalry and were of comparable size, cities they could neither subvert nor overwhelm with force. They had always depended upon their navy, and now it had been defeated, and they didn't know what to do."

The Syracusans were elated with their victory and decided to close off the harbor mouth (about a mile wide), using every sort of ship, chained bow to stern, to trap the whole Athenian fleet.

The crisis had arrived. The Athenians were low on supplies, and their ships were deteriorating. The generals conferred and decided to put everything into one last battle in the harbor, to defeat the Syracusans and break out of the harbor (or, if they failed, to burn the ships and march across land to a safe refuge). They decided to defend only the smallest necessary area and send every ship and every man, willing or not, whom they could spare from the land defense to sea. In this way they manned 110 ships and put archers and peltasts on board each ship, so they could grapple and board the enemy ships. Still, the Athenians were demoralized, and Nicias decided to encourage them with a speech.

"Men! Athenians and allies, the coming battle is the same for all of you because it is about your survival. If we win, we will see our homelands again, so don't be down-hearted. . . ."

After this not-very-inspiring beginning, he then explains that they will be fighting a kind of land battle in the harbor with almost the whole shore in enemy hands, and so they have put archers and peltasts on board "which we would never do in the open sea because their weight would unbalance the ship." He encourages the hoplites to clear the enemy decks "since, at least, we are strong in foot soldiers." And he addresses the allies in words that could hardly have been more patronizing—"you are almost considered to be Athenians, although you are not, and, because you speak our dialect and know our ways, you are admired throughout Greece." He went to each trierarch and begged him to do his best. Nicias's speech was more desperate than inspiring, and everyone knew this was the last throw of the dice. Nicias stayed on shore.

Nicias's dilatory leadership had infected the Athenians and robbed them of their famous characteristic to face a problem, quickly formulate a solution, and immediately act on it. Their plan to grapple the enemy ships was revealed to the enemy, and the enemy had plenty of time for a countermeasure—to stretch leather across their prows to fend off the grapnels.

Gylippus, for his part, also addressed the crews of the Syracusan ships by reminding them of their past victories, and of the Athenians' objective to conquer the whole of Sicily and then the whole of Greece. He suggested that the Athenians, unused to being defeated at sea, were now even more depressed than they needed to be and ready to be defeated again. Here now was their chance to get revenge against their deadliest enemy, who had sailed here to enslave them, their wives, and their children. Now was their chance for vengeance, and "Nothing is sweeter than vengeance."

The Syracusans stationed their infantry along the shore where ships might beach, and they spread their naval forces through the Great Harbor with the intention to attack the Athenian ships from all directions. The Athenians let them take up their positions without interference. With no room to maneuver— there were more than two hundred ships engaged—the battle would simply be courage against courage and will against will. The first Athenian charge carried them to the barrier, but the Athenians had failed to plan what to do if they reached the barrier, they had not brought the necessary tools, and they got bogged down trying to break it apart, while the Syracusans and their allies . . .

. . . bore down on them from all sides—the sea battle was fought not only at the barrier but in the harbor, too, and it was fiercer than the earlier battles. A great deal of zeal was shown by the sailors in rowing wherever their kybernetes ordered.

The steersmen used all their skill against each other and competed with each other. The marines strove, whenever ship struck ship, not to fall short of others. Everyone, wherever he was stationed, wanted to excel. Many ships crashed together in the small space. There were no opportunities for ramming and sailing through an enemy line and turning back on it. Ships were smashing together as one fled, or pursued, and they became ever more tightly packed.

Sometimes when one ship charged another, the deck men fought with javelins, arrows, and slung stones, and, when they grappled, the marines tried to board the other ship. Many times it happened, because of the narrow waters, that they collided with each other, two on one, and many ships were forced together, now to attack, now to defend. Everything had to be done at once. The noise of the collisions made it impossible to hear the keleustes' orders.

There was confusion from the multiple orders and shouts from each of the keleustes calling upon their men for victory: the Athenians shouting to force their way out and to fight for the safe return to their homeland and, now if ever, to fight with all their hearts; and for the Syracusans and their allies, to stop them from escaping and to save their homelands. And the generals on either side, if any saw a ship retreating, called out the name of the trierarch—the Athenians calling out, "Do you prefer this most hostile shore to the open sea?" The Syracusans, "Why are you fleeing from those who are desperate to flee?"

The soldiers on land, watching this battle, were seized by shifting emotions.

"The Athenians were afraid of what was going to happen. If some saw their side winning, they cheered and called upon the gods, not to deprive them of salvation, while others, who saw their side losing, cried out at the sight; they were all transfixed by the spectacle, as they knew their safety depended upon victory."

At last, with shouts and cheers, the Syracusans turned the Athenians and drove them to land. The Athenians landed wherever they could, regardless of whether it was within Athenian lines or not. Some of the Athenian foot soldiers roused themselves to rush to the defense of the men in the ships or the walls, and some were so sunk in despair that they did nothing.

The Athenians were totally demoralized. Demosthenes suggested that since the Athenians still outnumbered the Syracusans in ships, sixty to fifty, they man their ships and try once more to break out. The men absolutely refused. They were exhausted and they were terrified of being trapped in the lower rowing benches with no way of escape, but, even more, they had lost all confidence in their leaders. Demosthenes then proposed that they march out immediately and escape to some friendly place, but Nicias, still filled with hope that some Syracusans would betray the city to him, delayed two days. Then, too late, they left the dead unburied and abandoned the sick and wounded and their ships and much of their equipment and tried to escape. Few did. Demosthenes and Nicias were captured and executed. Their bodies were displayed by the city gate.

The Athenians had violated the main lesson the Old Oligarch had set forth—to attack only where they had overwhelming force and to withdraw in the face of organized resistance—and, even more importantly, they had ignored Pericles's dictum to do nothing to imperil the fleet.

And so the Athenians lost their fleet, the finest fleet in the history of the ancient Mediterranean, the source of their power and prosperity, and the basis of their democracy.

Athens at Bay

When the news reached Athens, the Athenians refused to believe that their whole expedition could have been lost, they were furious with everyone who had promoted the idea, they beat up the soothsayers who had predicted success, they mourned their friends and relatives, and then they got down to the business of continuing the war—raising money, curtailing expenses, and building new ships. They voted to use the one thousand talents, put aside as a reserve at the beginning of the war, to hire crews. They still had an advantage in the power of their "owls," the beloved coins they had never devalued. They could hire rowers for a third of what their enemies had to pay (partly because of confidence in the "owl" and partly because rowing for the enemy was three times as dangerous as rowing for the Athenians).

On the other side, the Spartans, their allies, and many of the Athenians' subjects believed that the war was already won. They expected that the Syracusans would now bring their fleet to join Sparta and fight Athens in the Aegean. Neutral Greeks hastened to join the winning side. The Persians offered Sparta an alliance, if the Spartans would pledge to return to the Persians all the Greek cities that had previously been under Persian rule. The Spartans agreed (in secret). A congress at Corinth set forth a plan to build a fleet with Persian financial support and formulated a strategic plan, but the allies, with no sense of urgency, allowed the Athenians time to recover and prepare.

The first major Athenian subject to revolt was Chios, but many others secretly approached the Spartans and requested help. The initial Spartan attempt to aid Chios was thwarted by the Athenians—the Peloponnesians were still afraid to fight the Athenians at sea, and as soon as they saw an Athenian fleet, they anchored near shore; the Athenians attacked on land and sea and disabled the whole fleet. The Athenians also intercepted a small Peloponnesian fleet returning from Syracuse, sank one ship, and forced the others to flee to Corinth. The Athenians suppressed a revolt in Samos and made Samos their base and, from there, attacked the Chians, defeated them in three battles, forced them back into their city, and then ravaged their land

Then they learned that Miletus had joined Chios in revolt. They immediately sailed to Miletus and defeated the Milesians, but when a fifty-five-ship combined Peloponnesian and Syracusan fleet arrived, the Athenians withdrew. The Athenian commander declared that the Athenians could no longer afford to take chances, although, in hindsight, taking chances was just what the Athenians needed to do, to send a signal through the Aegean that they were still formidable.

All this while, Alcibiades had been actively campaigning for the Spartans at sea, but now an order was sent out from Sparta to execute him. Agis, the Spartan king, hated him, because Alcibiades had seduced his wife (whose name by the way was Timaea, i.e., "Chastity"). In his own defense, Alcibiades said that he wasn't really interested in her, he just wanted his sons to be kings in Sparta. Alcibiades escaped to the satrap, Tissaphernes, and tried to convince him to withdraw his support from the Spartans as, at the same time, he, Alcibiades, appealed to the Athenian fleet in Samos to support him, because he could bring the Persians, or at least the one satrap, to the Athenian side, if the Athenians would dissolve the democracy and establish an oligarchy.

In the first half of 411, the Athenian assembly in desperation—and influenced by a series of murders of the leading supporters of the democracy—voted to replace the democracy with an oligarchy of four hundred, which would recall Alcibiades and thereby (they thought) win Persian support. The government of the four hundred tried in vain to open peace negotiations with Agis at Decelea and also approached the fleet at Samos, which repudiated the new government. These failures discredited that government, and it gave way to the government of the five thousand, which recalled Alcibiades. But in the meantime, the whole of Euboea revolted, and also Rhodes, and the Athenian supply route through the Hellespont was threatened by a Spartan fleet of eighty-six ships, stationed there to interdict supplies flowing to Athens and to force the Athenians to react.

The Athenians sailed to the Hellespont with a fleet of seventy-six ships; both sides wanted to fight—they exercised their crews for five days, checked the fitness of their ships, and then set out to engage each other. The battle (of Cynossema) took place between Abydos and Sestos, where the strong, swift current complicated maneuver. The Spartan fleet was larger, their marines were superior, but the Athenians were far more experienced and skillful in ship-handling. Both sides rowed south, the Spartans along the Asian shore, the Athenians hugging the western, European shore. The Peloponnesians, under the command of Mindaros, tried to overreach the head of the Athenian column, but the Athenian ships outrowed the Spartans, until the point of the Athenian column passed the headland of Cynossema, from where the Athenian commander could no longer see the center of his line, which had fallen into some confusion.

Mindaros ordered his ships to close, grapple the Athenian ships, and board, but the Athenian keleustai avoided the grapnels, outmaneuvered the attackers, and rammed them in the thwarts, though some ships did collide and engage in hand-to-hand combat. The Peloponnesian fleet lost its cohesion as it pursued individual ships and the Athenian commander at the head of the column turned and attacked the enemy coming after him, routed them, then attacked the center, routed it, and captured or destroyed twenty-one enemy ships. They would have destroyed more, but the enemy beached their ships in territory protected by their army. The Athenians lost fifteen ships.

The Athenians were so elated by their victory that they regained their old contempt for Peloponnesian navies and believed that they could recover the whole of their empire. They continued to operate successfully in the Hellespontine region, where they captured a small Peloponnesian fleet. A sizable Peloponnesian fleet sent to the Hellespont was destroyed in a storm off Mt. Athos—only twelve men survived—and a second fleet was driven on shore by the Athenians. (As a measure of just how much more competent the Athenians were than their enemies, Persian or Peloponnesian, Athens never lost a fleet to a storm.)

The Athenians intercepted a detachment of Peloponnesian ships, sailing up the Hellespont to join Mindaros, and drove them into a port, pursued them, and, despite the best efforts of the defenders, grappled the ships, and began to tow them off. Mindaros heard of the situation and brought his fleet of ninety-seven ships from Abydos. The Athenians, although they were outnumbered by twenty ships, prepared to fight.

"The trumpeters blew the signal to attack. The rowers strained at the oars enthusiastically, the keleustai showed their skill. Whenever the triremes went on the attack to ram, the steersmen in the very moment of impact turned their ship so that they met ram to ram. The marines, when they saw their own ships sideways to the enemy, cried out in fear and alarm, as they thought they were going to be killed, and, whenever the steersmen by their experience and skill avoided the attack, the marines shouted approval. The archers fired at a distance and filled the air with arrows; then, as the ships drew closer, the peltasts threw their javelins—they aimed particularly at the enemy steersmen; and, finally, when ships collided, marines fought first with their spears and then they boarded and attacked with their swords. As the victors gave a victory shout and the defeated cried out in despair, the sound of the human voice spread over the whole scene of combat."

They fought until it was almost dark, when, by chance, Alcibiades appeared in the distance with twenty ships, raised a purple flag to identify himself, and the Peloponnesians broke and fled. The Athenians captured ten ships, but a storm made it impossible to do more, and Mindaros got safely away to Abydos.

Over the winter of 411/410, the Athenians divided their Hellespont fleet into three squadrons to carry out separate operations against the rebels in the Aegean. At the beginning of the sailing season they gathered again with the intention of fighting Mindaros (and his ally, the Persian satrap Pharnabazos). The Athenians slipped past Abydos at night so that Mindaros would not know the size of their fleet. Alcibiades, who had assumed the overall leadership, told the troop, "We must fight them on the sea, on land, and in their fortifications," and he announced that the crew of any vessel caught sailing toward the other shore would be put to death. After feeding the crews breakfast, they set out under the cover of a heavy rainstorm to engage the enemy fleet. Alcibiades's detachment sailed past the port and lured out the fleet of Mindaros.

The Athenians pretended to flee and the Peloponnesians pursued as fast as they could with the happy thought that they had already won, but Alcibiades, when he had drawn the enemy away from the city, gave a signal and his triremes, as one, wheeled around, prows to the enemy. The two other Athenian commanders, Thrasyboulos and Theramenes, had already sailed past the city and cut off the enemy's line of retreat. Mindaros's crews, when they saw the number of Athenian ships and realized that they had been cut off, were struck with fear. Mindaros tried to escape to a stretch of the coast controlled by the Persian satrap, Pharnabazos.

Alcibiades pursued vigorously, rammed and put some ships out of action, grappled others, boarded, and seized them in hand-to-hand combat, but most of the enemy ships beached along the coast. Alcibiades attacked them with grapnels and began to drag some out to sea. Pharnabazos reinforced the Peloponnesians there and the ensuing battle was fought with considerable bloodshed, because the Athenians were elated by their victory and eager to fight, even on land, and even against a superior enemy, Peloponnesians reinforced by Pharnabazos. When the Athenian commander Thrasyboulos saw the reinforcements coming to the aid of the enemy, he landed his hoplites and archers and hastened to bring aid to Alcibiades. And he sent a message to the other Athenian commander, Theramenes, to come as quickly as possible.

Mindaros, the commander of the Lacedaemonians, himself, advanced against Alcibiades to prevent his dragging the ships off and he sent a subordinate with part of the Peloponnesians and the mercenary soldiers of Pharnabazos to engage Thrasyboulos. Thrasyboulos's hoplites and archers were able, at first, through their courage to withstand the enemy and kill many, although not a few of his own men were killed. Pharnabazos's mercenaries used their greater numbers to attack the Athenians from all directions. Just as Thrasyboulos's troops were being hard pressed and they had about given up hope, all of a sudden their spirits were revived by the appearance of Theramenes with his own troops and other troops he had gathered. For a long time the battle was fierce, and then, first, the mercenaries of Pharnabazos began to flee, and the cohesiveness of their battle line began to fray, and then finally Clearchos's Peloponnesians, who had stood their ground and inflicted great casualties on the Athenians and had suffered many themselves, were pushed back and fled. Theramenes then brought his troops to Alcibiades, who was in danger.

Mindaros kept his head despite the sudden approach of Theramenes's troops. He split his force of Peloponnesians in two and dispatched half against the approaching Athenians and he kept half. He called on them not to disgrace the reputation of Sparta, especially not in an infantry battle, and he advanced on the troops of Alcibiades at the ships. There he fought heroically and ran every risk in front of his own troops, he killed many of the enemy before he, himself, was killed by Alcibiades's troops in a heroic death worthy of his native land. When he fell, the Peloponnesians and all their allies broke and ran in panicked flight. The Athenians pursued their enemies vigorously until they learned that Pharnabazos was fast approaching with a cavalry force. Then they turned back to the ships and seized the city. They set up two trophies, one for the victory at sea and the other for the land battle. (All their enemies had fled to the camp of Pharnabazos.) The Athenian generals captured all but a few of the enemy ships, many captives, and heaps of loot.

Subsequently, they intercepted a Spartan message, which read (in quaint Laconian dialect), "Logs [the ships] lost, Mindaros gone, soldiers starving, we don't know what to do." With this action the Athenians regained control of the Hellespont and reestablished their reputation. In response, the Spartans offered peace on the basis of the status quo. The Spartan envoy laid out the exact situation to the Athenians in a blunt and realistic appraisal.

"You can farm only a small part of Attica, we the whole of the Peloponnesus. The war has brought Laconians many allies, who once were your allies. The richest king in the whole world is now our paymaster, you are supported by the poorest of the poor. Wherefore our troops eagerly campaign because of the size of their pay, yours, because you have to pay out of your own resources, dodge this misery and expense. And when we fight at sea, we risk only the hulls of ships, while you have many citizens on board your ships and, most importantly, when we lose a battle at sea, we still have the same mastery of the land as before, we still have the Spartan army, but you, if you lose at sea, lose everything."

The Athenians rejected any peace that acknowledged the loss of even a part of their empire. In the light of what was going to happen, it was a tragic decision, but, still, a peace on those terms would not have been a peace at all: the Spartans would have had ample time to rebuild a fleet, and the Athenians certainly would have continued operations against the rebels.

From 409 to 407, the Athenians had effective control of the Aegean. Alcibiades and other Athenian commanders raided Persian territory to raise money, now an absolute necessity for the Athenians, but also a policy that ensured continuing Persian enmity. The Athenians, in general, were on the attack and victorious. They had complete control of the Hellespont (except for Abydos), and they levied a 10 percent tax on all cargo moving through the strait. In 407, Alcibiades returned to Athens. His first act to raise the morale of the Athenians was to lead a procession to Eleusis to participate in the Eleusinian mysteries (in abeyance since the Spartan occupation of Decelea) and to raise fifteen hundred hoplites, one hundred fifty cavalry, and one hundred ships.

At this crucial moment of the war, the Spartans sent out a new naval officer, Lysander, to take command of a new fleet of ninety ships built with Persian money at Ephesus. There he met the younger son of the Persian king, Cyrus, who had been ordered by his father to oversee the war. Lysander and Cyrus hit it off immediately and became friends or, as some would have it, lovers, and Cyrus put his full support behind Lysander and the Spartans.

Alcibiades returned to the fleet and his headquarters at Samos, but in his absence, his second-in-command violated his orders, bungled an operation at sea, and lost twenty-two ships in the Battle of Notium (406). The Athenians withdrew to Samos because of this defeat, and rejected Alcibiades's bid to be re-elected general. (He sailed away in self-imposed exile to his castle in the Chersonese.) The Athenians raised a new fleet, elected a new commander, Conon, and sent him to Samos. He was shocked to find how low the sailors' morale was and decided to raise it by consolidating the fleets and leading a series of small, safe raids, which gave the sailors a chance to enrich themselves with plunder and recover their confidence.

In 406, at the conclusion of Lysander's year in command, the Spartans sent a new commander, Callicratidas, to replace him. Lysander was so elated by his victory at Notium that when he handed over the command to his successor, he boasted that he, Lysander, was the master of the sea. Callicratidas replied, "I will concede that title to you, if, before you hand over the fleet, you will sail it past the Athenians at Samos." Lysander's supporters and friends, including Cyrus, tried to undercut Callicratidas, because, even though he was ready to conduct an aggressive campaign against the Athenians, still he believed that Sparta should reject Persian involvement and reach an accommodation with Athens.

With a fleet more than twice the size of Conon's he sent him a message—"I am going to break up your dalliance with the sea"—cut him off, and forced him to fight his way into the harbor of Mitylene. Conon lost thirty ships in the battle, but their crews escaped to land, and the rest found refuge in the harbor. Conon sank some boats to constrict the entrance and placed merchant ships with large stones hanging from their yardarms, which were to be dropped on the enemy ships trying to enter the harbor. He beat off Callicratidas's first attempt, but Callicratidas succeeded on the second, entered the bay, and put Conon under siege by land and sea. Conon's situation was precarious—his supplies were short and Athens was unaware of his situation.

Conon anchored two triremes in the inner harbor and rotated their crews by night, so they would be fresh. As day after day passed, the enemy grew accustomed to seeing the ships at anchor there, and then, one day, at noon, the crews threw off their anchor ropes and rowed as fast as they could through the enemy and into the open sea. The enemy were taken completely by surprise, but soon set off in pursuit and captured one of the two ships; the other escaped and carried the news to Athens, where the Athenians took immediate action—outfitting and manning as many ships as they could (eventually 150) with all classes of Athenians—foreigners (who were offered citizenship) and slaves (who were offered their freedom, but not citizenship). Callicratidas lifted the siege on the approach of the Athenian fleet.

Both commanders were eager to fight, and both knew that this was going to be a close thing. The weather was stormy, and the soothsayers on both sides read signs that suggested caution. For the Spartan commander, a sacrifice on the seashore, in which the victim's head was covered by the waves, suggested that he would die in the battle. For the Athenians, the commander had a dream in which he played a hero in a tragic performance of the "Seven against Thebes" (during which all the heroes are killed).

The next day, the Spartan admiral drew up his fleet opposite the Athenians, who incorporated the Arginusae Islands into their tactical formation to extend their line and protect their center. The battle of Arginusae was a long, drawn-out affair, in which formations broke into separate melees and individual combats. The Spartan Callicratidas, advised by his second-in-command to break off the battle, instead rammed an Athenian ship and fell overboard, never to be seen again. His death was the turning point of the battle. The Spartans lost seventy ships, the Athenians twenty-two, but the Athenian generals failed to rescue the crews in the water or pick up the dead—corpses and wreckage littered the coast for miles—and, subsequently, were sentenced to death. Ships could, with difficulty, be replaced; crews could not.

The stunning victory of the Athenians proved, nonetheless, the truth of what the Spartan envoy had told them. The Spartans had only lost hulls, the Athenians irreplaceable citizens. In the year 405, the Persians, after the Spartans acceded to requests from Cyrus and the Ionian cities to reappoint Lysander to command the war at sea, rebuilt the fleet. At the end of the summer of 405, Lysander sailed to the Hellespont to interdict the supply ships carrying grain to Athens and to force the Athenians to respond.

In the spring, the Athenians had watched Aristophanes's play *Frogs*, an inspiring, patriotic play that they enjoyed so much that they voted to have it put on again the next day. In the play, which features a contest in the underworld between the great tragic writers Aeschylus and Euripides, they are asked to give the best advice they could to the Athenians; Aeschylus said, *think of the enemy land as your land, and your own land as nothing; your power is your fleet, nothing else matters.* Unfortunately, the Athenian commanders ignored this advice.

Lysander stationed his fleet in Lampsacus, while the Athenians beached their ships roughly opposite by the river Aegospotami. Supposedly, Alcibiades came down from his castle and warned them that they were putting the fleet at risk and should use the port of Sestos as their base. He was mostly right, but to protect their grain fleet and confront Lysander, they would have had to row up the Hellespont against the current every day and then, already tired, prepare to fight a battle.

For four days they rowed out from Aegospotami, offered battle, and for four days Lysander kept his fleet close to port. On the fifth day, when the Athenians had grown accustomed to this routine, they returned to Aegospotami, beached their ships, and set about gathering firewood and supplies. At this moment Lysander attacked and caught them unprepared. This was the battle of Aegospotami, which wasn't a battle at all, only an ignominious end to the Athenian fleet. Conon, alone, got to sea with a small detachment. When he saw that the fleet was lost, he sent one ship to carry the news to Athens, and then he sailed away into the Aegean and became a pirate.

The ship with the tragic news reached the Piraeus, and the news passed from the Piraeus up the Long Walls to Athens; as they heard the news, Athenians wailed in despair. That night they went to their beds with the fearful expectation that they would now suffer what they had caused so many others to suffer. Many of the Spartans' allies wanted to do exactly that, to do to the Athenians what the Athenians had done to others, to execute the men and sell the women and children into slavery, and they could have done it—the history of Athens would have come to an end right then—but the Spartans said *no.*

The Peloponnesian War continues to fascinate us for many reasons: the vivid accounts, a war between a navy and an army, an amateur war with few creative leaders, strategies based on erroneous expectations, and an outcome reached more by blunders than strategy. However, no one should weep for the Athenians. Although they were a democracy at home, they were a tyranny abroad, utterly ruthless, murderous even, and indifferent to the suffering of their subjects.

In the next half-century, the Spartans, liberators of Greece, would become more hated than the Athenians.

Illustration 10. Illustrations 10–17 depict battles at sea, boarding, and the landing of troops. Illustration 10 shows a geometric fragment of a ship battle. (Adapted and redrawn by Alfred S. Bradford)

Illustration 11. Athenian fragment (from a krater) of a sea battle with dead upon the deck. (Adapted and redrawn by Alfred S. Bradford)

Illustration 12. The Dipylon vase. Men straining at the oars. (Adapted and redrawn by Alfred S. Bradford)

Illustration 13. Attic geometric (8th century BCE). Either a boarding battle or a raid. (Adapted and redrawn by Alfred S. Bradford)

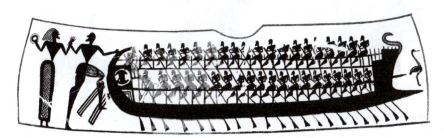

Illustration 14. The Paris and Helen ship (spouted krater from Thebes). The ship is probably not a bireme, but rather reflects the artist's attempt to show both sets of oarsmen. (Adapted and redrawn by Alfred S. Bradford)

Illustration 15. This painting (a krater from Thebes) may be an artist's attempt to depict a penteconter, a long ship packed with oarsmen. (Adapted and redrawn by Alfred S. Bradford)

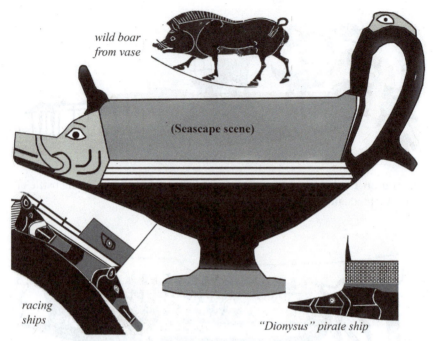

wild boar from vase

(Seascape scene)

racing ships

"Dionysus" pirate ship

Illustration 16. The cup is shaped like a ship with a boar's snout. Compare the ships' prows. A wild boar from a vase painting is included for comparison. (Adapted and redrawn by Alfred S. Bradford)

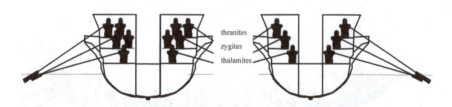

thranites
zygites
thalamites

Illustration 17. The rowing schemes of a quinquereme and a trireme. (Adapted and redrawn by Alfred S. Bradford)

PART 5

The Rise of Superpowers

Illustration 18. Black-figured Hydria. This painting makes clear that boarding was done bow to bow. (Adapted and redrawn by Alfred S. Bradford)

Hanging by a Thread

Dionysius of Syracuse was the quintessential tyrant. If he was not quite Plato's monster who ate his own children, nonetheless, he was one of those whom Plato wished would be skinned, dragged through thorns, and thrown down into Hell—paranoid, power-mad, and avaricious. Worse, he was restless and active. Asked once by a friend if he had some spare time, Dionysius said, "Never." He turned Ortygia (the little peninsula jutting out from Syracuse) into a fortress, where everyone who approached him was body-searched. Once, as a joke at a feast, to demonstrate the risks of tyranny, he suspended a sword by a single horsehair over the head of his friend Damocles, who thought being a tyrant was a sweet deal.

Next to his personal security, his primary objective was to expand the power of Syracuse throughout Sicily and Italy. To that end he convened a conference of military engineers (attracted by lavish pay) to develop new weapons of war. His engineers created all the accoutrements of siege warfare—catapults, towers, battering rams in sheds—and manufactured and tested every type of armor, by one count producing 140,000 shields. This convention of military engineers introduced siege craft to Greeks. (Philip and Alexander, and after them almost all commanders, had a siege train as part of their armies.) And his engineers also developed new kinds of warships.

To the original warship with one bank of oars the Greeks had added a second tier—creating the bireme—and then a third resulting in the trireme, which dominated naval warfare for close to two hundred years and continued to provide significant service to the end of the Roman empire. The logical next step, taken first by the Carthaginians, was the *quadrireme* (in Greek the *tetreres*), not four banks of oars, as the name could imply, but two men to each oar in a two-tier ship. (The limits of human muscle rule out a four—or greater—tiered ship.) The "Four" required a widening of the bireme to accommodate more oarsmen, who provided enough extra power and speed to compensate for the increased drag.

Dionysius's naval engineers applied the concept of the quadrireme to the trireme and created the *quinquereme* (a "Five"), three tiers of oars with two men to the oar at the two upper levels and one at the lowest. The quinquereme was decked, about 160 feet in length, twenty-four feet wide, and nine feet above the waterline. The quinquereme's main disadvantage was that it required three hundred oarsmen (and up to 120 marines).

Dionysius, in preparation for his war against the Carthaginians in Sicily, built a new fleet of triremes (mostly) and quinqueremes, which, added to his old fleet, gave him over three hundred ships. (He also constructed within the Great Harbor 160 ship sheds, each of which could hold two ships.) He manned his ships, half with citizens and half with mercenaries.

All this took money, lots of money, and he sent his soldiers out to collect it from the citizens of Syracuse. The citizens protested volubly that they had nothing, but the soldiers rooted out and confiscated piles of valuables. Once was not enough, and, later, he had the soldiers search again and the citizens protested again. But the third time he sent the soldiers, the citizens just laughed at them; and, then, Dionysius said, "Now I know I have gotten everything there is."

Dionysius Triumphant

In 397, he declared war on the Carthaginians. His first objectives were the Carthaginian strongholds of Eryx and Motya in western Sicily. In all he had eighty thousand infantry, over three thousand cavalry, about two hundred warships with at least thirty-four thousand rowers, and five hundred transport vessels with supplies and siege equipment. His massive armament overwhelmed Eryx, but Motya was a different matter—it was a prosperous city, located on an island connected to the shore by a narrow causeway twelve hundred yards long (which the inhabitants destroyed), it expected aid from the Carthaginians, and it wanted nothing to do with Dionysius.

Dionysius's siege of Motya was the first use of his new siege equipment and his new fleet. He beached his warships at the front of the harbor, anchored his transports beside them, and began to run several moles out to the city. Meanwhile, the Carthaginians made a night-time diversionary raid on the harbor of Syracuse with a fleet of ten triremes, rammed and sank all the ships moored there, and then withdrew. Dionysius ignored the raid and pressed his siege of Motya with all his resources, increasing the size of the mole and pushing his siege engines forward along the mole, as it stretched toward the walls of Motya.

In response, a Carthaginian fleet of one hundred triremes made a surprise attack on the beached fleet; it sank some transports and burned some of the ships on shore, but Dionysius chased it off with his army. The Carthaginian admiral then withdrew to the mouth of the harbor, where he could pounce on any ship trying to escape, but Dionysius had his troops haul his fleet overland, out of the harbor, and launched them into the sea. The Carthaginians destroyed a few of the first into the water, but Dionysius had armed his ships with a multitude of archers and slingers, while, on shore, he drew up his new catapults and employed them against the Carthaginian ships. The Carthaginian admiral was dismayed by this new and unexpected kind of attack and withdrew his fleet.

Now Dionysius finished the mole and began his assault on the city. The inhabitants knew that they were fighting for their lives with no possibility of escape or quarter. The siege dragged on. The Greek troops grew weary of fighting all day, withdrawing at dusk and fighting the next day with no apparent end to the siege in sight, and Dionysius was getting worried about their flagging spirits. So one evening, after this routine had been firmly established, Dionysius had the usual trumpet signal blown for his troops to pull back, at which the enemy relaxed, and an elite Greek force threw up siege ladders on an undefended wall, climbed over, gained a foothold inside the city, and let the rest of the army in. The Greeks poured in, slaughtered the inhabitants, and plundered the whole city. Dionysius was furious at the savagery of his troops, because there is no profit in dead people.

The tyrant left a force of 120 triremes to ambush any Carthaginian fleet attempting to recover Motya, he sent Leptines (his brother) to take the last hostile cities in western Sicily, and he returned to Syracuse.

Carthage Triumphant

The Carthaginians prepared a massive armament—one hundred thousand men, four hundred warships, six hundred transports, four thousand cavalry, and four hundred chariots—under the command of an admiral named Himilco. He fought past the fleet of Leptines and landed his army in western Sicily. In quick succession he recovered Eryx and Motya and then advanced along the northern coast, army and fleet together, to a site not far from Messana. The Messanan army marched out to block his approach, and he used his fleet to leapfrog it, land by the undefended Messana, take it, sell the population into slavery, and then raze it. (It was later rebuilt.)

Meanwhile, Dionysius organized a fleet of 180 ships of war, 60 of which were manned by freed slaves, and "of which only a few were triremes" (i.e., most were Fours or Fives). Dionysius sent his fleet under the command of his brother, Leptines, to engage the Carthaginian fleet while it was separated from its land army—an eruption of Mt. Etna had made it impossible to march along the coast—and Leptines attacked with his thirty quadriremes as soon as he came in sight of the Carthaginians. "And he sank not a few of those drawn up against him, but the Carthaginian forces, far outnumbering him, crowded around his detachment. The courage of the crews of Leptines's ships sustained them, while the number of Carthaginian ships encouraged them.

"Wherefore there was a brisk battle and the helmsmen steered their ships broadside to the shore, because of the risk to them of the soldiers drawn up on shore [if they charged and happened to get too close to shore]. They did not charge from a distance to ram the enemy, but they grappled the ships and fought hand-to-hand. Some of the marines, jumping from ship to ship, fell into the water. Some succeeded in boarding the enemy ships and fought there. But in the end Leptines was overwhelmed and forced to flee to the open sea. The rest of his ships had arrived in no particular order and were defeated piecemeal by the Carthaginians."

The Carthaginians destroyed more than a hundred ships, killed twenty thousand men, and left Dionysius worse off than before his campaign against Motya. Himilco [in 396] sailed into the Great Harbor of Syracuse with a massive fleet of 250 men-of-war and three thousand merchantmen. He built three forts, set up a siege, and plundered the countryside. All Dionysius's allies deserted him, and the tyrant was besieged in his stronghold by a Syracusan mob; an adviser recommended that he flee, but Dionysius pointed out a butcher killing a steer with a single blow and said, "Shall we let the fear of a quick death lose us a long reign?"

Dionysius Triumphant

A plague struck the Carthaginian forces; so many soldiers died so quickly that the survivors were unable to bury them, and, at the depths of their despair, Dionysius, who had plenty of courage, led a concerted attack by land and sea. As the Carthaginians were defending their fortifications from Dionysius's land attack, his fleet attacked their ships and rammed and sank many of them. Himilco begged for terms, and Dionysius offered to let him escape with his fellow citizens for a payment of three hundred talents. Himilco took the deal and abandoned his army. Some enemy soldiers scattered across the countryside, some—the Iberians—told the tyrant that they would fight to the death unless he enlisted them in his own forces as mercenaries, and the rest surrendered on the one condition that their lives be spared. Dionysius sold them into slavery, reconquered and resettled Sicily, and wiped out all the Carthaginian gains.

In this period Plato visited Syracuse and met the tyrant. Dionysius asked him what he was doing in Sicily, and Plato said that he was looking for a virtuous man. Dionysius said, "Well, obviously, you think you have not found one." He was so outraged at Plato's arrogance that he arranged to have him kidnapped on his return to Athens and sold into slavery, with the comment, "Since he is only interested in justice, he can be as just as a slave as he can as a free man."

Dionysius may not have been a philosopher, but he understood human nature as well as anyone of his time. He understood that he was hated, and feared, and the constant object of conspiracies. Once he was approached by a man who told him that he could instruct him in a simple method of detecting conspirators, just by looking at them. When Dionysius took him aside and asked him how, the man said, "Pay me a talent and everyone will believe that I did give you such a method." Dionysius paid him.

Carthage Triumphant

The Carthaginians sent a new general named Mago to take charge of their Sicilian affairs, and he tried a new tactic—generosity—and won over a considerable part of Sicily without fighting. When Dionysius advanced against him, he withdrew into a strongpoint, from which Dionysius could not dislodge him, so the tyrant gave up on Sicily. and between 391–387 attacked the Italian city of Rhegium and, finally, took it after repeated efforts. (He had a particular grievance against Rhegium, because, when he had tried to arrange a marriage there, he had been offered the hangman's daughter. Dionysius already had two wives, whom he had married on the same day at the same time; on the wedding night he concealed which he had visited first, so no one, not even his brides, would know which had priority.)

In 384, in response to an attack on the Greeks by Illyrian pirates, Dionysius campaigned up the Adriatic, destroyed many of the Illyrian small craft, and took a number of prisoners. He also used alleged Etruscan piracy as an excuse to pillage an Etruscan temple, where he took one thousand talents of gold and captured enough prisoners to raise another five hundred talents.

He used money not just to pay his troops and build his military machines, but also to make personal connections. When he saw that his son (Dionysius the Younger) had amassed large quantities of gold and silver, he berated him for not using it to win friends.

Dionysius Triumphant

In 383, having amassed enough money to recruit a large army of mercenaries, Dionysius supported revolts by the Greek cities under Carthaginian control and used the revolts as a pretext for war. Dionysius won a major engagement against the Carthaginians and killed thousands of Carthaginians, including their general, Mago.

Carthage Triumphant

Thereupon the Carthaginians (commanded by Mago's son) won a major engagement and killed thousands of Greeks, including Dionysius's brother, Leptines. Dionysius made peace on the basis of the status quo and a payment of a one thousand-talent indemnity.

Dionysius Triumphant

While the Carthaginians were attempting to restore their position in Sicily and Italy, a plague broke out in Carthage, the Libyans rebelled, and a panic swept the city of Carthage. In 368/7, Dionysius, encouraged by the troubles the Carthaginians found themselves in, mustered a fleet of three hundred triremes and campaigned successfully in western Sicily . . .

Carthage Triumphant

. . . until the Carthaginians unexpectedly arrived with two hundred triremes, caught his fleet in harbor, attacked, and towed off a number of his ships.

A Truce

Exhausted, the two sides agreed to a truce.

Dionysius's Final Triumph

Dionysius, among his other interests, composed tragedies and had a lifelong ambition to have one of his tragedies performed in Athens. Year after year the Athenians rejected his efforts, and even mocked them, but, finally, in the winter of 368/7, he received news that the Athenians had accepted his latest submission. He was so excited, he dropped dead.

Dionysius introduced siege warfare and the quinquereme to the Greek world, but he used them to fill Greater Greece with war to satisfy his own personal ambition. And the result? . . . Civil war in Syracuse, the depopulation of Sicily, and the destruction of cities—not to mention the large numbers of people killed or enslaved amid the general misery of Sicily.

Conon the Athenian

The Long Walls of Athens came down to the sound of flutes while Greeks everywhere celebrated because "now they would be free." The victorious Spartans were so revered that, as Xenophon wrote, "a Spartan anywhere could give an order and it would be carried out." Within ten years, the Spartans would become more hated than the Athenians had ever been.

The Spartans established an oligarchic government in Athens, which came to be called the Thirty Tyrants. The Thirty Tyrants set out to execute everyone they blamed for the war and for the democracy. Their brutality led to a civil war, which the Spartan king, Pausanias (the grandson of the victor of Plataea), let play out—ultimately the Thirty Tyrants were defeated, the Athenians reconciled, and their democracy was restored.

Pausanias believed that the Spartans should withdraw back into the Peloponnesus, resume the kind of life they had led before, and allow Greek cities to settle their own affairs. Lysander, on the other side, proposed taking over the Athenian empire; he prevailed, and for thirty years the Spartans strove to hang on to, and rule, what once they had fought to dissolve.

They had received Persian help by agreeing to surrender all of the Greek cities of the Ionian coast to Persian rule, but the younger son of the Persian king, Cyrus, proposed to the Spartans that if they would help him defeat his brother, Artaxerxes, and gain his father's throne, he would not insist upon their fulfilling the agreement. Cyrus almost succeeded, but in the decisive battle, on the verge of victory, he yelled, "I see the man himself," charged his brother, caught a javelin in the eye, and fell dead.

The Persian king—still king—Artaxerxes, now demanded that the Spartans return the cities they had pledged to return to him. The Spartans refused and for several years fought against the Persians in Asia Minor, until the Persian king sent envoys to Greece with bags of gold coins to see if his "golden archers" (the coins displayed an image of an archer) couldn't work up an alliance against the Spartans. The "archers" succeeded, and for the next twenty-five years the Spartans were at war with different combinations of Greeks (usually led by Thebes).

Artaxerxes had committed five hundred talents to building a fleet, and his satrap Pharnabazos ordered the kings of Cyprus to construct one hundred triremes. Artaxerxes hired a commander for the Greek division of his new navy, and the man he chose was none other than the Athenian Conon. Conon had supported himself as a pirate and a mercenary; he had gained a considerable reputation and had found refuge at the court of a Cyprian king. As commander of the Greek contingent of the Persian fleet, Conon gathered forty triremes and began immediate operations against the Spartan fleet based in Rhodes.

Such was Conon's reputation that when the Spartan king, Agesilaus, was recalled—driven out by "10,000 golden archers," he said—to Greece to support Sparta in its wars against Thebes, he had to march up the coast of Asia Minor, across Thrace, and down through Macedonia and Thessaly to get into Boeotia (where he defeated the Theban army).

Conon convinced the Rhodians to expel the Spartans, which they did—and they profited immediately by capturing an Egyptian fleet laden with supplies for the Spartans. After this coup, Conon went to visit the Persian king in Babylon and promised if the king would furnish the resources, that he would defeat the Spartans. The king agreed and allowed Conon to select any Persian he wished to be his co-commander. Conon chose Pharnabazos.

With their new fleet, Conon and Pharnabazos sailed to Cnidus to engage the Spartan fleet under the command of the Spartan admiral, Pisander. Pisander sailed out from Cnidus (a few days before August 14, 394). He had eighty-five triremes—Conon had ninety—and he was ready to fight, but his allies took one look at the Persian fleet and turned tail. Pisander's ship was rammed and driven on shore, where he died fighting. The rest of the Spartan's fleet fled. Most of the crews jumped overboard and swam for it, but Conon still captured about five hundred men and fifty triremes. The Spartans had held command of the sea for ten years.

Conon convinced Pharnabazos that he could win the Greek cities over, if he presented himself as a liberator and not as a new master, and the two of them drove Spartan commanders and garrisons out of all the cities of the Aegean coast and islands. The expelled Spartans gathered at Abydos and Sestos on the Hellespont.

Pharnabazos and Conon next raided Laconia, seized the island of Cythera as a base, and left an Athenian there as commander. They sailed to the Isthmus of Corinth, addressed a council of Greeks meeting there, and encouraged them with persuasive words and cash to continue their war against Sparta—the Corinthians used the cash to build a fleet to contest Spartan control of the Gulf of Corinth. After this, Pharnabazos wanted to return to

Asia Minor, but agreed to let Conon use the fleet—he said he could support it on his own by contributions—and he proposed to help the Athenians rebuild their Long Walls. Pharnabazos welcomed the proposal and gave Conon extra funds for the project. Conon used his own crews to work on the walls alongside the Athenians.

The Spartans were appalled—they could see Conon undoing everything Sparta had gained in the Peloponnesian War, and they sent an embassy to the Persian king. (So did the Athenians, and Conon was one of their envoys.) They complained to the Persian king that Conon was using Persian money to further Athenian ambitions to recover their empire and that they, the Spartans, wanted peace with the king—they were ready, finally, to hand the Greek cities over to him. Conon argued his side, that he was only bringing war—at the behest of the king—on the Spartans who had brought war on the Persians, but the king imprisoned him, while he determined what to do. (Conon escaped to Cyprus and died there.)

The Athenians, despite the catastrophic defeat in the Peloponnesian War, still possessed the best natural harbor in the Aegean—harbor dues brought them a significant amount of revenue—and Athens, while far poorer than it had been as the center point of an empire, was, nonetheless, prosperous enough, and, in truth, the Athenians were taking advantage of the war between the Spartans and the Persian king to try to regain control of the Aegean.

The commander of the Athenian fleet, Thrasyboulos, installed a democratic government in Rhodes and then sailed to the Hellespont, reconciled the different factions of Thracians there, won over Byzantium by installing a democracy, won Chalcedon, too, and sailed from there to Lesbos, where, at first, only Mytilene favored the Athenians. He collected the four hundred hoplite-marines of the fleet and convinced the Mytilenaeans, and also the exiles from the other cities, to join his army. This army defeated and killed the Spartan commander, routed his troops, and caught and killed many in the pursuit. He won over some of the cities and plundered the rest, but as he continued on his way to Rhodes, he raided Aspendus and was killed. Meanwhile, in the north, the Athenian Iphicrates ambushed the Spartan commander and his staff and killed them.

Closer to home, in the Saronic Gulf, the Athenians were not so successful. The Spartans encouraged the Aeginetans to raid Attica and interdict supplies bound for Athens. After one abortive counterattack, an Athenian fleet drove the Spartans into a harbor, but it was just at sunset, the Athenians moved on, and the Spartan commander kept his crews at their oars; as night fell, he followed the Athenian fleet. He set a light on his ship for the other ships to follow; he had the timekeepers clap their hands rather than call out the time or beat a drum; and, just as the first Athenian ships were entering their harbor, he attacked under the moonlight, caught them completely by surprise, and captured four triremes. Later, the Athenians ambushed the Spartan commanders on Aegina and killed them. The new Spartan commander ran out of money and failed to persuade his crews to serve without pay.

The Spartans replaced their unpersuasive commander on Aegina with an experienced and resourceful commander named Teleutias, who convinced the unpaid men to trust him just once; and so, one evening after dinner, he led out his fleet of twelve triremes toward the Piraeus. They rowed for a stretch and rested and then rowed some more, until he gave them one final break a mile from the Piraeus. Then he ordered them to ram any Athenian warship (and put it out of action) and take loaded transports under tow, and he led his fleet into the harbor. He caught the Athenians completely by surprise and had things his own way until the Athenian cavalry and hoplites could respond. He returned to Aegina with enough money to pay his men's back wages plus a month's advance, as well as feed them from the captured cargoes.

The Athenians were hard-pressed both by the Spartan fleet at Aegina and also by a new fleet of eighty triremes, which blocked the Hellespont; the two adversaries, however, were running out of money. Therefore, when the Spartans, in the name of the Persian king (who preferred the Spartans to the Athenians, if not by much), offered peace, the Athenians were ready to accept it. The conditions of the peace (the Peace of Antalcidas, 387 BCE) were relatively simple: all Greek cities were to be free and autonomous (except, of course, the cities in Laconia and Messenia); the Athenians were allowed to keep the islands of Lemnos, Imbros, and Scyros. Everyone, including the Athenians, now demobilized, and the Athenians gave up any plan to refound their empire . . . for the moment.

From 387 to 382, the Spartans tried (largely successfully) to break up every attempt by Greek cities to form associations for collective security—Mantinea, Elis, the Boeotian League, the Chalcidian League—in the belief that by reducing others they themselves would become stronger. In 382. in a time of peace, they seized the acropolis of Thebes and held Thebes with a garrison until it was liberated in 379. Shortly after the liberation of Thebes, a Spartan commander, again in a time of peace, attempted to seize the Piraeus. He failed dismally, and the Spartans now found themselves at war again not only with Thebes but also with Athens. The Athenians reinforced the defensive measures of the Piraeus, refitted their fleet, and sought naval allies (in addition to Thebes). The Spartans, by their foolish and shortsighted actions, spurred the formation of the Second Athenian Confederacy and of the Boeotian League, both created in response to the Spartan threat.

Spartan strategy was to blockade Athens and Thebes. The Athenians manned a fleet and fought a battle with the Spartans at Naxos in September 376, where the Athenians had interceded in a war between Naxos and Paros. The Spartan commander, Pollis, entered the harbor, and the Athenian commander, Chabrias, met him with his fleet. The Spartans overwhelmed the

Athenians on one wing, but Chabrias, on the other wing, charged the Spartans and drove them off. In all he lost eighteen triremes and destroyed twenty-four. He would have done more, but he stayed in place to collect the survivors in the water and the bodies of the Athenian dead. This was the first major sea battle an Athenian fleet had won since the Peloponnesian War.

Once again, however, the Athenians were running out of money, and they had become as concerned about the increase of Theban power as they were about the Spartans, so in 375, the Athenians offered to make peace with Sparta on the basis of the King's Peace except that the Athenians' second confederacy would be recognized and they were to be acknowledged as co-guarantors of the peace. The Spartans, in reply, began operations at Corcyra to which the Athenians responded by dispatching a fleet under the command of their foremost general, Iphicrates. During the voyage, he demonstrated his own ability but also the new reality that an Athenian commander needed to train and condition Athenian crews before they would be fit to fight an anticipated battle.

Iphicrates left the mainsails on shore and had his crews row all the way around the Peloponnesus. When it was time to beach and prepare a meal, he had the ships race for the shore and the first there got first pick of water and fuel, but all ships had to leave at the same time, so the losers got less time on shore. This led to a competitive spirit in the fleet. The fleet mostly had to beach in enemy territory (in the Peloponnesus), so when they were on shore, he posted scouts and had other men climb to the tops of the masts to watch for enemy ships. He practiced maneuvers while under way and sometimes sailed (with the smaller sails) at night or had one or two tiers of oarsmen row while the others rested.

When he arrived at Corcyra, he discovered that the Spartan operations had been a miserable failure and the Spartans had withdrawn. The Athenians again initiated peace talks with the Spartans (under the aegis of the Persian king), and all parties met in Sparta in 371 and agreed to a general peace except that the Spartans excluded the Thebans and continued the war against them. The Spartans fought the Thebans at the battle of Leuctra (371 BCE), lost the battle, lost their allies, and suffered invasion. Greeks everywhere celebrated the Theban victory, up to the moment when they realized that the Thebans intended to replace the Spartans at the head of the empire. The Athenians, and others, joined the Spartans at the battle of Mantinea in 362 to fight the Thebans. The battle was a draw, which left Greece impoverished, riven with factions, and leaderless.

Three years (359 BCE) after the battle of Mantinea, Philip became king of the Macedonians when his brother was killed in a catastrophic battle with the Illyrians and the Macedonian army was almost wiped out. At the time, Philip seemed to be just another petty Macedonian king, and the Athenians attempted to replace him with their own candidate. Philip trapped their small army and then let them go without conditions (except that they hand over his putative rival). For the next twenty years, he flummoxed and bamboozled the Athenians, as their two leading orators, Aeschines and Demosthenes, argued about what Philip really intended and how they should react to him.

He made an alliance with Athens and, at the same time, attacked and took Potidaea (their possession); then he promised if they would not defend Pydna (an Athenian possession on his coast), he would take it and give them Amphipolis in exchange for Pydna. They agreed and he captured both and kept both. He took advantage of an Athenian war with their allies (which the Athenians lost), and he took advantage of a sacred war, which embroiled the whole of Greece. The Athenians relied upon their navy to wage their off-and-on-again war against him—Philip said that they "waged peace as though it were war." At one point, they listed four hundred ships, but their navy was underfunded, and every campaign began with raids to acquire enough plunder to pay the crews. One general complained that his men, unpaid for two months, had deserted for service as mercenaries in other navies. Relations between Athens and Macedonia deteriorated so profoundly that when Philip offered to give the Athenians an island he had captured from pirates, the Athenians insisted that he state that he was giving it *back*.

Nonetheless, their activities forced him to maintain a fleet to respond to their activities. Although he engaged in no major ship actions, he interdicted grain transports headed for Attica, and he invaded Euboea. In the end, he marched his army down into Boeotia as a jumping-off point for Athens, but the great Athenian orator Demosthenes convinced the Thebans that Philip was as great a threat to them as he was to Athens, and the two formed an alliance that fought Philip at Chaeronea (338 BCE) and lost. Athens had to capitulate and swear an oath to obey Philip and the heirs of his body in a new league designed to fight the Persians. In 336 BCE, Philip was assassinated by a jilted lover, and Philip's son, Alexander, succeeded him.

Giant Men, Giant Ships

Alexander's conquest of the Persian empire was almost exclusively fought on land, because Alexander determined that it would be so. Alexander had a Macedonian fleet of sixty ships and numerous ships from his Greek allies, but he was heavily outnumbered by a Persian fleet of four hundred Phoenician ships, commanded by Memnon of Rhodes (a member of the Persian royal family by marriage). Memnon intended to use the fleet to foment rebellion among the Greeks and thus force Alexander to turn his attention back to Greece and withdraw from the Persian empire.

Alexander ferried his army across the Hellespont in 334, defeated the Persians at the Battle of the Granicus River, and advanced down the coast of Asia Minor without significant resistance until he reached Miletus, where Memnon and his fleet were stationed. Here at Miletus Alexander made a crucial decision about future naval operations. In response to a significant omen— an eagle, the bird of Zeus, had landed on the prow of Alexander's flagship— his second-in-command, Parmenion, urged him to fight the Persians at sea, as the omen was a clear indication that Zeus supported a naval battle.

To the contrary, Alexander replied, the fact that the eagle had landed on his ship while it was beached was rather a sign that he should keep his ships beached. Yes, in theory, if he fought a sea battle and lost, still, his main strength, his army, would not be diminished, but his reputation of invincibility would be. And, win or lose, he would still have to march down the Phoenician coast and occupy the Phoenician cities, and thus, in any case, eliminate the enemy fleet. He was king, his opinion prevailed, and, in the end, his strategy succeeded. He defeated Darius in person, on the battlefield of Issus in 333. Darius fled back to the heart of his empire, and Alexander continued down the coast, accepting the surrender of all the Phoenician cities, until he came to Tyre. The Tyrians refused to capitulate and foolishly antagonized Alexander.

The siege of Tyre is a culmination of the innovations in siege craft introduced to the Greek (and Macedonian) world by Dionysius. Tyre had strong walls, fortified harbors, every sort of defensive machine the ingenuity of man had devised for the destruction of his fellow man, and it lay half a mile (880 yards) off the mainland. Alexander employed the whole labor force of the surrounding area to demolish "Old" Tyre and begin the construction of a mole two hundred feet wide. At first, Tyrian ships sailed up to the work without opposition—Tyre had a fleet of eighty triremes—and the crews shouted out taunts: "Do you expect to defeat Poseidon?" Nonetheless, the work progressed amid ambiguous omens. As the mole came within range of the catapults, a "sea monster" threw itself upon the mole, rested there a brief time, and then heaved itself back into the sea. The Tyrians concluded that Poseidon would destroy the mole, the Macedonians that Poseidon, so to speak, was putting his imprimatur on it.

The Tyrians manned boats with catapults, archers, and slingers, and attacked the laborers on the mole from front and flanks and killed or wounded many of them. Alexander took immediate command of his fleet and rushed to cut the Tyrian boats off from their harbor in a race, which the Tyrians barely won. Now Alexander's naval strategy paid off. The fleets of the other Phoenician cities and Cyprus joined him and were ready to fight the Tyrian fleet. The Tyrians, heavily outnumbered, refused battle and closed off their harbors to prevent Alexander's allies from entering.

When the end of the mole was within artillery range of the city, Alexander pushed out his heavy catapults and began a continuous barrage of stones on the city. The Tyrians doubled the thickness of their walls by building a second wall behind the first and filling the space with rubble. They could not concentrate their countermeasures solely on the portion of their walls abutting the mole, because Alexander sailed around the island with a fleet of triremes lashed together and decked to hold towers and catapults; and, as he was searching for a weak spot to assail, he threatened every spot.

Alexander's catapults knocked down a portion of the wall. The Tyrians defended the opening ferociously with missiles until night fell, and then they rebuilt that section. Meanwhile, the siege towers on the mole approached close enough to the walls to lower their bridges for an assault. The Tyrians threw nets over the attackers and dragged them down to their death; they fixed barbed tridents in the Macedonians' shields and either pulled the soldiers off the towers to fall to their death or forced them to cast aside their shields which exposed them to missiles; they poured superheated sand over the Macedonians; and they fired masses of red hot metal into their ranks. Both sides used axes as well as swords and spears.

At last, when Alexander observed that the Tyrians had weakened, he brought his linked triremes within range of the walls, lowered a bridge from one of the trireme's towers, and personally led the Macedonians across onto the wall. Meanwhile, the Macedonians on the mole broke into the city with their battering rams and rushed forward. The Tyrians continued to fight within the city, but the city had fallen, and they all were either killed or captured and sold into slavery. Alexander had shown to the world that no city, not even a city on an island, could withstand a tenacious siege by land and sea.

Alexander's particular combination of ruthlessness, perseverance, and personal example had accomplished his objective of closing off the Phoenician coast. Only Egypt remained, and the Egyptians hated the Persians and were anticipating his arrival, while the Persians themselves were not prepared to fight. Alexander sent his fleet up the Nile to Memphis at the same time as his army entered from the east; resistance collapsed in the face of the double onslaught.

After he had organized Egypt and rested his army, he advanced on Persia, met and defeated Darius at the battle of Gaugamela, took Persepolis, pursued and caught Darius, and continued on into India (over the course of five years). When he reached the Indus River, he ordered a fleet of triaconters, hemioliai, and horse transports built, partly to construct a bridge over the Indus and partly to ferry his army across. He had the boats dismantled and transported up the Hydaspes River, where he made a surprise crossing against the Indian king, Porus. He defeated Porus (at the battle of the Hydaspes, 326 BCE), and he wanted to follow up his victory by advancing into the interior of India, but he was forced—grudgingly—to accept that his men just would not advance any farther. And after he had recovered from a serious wound, he decided to travel down the Indus River by boat and then, while he himself marched through the Gedrosian Desert, to send an expedition to sail from the mouth of the Indus to the Persian Gulf. In all, his fleet had come to number two thousand vessels.

The voyage was considered so risky that nobody wanted any part of it until Nearchus, his boyhood friend, volunteered to command the expedition and thus reassured the crews—*surely Alexander would not send a friend to certain death*. Indeed, the fleet endured privation of food and water, suffered from contrary winds, and encountered tides with which they were completely unfamiliar. They saw odd sights: strange waterspouts, which turned out to be monstrous whales. Nearchus formed up his fleet in battle line, ordered everyone to give the war cry, and charged. The whales submerged. Another day, for the first time in their lives, the crews saw someone paddling a boat. They were so used to oars that the paddler appeared to be "shoveling the water." They encountered strange, and hostile, people living in inhospitable terrain.

Nearchus was expected to explore the coast, find harbors, watering spots, and sources of food. He found some water, but the local people, the "Fish-Eaters" (so called, Arrian tells us, *because they ate fish*), were unfriendly, and he had to do some fighting along with his exploring. The voyage took eighty days, so long that Alexander was sure that the whole expedition had been lost, and when he first saw Nearchus, he didn't recognize him because of the tolls of privation—half-starved, his skin crusted with salt, and his hair wild and unkempt.

Alexander returned to Babylon and made plans for future communications within his empire. He was always concerned with routes, to India by land and water, to Egypt around Arabia, and, with the exploration and exploitation of the coasts of his empire, by building a string of forts and harbors along the trade routes. He grasped the obvious advantages of communication and transport by sea, but before he could finish that work, he fell ill and died (323 BCE).

Upon the death of Alexander, a board of generals decided to run the empire in the name of the royal family of Philip and Alexander (which culminated in the "reign" of Alexander's son, Alexander IV, until in his early teens he was murdered). These men, the "Successors," argued from the first over who should rule what and who should be included, or excluded, and soon they fell to fighting each other.

When the Athenians learned of the death of Alexander, they prepared for war. They had a substantial amount of money confiscated from the fugitive treasurer of Alexander and access to eight thousand battle-hardened mercenaries quartered at Taenarum. The Athenian assembly voted to build forty quadriremes and two hundred triremes; they mustered and organized citizens for military service on the borders of Attica and abroad; they appointed a man of real ability, Leosthenes, as general; and they sent envoys throughout Greece to remind Greeks of Athens's role in the Persian wars and to persuade them to join an alliance in the common bid to liberate Greece.

When Antipater, the Macedonian regent, heard of the Greek action—they were technically violating their oaths to follow Philip and the heirs of his body, which included the infant Alexander IV—he sent requests for help to two of the Successors and then marched south with an army accompanied by a fleet of 110 triremes. The Greeks, under the command of Leosthenes, defeated Antipater and drove him into the city of Lamia (hence the "Lamian War"). Leosthenes pressed the siege vigorously, but he was killed, and without him the Greeks settled into a passive siege, which dragged on through the winter of 323/2. In the spring one of the Successors brought a Macedonian army to relieve the siege, and Antipater broke out of Lamia. Now the issue of the war hinged on whether the Athenian navy—170 ships—could prevent more reinforcements from reaching him across the Hellespont. It couldn't.

The nature of the ancient warship, its inability to remain at sea and the necessity to beach at night, made it almost impossible for a fleet to maintain a constant position at sea twenty-four hours a day. The Athenians, for instance, in the Peloponnesian War had found it exceptionally difficult to intercept the boats of the helots crossing from the mainland to the island of Sphacteria to supply the Spartan troops there. Later the Carthaginians were unable to intercept the Romans, when they crossed the Straits of Messana to Sicily.

Antipater, with the reinforcements, defeated the Greeks, the alliance broke apart, and the Athenians were left on their own. Their fleet was defeated in two battles around Amorgos, although they were able to recover their ships and tow them all the way back across the Aegean. Nonetheless, with the defeat of the allied army and their own defeat at sea and with the enormous call upon their finances and manpower, the Athenians decided to negotiate peace terms with Antipater, accept a garrison, and undergo a political restructuring, which established a property qualification for citizenship and disenfranchised those Athenians who manned the ships. One hundred-sixty years of Athenian sea power came to an end.

Of all the Successors, the most successful proved to be Ptolemy. He seized Egypt and he and his descendants clung to it through different swings of fortune for almost three hundred years. No others of the first round of Successors established themselves in any segment of Alexander's empire. The most prominent of the first Successors was killed trying to break into Egypt—he was unable to force the line of the Nile. Another—Antipater, a highly respected contemporary of Philip—died of old age. Of the second round of Successors, Antigonus the One-Eyed, a general who had served with Philip and had been sent to campaign inside Asia Minor by Alexander, was the most able, but his first attempt to seize the empire in 318 BCE was momentarily thwarted when his admiral in the Hellespont near Byzantium was defeated, as he tried to force his way into Europe. He lost seventeen ships sunk and forty captured with their crews. The survivors took refuge in Chalcedon. Antigonus then took personal charge, exploited his enemy's assumption that he had been thoroughly defeated, and figured out how to fight a sea battle on land.

That night Antigonus gathered transport vessels from Byzantium and sent across archers, slingers, and a sufficient number of other light-armed troops. Before the break of day they attacked the crews who had disembarked from the enemy ships and who had camped on land and they threw the enemy and their commander into confusion. The panic-stricken enemy tried to board their ships and were further unsettled because their ships were crowded with the supplies and the prisoners they had left on board. Now Antigonus, who had prepared his warships and put many marines on board, set out, and called to them to be of good heart and that the victory was in their hands.

His admiral had already gotten under way at night and, as the day dawned, they fell suddenly upon the enemy ships which were in total confusion and with their first charge they routed them, ramming some of them, breaking the oars of others, while others surrendered, crews and all. This victory they won without risking themselves. They captured the whole fleet except for one ship, used by the commander to flee.

He was caught while trying to escape overland and executed.

In the years 318–306, Antigonus attempted to reunite the whole of Alexander's empire and found himself opposed by every other Successor. Antigonus and his son, Demetrius, assembled a grand fleet and army. In general, the Successors built the largest fleets and the largest ships in the ancient world—they had all the wealth of the Persian empire—and they experimented with larger ships, building even a "sixteen." (We have no idea what it looked like, except that it couldn't have been sixteen tiers high.) This was a golden age for naval engineers—they had the money and resources to build any ships they could conceive and see how they performed.

In the fleet of Ptolemy . . . "among *sixes* and *fives* and undecked ships there was one, an *eight* called *leontophoros*, because of its size. Its size and beauty made it a marvelous sight. Each tier of oarsmen contained one hundred rowers, so that on each side there were eight hundred men at the oars for a total of sixteen hundred oarsmen in all. And there were twelve hundred marines who fought from the deck and there were two kubernetai."

One of the descendants of the first Ptolemy had a "Forty" built. It was more than four hundred feet long, seventy feet above the water; it had four thousand oarsmen, eight to an oar, and 2,850 marines. It had three tiers of oarsmen, and the topmost oars were fifty-seven feet long, too unwieldy for a single man. It was double-hulled, like a catamaran, with ample space between the hulls to ply the oars.

Demetrius set catapults on his ships, which required a deck on which to fix them—his catapults fired a twenty-one-inch bolt with a range of four hundred yards. Soon everyone had adopted ship catapults. They also added towers from which they could pour missiles down on the enemy ships below. These unwieldy ships—the Sixes and larger—were less seaworthy than a trireme and could only fight by boarding, although the Fives still employed a ram. The impetus toward larger ships may have been driven by the increased use of ship-based siege equipment in besieging port cities. Demetrius became the master of such warfare.

Antigonus's first target was Ptolemy. Demetrius had under his command 240 warships: 90 Fours, 10 Fives, 3 Nines, 10 Tens, and over 100 Threes. In his first blow in spring 315, Antigonus drove Ptolemy out of Syria and won control of the whole of the eastern empire. He then turned to Macedonia and instructed his son, Demetrius, to remain on the defensive. As Antigonus was forcing the defensive line in Europe—and Ptolemy seemed intimidated into inaction—Demetrius decided to attack Ptolemy in Egypt. But in 312, Ptolemy unleashed a surprise attack by sea on Demetrius at Gaza, routed him, and thus threatened Antigonus's rear, so that he had to break off his attack in the north and return to save his southern position and his son. He quickly restored the situation, but Ptolemy's coup gave Seleucus, another of the second round of Successors (and friend of Alexander), the chance to establish control over the eastern part of Alexander's empire. Eventually, Antigonus had to accept that he had lost the east.

In 308, Antigonus resumed his campaign in the west. Ptolemy was allied with Cyprus and Rhodes and was competing in the Aegean and in Greece for allies, as were all the other powers bordering on the Aegean. (Greeks were all too aware that they were mere pawns in the struggle between greater powers.) The Successors' access to the recruiting grounds of Greece and Macedonia was absolutely vital and so, then, were substantial navies. In 307, Demetrius entered Athens in triumph, and the Athenians paid him divine honors. He restored "democracy" under the careful watch of his garrison, and since the Athenians had honored him as a god, he took them at their word and moved into the Parthenon with a coterie of prostitutes.

In the same year, Demetrius assembled a fleet to conquer Cyprus and from there to control the whole of the eastern seaboard with its shipbuilding supplies and shipyards. In 306 BCE, as Demetrius pressed the siege of Salamis (on Cyprus), Ptolemy brought his fleet to lift it. He had a fleet of 140 ships, all quinqueremes or quadriremes, and two hundred troop transports. He had an additional force of sixty ships in the harbor of Salamis, but Demetrius drew up ten quinqueremes across the mouth of the harbor to block their egress. Demetrius's main fleet was armed with ballistae and catapults as well as marines with javelins. He had a fleet of 110 triremes and quadriremes and about forty larger ships, including a Seven (a *hepteres*). The two sides came in sight of each other and drew up for battle. The keleustai, as usual, led the prayers to the gods, and the crews repeated them.

Demetrius, when he was about six hundred yards away from Ptolemy's fleet, raised a gilded shield, which flashed out the signal to charge. Ptolemy did the same. Both sides blew trumpets, and the crews shouted their war cries. As soon as the ships were in range, the marines fired the ballistae and catapults and then at closer range threw their javelins. When the orders were given to close by rowing as hard as possible, the marines crouched down and held on. Some ships smashed the oars of others and put them out of action; other ships rammed each other bow to bow, rebounded, and rammed again as the marines hurled their missiles, effectively, because they were so close to each other. Other ships rammed the enemy in the side, and the marines rushed to board the enemy vessel. Some fell into the water and were speared there, others boarded and fought hand to hand, and here the height of the ships mattered, whether the marines had to clamber up or could just shoot down and jump to the lower deck. They tried to clear the narrow decks.

"At sea luck seemed to play more of a part than on land, because the position of the ships and their sizes matter as much as courage."

The fighting was so severe that Demetrius himself, on his Seven, was locked in hand-to-hand combat. His three bodyguards were all wounded and put out of action. Demetrius dodged some of the missiles, but others struck his armor. At last he beat off his attackers, defeated the wing of the enemy opposite him, and flanked the middle of Ptolemy's line. Ptolemy, on the other wing, thought he was winning, but when he saw Demetrius bearing down on him, he realized that he had lost the battle and he sailed away.

Demetrius captured forty ships with their crews, and eighty disabled ships filled with seawater. He captured half the troop transports and eight thousand soldiers. He recovered all his own ships and was able to repair them and refit them for further action. Ptolemy gave up Cyprus and returned to Egypt. Demetrius effectively knocked Ptolemy out of the naval war.

Antigonus used this victory as the occasion on which to take the title "king," and all the other Successors, including Ptolemy, did the same. The assumption of the title "king" ended once and for all the fiction that the Successors were the quasi-regents of a legitimate dynasty in Macedonia. Antigonus was determined to press his advantage against Ptolemy. As the beginning shot at Ptolemy, Antigonus sent his son to capture Rhodes, a formidable Ptolemaic ally.

In the years 305–304, Demetrius lay siege to Rhodes, a lengthy and famous siege marked by outsize siege towers, ship-mounted catapults and towers, attacks by fireships, the tenacity of both sides (which earned Demetrius the epithet "Besieger"), and the empty result. Rhodes kept its independence, except that it agreed to become an ally of Antigonus with one condition, that it would not fight against Ptolemy (which had been the whole point of the operation). The Rhodians melted the enormous amount of bronze abandoned by Demetrius into a gigantic statue, the Colossus of Rhodes, which, according to legend, stood astride the Rhodian harbor entrance.

In 301, the Successors combined against Antigonus and Demetrius, defeated and killed Antigonus at the battle of Ipsus, and divided up the empire between them. Although Demetrius was eventually captured and held in captivity until he died, his descendants established the dynasty that ruled Macedonia down to the Roman conquest in the second century. Ptolemy had come late to the battle and received short shrift, but he, and his descendants, continued to defend Egypt and contest the sea until everyone, exhausted by the constant fighting and, in particular, by the insupportable expense, acknowledged that the situation had stabilized, more or less, in a balance among the kingdoms of Antigonid Macedonia, the Seleucid empire, and the Ptolemaic empire.

At this point, our sources for the history of Greece and the Successor kingdoms become scattered and fragmentary. As a kind of metaphor for the limits of our knowledge of this period, we know that the famous statue, the Nike of Samothrace (now in the Louvre)—Nike landing on the prow of the flagship of the victorious commander—was commissioned to celebrate a naval victory, but we cannot identify with certainty the commander or the battle. (A writer of the second century CE said that it was as though someone had purposefully suppressed the history of this period.)

The island of Rhodes, which had held out so heroically against Demetrius, as a free state that depended upon trade, set itself to protect the freedom of the seas against both pirates (they designed a ship specifically to fight them) and other states that tried to impose tolls—for instance, Byzantium on the trade passing through the Hellespont. Rhodes did not have a large navy, perhaps forty ships, most of them quadriremes; but they manned them with citizens, used ramming tactics, and generally allied themselves with the lesser of the great powers so as to preserve a balance of power.

The first Successors and *their* successors were giant figures at the very top of the craft of war—leaders who inspired loyalty in their armies and who had supreme confidence in themselves. The first generation pursued the dream of reuniting Alexander's empire; the next generation rather dreamed of being Alexander. Each of the kings had a fleet. Each had an army combining a Macedonian phalanx, cavalry, and elephants.

In the year 280 BCE, for the first time, one of those armies encountered Roman legions.

PART 6

The Roman Domination

Illustration 19. "Who is safe?" Black-figure painting (540–500 BCE) of a pirate ship attacking a merchant. (Adapted and redrawn by Alfred S. Bradford)

Illustration 20. Detail of the pirate ship. (Adapted and redrawn by Alfred S. Bradford)

Rowing on Land

In contrast to the Greeks, the Romans considered the blue on the map, if they thought about it at all, more as a barrier than a pathway. When the Romans looked at the world, they looked inland—first to the Latins, who were very like themselves, then to the north to the Etruscans, who had given them many of their institutions, to the east and immediate south to other Italic peoples who were similar to themselves, and to the far south to the Greeks, whose culture they admired and partly adopted. Only to the far north did they encounter a truly different people, the wild and savage Gauls, whom the Romans considered nothing more than beasts. In simple self-defense (they believed), the Romans organized Italy under their leadership, assimilating some, granting limited citizenship to others, forming alliances, and weaving the whole of Italy together in a federation unlike anything else in the world. For the willing, there were benefits; for the intransigent, there were the legions.

The earliest account involving a Roman warship relates a rather ignomini-ous event. In 394. the Romans sent three Senators to Delphi in a small war-ship. Inhabitants of the Lipari Islands thought it was a pirate ship and captured it. (When they learned their mistake, they made up for it by escorting the Senators on their way.) Later, the Romans won a small naval victory against the Latins (340–338), who were no more experienced at sea than the Romans, and in 338 agreed in a treaty with Tarentum that they would never sail a fleet into the Gulf of Tarentum.

As time passed, the Romans forgot all about that treaty, and, when they were asked to help some Greek cities in the Adriatic against pirates, they sent a small fleet, which entered the Gulf of Tarentum and was attacked by the Tarentines. The Romans demanded redress, but their Senatorial envoys arrived during a festival, when the Tarentines were drunk, and the Tarentines mocked them and one of them pelted the Senators with ordure. (Actually, it was worse than that—the miscreant produced the ordure himself.) The besplattered Senator said, "You will wash this garment clean with your blood."

The Senators departed, the Tarentines sobered up, and they called upon Pyrrhus, the king of Epirus, to come to their rescue. He arrived in Italy with cavalry, a deep "Macedonian" phalanx, and war elephants. Thus began the Pyrrhic War. It was fought on land, although, after two victories, Pyrrhus abandoned Tarentum, sailed to Sicily, and tried to create a league of Greek poleis there under his command. The Carthaginians were alarmed enough by the prospect that they offered to transport Roman troops to the island. An alliance was struck, but the Romans stuck to Italy and, in his absence, reduced Pyrrhus's Italic allies. Pyrrhus, thwarted in his expectations in Sicily, returned to Italy, and after one more battle—a draw—he withdrew from Italy. Once Pyrrhus left, the Romans were free to continue the organization of the whole of Italy, and by the mid-260s, they had Italy, including Tarentum, firmly under their control. The Pyrrhic War is odd in one respect—the Romans won the war without ever having won a battle against Pyrrhus himself.

The Romans' next challenge came from Sicily. After the death of Dionysius the Elder, Syracuse fell into a period of civil war, which spread destruction and depopulated the island. Carthage was poised to take advantage of the Greek weakness, when the Corinthians sent a single man, Timoleon, to restore the situation. Timoleon had killed his own brother to stop him becoming tyrant, and he worshipped a peculiar and personal divinity. By every means, including a battle against the Carthaginians won only because of a providential storm, he did restore stability to Syracuse and Sicily, but after his death the situation degenerated again. The problem, stated in the simplest terms, was that the constant wars against other Greeks and against the Carthaginians gave rise to generals, who, the more capable they were, the more likely they were to become tyrants. One of them was Agathocles. His origins are obscure, but his military ability and his courage carried him to the top.

After Timoleon died (in 337), the democracy he had established flourished for only a brief time and then was replaced by an oligarchy. Agathocles established a position in the Syracusan oligarchy by his courage and his leadership and also by his marriage to a wealthy widow. He was exiled by the oligarchs and brought back because of his military ability and then exiled again. By the time of his last exile, the oligarchs had become so afraid of him that they made an alliance with the Carthaginians, but Agathocles used his wealth to bribe the Carthaginian general to withdraw and the oligarchs now found themselves doubly isolated, tainted by their approach to the Carthaginians and hated by the democrats. Agathocles was invited to return to Syracuse, providing only that he swear an oath not to work against the government; and upon taking the oath, he was appointed "general and protector of the peace."

In 319/8, he became commander-in-chief, and, using his new powers and the troops he had raised personally, he overthrew and murdered four thousand oligarchs and drove six thousand into exile. He became tyrant in 316/5, and he immediately initiated a building program, which created jobs for his supporters and expanded the fleet. He carried on a series of wars against his opponents, the exiled oligarchs, and captured Messana, but his successes alarmed the Carthaginians; and in July 311, the Carthaginians landed near Himera in the rear of the Greek forces, trounced Agathocles's army, inflicted seven thousand casualties, and forced Agathocles to retreat to Syracuse. The Carthaginians lay siege to Syracuse by land and sea.

In response, Agathocles undertook one of the most imaginative and daring campaigns in the whole history of warfare (and one the Romans studied later). In 310, still under siege, he gathered his infantry and naval forces in Syracuse, and, waiting for the right moment, sailed out of Syracuse and, taking the Carthaginians completely by surprise, landed in Africa, burned his ships, and began operations. Between 310 and 307, he waged war with varying degrees of success, until he had achieved his primary objective—he forced the Carthaginians to lift the siege of Syracuse and agree to negotiate with him. Under the terms of the final agreement, he abandoned his army in Africa—like most tyrants his only loyalty was to himself—and slipped back to Syracuse. In 304, Agathocles adopted the title *king*. He died in 289/8 and—because of a family feud—bequeathed the city of Syracuse to the people of Syracuse.

The popular government gave way to a new leader, Hiero, and Syracuse became, once again, an aggressive power in Sicily. Hiero turned his attentions to the prosperous city of Messana. Messana hired as protection an Italic mercenary company, who called themselves Mamertines ("dedicated to Mamers," i.e., Mars). The Mamertines arrived and discovered that they liked Messana, so much, in fact, that they expelled all the adult males, divided up the property and wives and families among themselves, and made the city their own.

Hiero took the side of the expelled Messanan men and fought and defeated the Mamertines in a battle outside the city. The victory had two results: Hiero was proclaimed king and the Mamertines sought help. One delegation went to the Carthaginians and requested a garrison (which the Carthaginians sent); another went to Rome. The Roman Senate could not reach a decision: should they support men, even if they were Italian men, who had unjustly seized a city? Or, if not, should they let Carthage gain a strong position just across the strait from Italy? The Senate referred the matter to the People's Assembly, and the People voted to aid the Mamertines.

Under pressure from the Mamertines and the threat of a Roman invasion led by the consul Appius (the "Log"), the Carthaginian commander withdrew—he was crucified for this error of judgment—and Appius prepared to cross to Messana. The Carthaginians sent a fleet to stop him, and Hiero made an alliance with the Carthaginians to eliminate the Mamertines. As the Carthaginians blocked the sea approaches—the Carthaginian commander had told the Roman commander, "We will not even let you wash your hands in the sea"—Hiero blocked any possibility of the Mamertines escaping overland. The Romans, while they were not complete lubbers, had no warships, neither the modern quinquereme nor even the lowly bireme; they had no supply ships;, and they had to borrow transports from their Greek allies. Appius chose a dark and unsettled night to ferry his force across the straits and into Messana. Even so, the crossing was highly risky, and the Carthaginians almost caught him. In the ensuing pursuit, one Carthaginian quinquereme crashed on the Italian shore and fell into Roman hands.

Once in Messana, Appius the Log assessed the tactical situation, which was hardly encouraging, and tried to negotiate a settlement. The opposing forces refused, and so, first, he engaged and defeated Hiero. Hiero burned his camp and retreated as quickly as he could to Syracuse. Next, Appius attacked and scattered the Carthaginians—the rank and file refused to fight the Romans—marched down to Syracuse, and put it under siege.

In the next year, the Romans sent both consuls and their armies to Sicily. Many of the cities came over to the Romans, and Hiero, seeing the new situation and having experienced Roman abilities, negotiated an alliance with the Romans. The Romans, in their turn, had recognized that their greatest problem in Sicily was supplying their army, since they had no credible fleet. With such an ally—Syracuse would open up a supply route for them—the Romans thought that they could reduce their forces in Sicily, and one consul and his army returned home.

The Carthaginians, on the other hand, hired mercenaries and prepared from their base in Agrigentum to fight for Sicily. The Romans, in turn, concentrated their efforts on Agrigentum. In the initial skirmish, the Carthaginians caught them by surprise, but the Romans reacted swiftly and drove the Carthaginian forces back into Agrigentum, whereupon the Romans constructed siege works around the city. For five months, the siege went on. The Carthaginians were able to communicate with Carthage by sea and obtain supplies in the same way. Then a second Carthaginian force with fifty elephants (brought by sea) concentrated on the landside of the Roman forces and, in effect, put the besiegers under siege.

Deprived of supplies, the Romans almost withdrew, but their new ally, Hiero, proved his worth by breaking through the Carthaginian forces with enough supplies to keep the Romans going, and they persevered even when disease started killing them. The two forces faced each other for two months before the Carthaginians brought on a battle. The Romans routed them and captured most of the elephants, but that night, as the Romans relaxed, the Carthaginian army in Agrigentum broke out of the city and escaped. The Romans entered the city, systematically sacked it, and sold the population into slavery.

By 261, the Romans appeared to have the situation under control in the heartland of Sicily, but the Carthaginian fleet controlled the coastal regions.

Moreover, the Carthaginians used their bases on Sardinia (as well as Sicily) to ravage the coasts of Italy. This was a new kind of war for the Romans. Their shipbuilders had no experience building a quinquereme, and they had to use the one they had captured as a guide. In addition, the Romans had to train crews from scratch. They built mock-ups, so that the crews could practice on land to win at sea. (The trick to rowing a tiered-ship is for each separate tier to learn to work together—in this case, a tier of three oars and five oarsmen—and, of course, to condition themselves for the physical labor.)

As soon as the ships were built, they were sent down the coast to join the Roman forces in Sicily. The very first contingent of seventeen ships was captured by the Carthaginians. Despite this setback, the Roman consul, Gaius Duilius, gathered a fleet; and when he heard that a Carthaginian fleet was near, transferred the command of his army to a subordinate, took command of the fleet, and went out to engage the Carthaginians near the Lipari Islands at Mylae (hence, the battle of Mylae). When the Carthaginian commander, Hannibal (not the famous Hannibal, of course—it was a common Carthaginian name), heard that the Roman fleet was approaching, he put to sea with 130 ships, fully confident of victory. He had nothing but contempt for the Romans and their seamanship. The Carthaginians were supremely confident because of their experience at sea and also because the Roman ships were slow and poorly constructed, but the Romans had one advantage of which the Carthaginians were unaware, the "raven" (in Greek, the *korax*).

"Hearing that the enemy fleet was not far distant, the Romans prepared for a sea battle; because their ships were poorly constructed and slow and clumsy, they had added a device to them called the 'raven,' which is like this: on the prow was an upright pole, in height twenty-four feet and in width about nine-to-twelve inches. At the top was fastened a pulley and around it was a gangway, four feet wide and thirty-six feet long and there was a knee-high railing along each length."

At the top was a sharpened iron spike. When the Roman ship was within range of an enemy ship, the raven was raised by means of the pulley and dropped on the enemy, either prow to prow, in which case the soldiers ran across it, two abreast—the two in front holding up their shields to protect those behind them and those behind them holding their shields to the side as protection—or, if the ships had collided side to side, the raven was dropped to grapple the enemy, and the soldiers poured over the whole length of the enemy ship.

The Carthaginian ships pulled as hard as they could, and in no particular order, to attack the Romans, "as it seemed perfectly clear that they were not going out to fight but to gather booty, as though the Roman ships were a herd of cattle." The Carthaginians then for the first time noticed the "ravens," and they were surprised at this novelty, but still fully confident and they attacked, only to find as they closed, regardless of the position of the ships, the ravens fell and held them fast, the sea battle was transformed into a land battle, and the Roman soldiers stormed onto the Carthaginian ships, massacred the crews who resisted, and forced the rest to surrender. The first thirty Carthaginian ships to engage were captured, and Hannibal barely escaped by jumping into a skiff and rowing away as fast as he could.

Now the rest of the Carthaginian fleet came up and observed what had happened. They tried to row around the Romans and attack from another direction, but each and every ship that came close was impaled with the spike of the raven and thus put at the mercy of the legionnaires. The ships that could, fled. In all, the Romans captured fifty ships. Duilius was the first Roman ever to celebrate a triumph for a naval victory. Hannibal withdrew his fleet from Sicily and concentrated on Sardinia, where a Roman fleet caught him in the harbor and inflicted devastating losses on the Carthaginian ships. The surviving Carthaginians crucified Hannibal.

Sacred Chickens

By 257 BCE, the situation at sea had completely reversed. The Romans now were supremely confident of victory in any sea battle, and they became aggressive to the point of recklessness. When the consul C. Atilius Regulus, stationed at Tyndaris, observed a disorganized Carthaginian fleet sailing by, he set out to attack it with his flagship and nine other ships. He lost his nine ships and almost was captured himself, but he kept the enemy occupied just long enough for the rest of the Roman fleet to catch up, sink eight ships, and capture ten.

In 256 BCE, the crisis of the war seemed to have arrived. The Romans planned to land in Africa (as Agathocles had), detach the subjects of Carthage, and attack Carthage itself. They had prepared a fleet of 330 decked ships of war, commanded by the two consuls, M. Atilius Regulus and Lucius Manlius. The Carthaginian fleet, numbering 350 ships, had no choice but to try to stop the Romans.

The Romans selected the best of their infantry and divided them into four legions corresponding to the different squadrons in the fleet's battle formation and designating them first legion of the first squadron and so forth. Each ship had a crew of some three hundred men and a marine force of 120 legionnaires. The total manpower of the fleet was about 140,000 men. For their part, the Carthaginians put about 150,000 men to sea.

The Romans were quite conscious of the risks they were running—they had to both protect the invasion force and also be prepared to fight. The two consuls led the way in two Sixes (hexereis—three tiers, two men to each oar in each tier). The first and second squadrons followed behind the leading ships in single file, but spread out so that they formed a wedge. The third squadron advanced in a line closing off the base of the wedge and forming a triangle. These ships towed horse transports. The fourth squadron formed a line behind the third, but extending somewhat beyond it.

For their part, the Carthaginians still believed that they had a chance at sea, and, moreover, they knew that if they were defeated now, the Romans would invade their homeland, and so they prepared to fight. The Carthaginian commander reacted to the Roman formation by extending his ships in a single line, with the left stretching almost to the coast and the right, having the swiftest quinqueremes, far to the left of the Roman fleet. The Romans noticed that the Carthaginians were at their most extended in the center, and they accelerated and attacked there. The Carthaginian commander, however, ordered those ships to retreat, in order to draw the Romans out and split their formation.

At first, the situation developed as the Carthaginian had hoped. The Romans pursued vigorously and the third and fourth squadrons were left behind (as the third was slowed by the horse transports). The retreating Carthaginians now received the command to turn and fight. The Carthaginians had the advantage in speed and maneuverability, but if a ship failed to ram and back water quickly enough, the ravens grappled it and it was finished.

The Carthaginian right wing engaged the fourth squadron of the Romans, and the left wing attacked the third squadron, which released the towropes and engaged in battle. Thus the sea battle devolved into three separate engagements, widely separated so that no ship of any engagement could help any other part of its fleet. The two consuls defeated the fleet opposed to them, and the surviving Carthaginian ships fled. Lucius occupied himself in towing off the captured enemy ships, but Marcus observed that the fourth squadron was in real difficulties, turned to help it, and by his approach gave new heart to the struggling crews, who renewed their attack. The Carthaginians found themselves fighting in two directions, and they broke off the battle and tried to escape into the open sea.

In the third engagement, the Carthaginians had managed to force the Romans back toward shore, but hesitated to close with them because of the ravens. The two consuls, now together, turned their attention there and surprised the Carthaginians, who had been concentrating on their efforts to drive the Romans onto the rocks. In this engagement, the Romans captured fifty ships with their crews. Only a few Carthaginians managed to escape by hugging the coast. In all, the Romans lost twenty-four ships, but had no ship captured. The Carthaginians lost more than thirty ships sunk and sixty-four captured.

The Romans refitted their ships, rewarded the crews for their efforts, and resumed their voyage to Libya, rendezvoused off the Hermaeum Promontory, and sailed from there to Aspis, where they beached their ships, put up a defensive trench and palisade, and lay siege to Aspis. The Carthaginians, meanwhile, convinced that the Romans would attack Carthage directly, had deployed their fleet there and thus were in no position to contest the Roman landing.

The Romans were surprised their operation proceeded so easily. They sent to Rome for instructions, and, while waiting for a reply, ravaged the countryside and captured twenty thousand slaves and a fortune in booty. Instructions arrived from Rome that Regulus should remain in Africa with the army and forty ships, while the other consul should return to Rome with the slaves and the booty. In the course of the campaign that year in Africa, the Roman army defeated the Carthaginians (despite their superior cavalry and their elephants), and the Carthaginians withdrew into Carthage and abandoned the countryside to the Romans.

Regulus seemed to have peace within his grasp, but he demanded such severe terms that the Carthaginians rejected them and hired a Spartan mercenary, Xanthippus, to train and lead their army. He used their superior cavalry and a hundred elephants to break the Roman legions. (Xanthippus is the only *Greek* ever to defeat a Roman consular army.) Regulus himself was captured, and only a remnant of the Roman force escaped and took refuge behind the walls of Aspis. The Carthaginians stormed Aspis, but were beaten off and abandoned the siege.

In the next year (early summer, 255), the Carthaginians received intelligence that the Romans had collected a fleet to remove the soldiers from Aspis. They repaired the ships that had escaped the last engagement, and they put to sea to intercept the Romans. The Romans ran into the Carthaginian fleet near the Hermaeum. In the ensuing battle, the Romans captured 114 ships with their crews, and they brought off the troops at Aspis, but on their return and against the advice of the ships' captains familiar with the sea, the rugged coast, and the weather at this time of year (July 4–24, 255), they sailed along the coast of Sicily and were overtaken by a storm of such ferocity that only 80 ships out of a total of 364 survived. Wreckage and corpses were scattered for miles up and down the coast. The loss of life, perhaps as many as one hundred thousand men, is the largest ever in a single shipwreck.

Polybius described the Roman strengths and deficiencies of character:

"In general, the Romans use force in every situation and they think that they must carry everything out to its conclusion regardless, and, in many cases, they succeed by this tenacity, but, in some cases, obviously, they fall short, and, in particular, in sea operations. On land against men and the constructions of men they are usually successful in their application of overwhelming force, although they do fail from time to time. But when they fight against the sea and weather, they often meet disaster. This will continue to be the case and they will continue to suffer, until such time as they correct their reliance on their aggressive spirit and force, relying on which, they believe that every time, no matter what, is the proper time for them to sail."

When the Carthaginians heard of the disaster, they believed, after their victories in Africa, perhaps they could be successful in Sicily as well; they mustered their forces, undertook the construction of two hundred new ships, and sent an army with 140 elephants to Sicily. The Romans reacted by building 220 ships in three months—"a thing not easily believed." The two consuls who commanded the new fleet picked up the ships that had survived the storm and transported an army to Panormus, attacked it, took it, left a garrison, and sailed back to Rome.

In the next year, the consuls brought the fleet to Africa, raided here and there to no great consequence, and, upon their return voyage to Rome, ran into another storm, which wrecked over half their fleet (150 ships). In the next two years, the Romans conducted a desultory campaign in Sicily; the Roman troops were terrified of elephants, and at Panormus their consequent hesitancy encouraged the Carthaginians to press an aggressive siege. The consul in the city exaggerated his own and his troops' fear of elephants and convinced the Carthaginian general that his troops were so fearful of the elephants that they would not come out from behind the walls to fight no matter what and, in fact, if confronted by elephants, would run away. The Carthaginian general was so completely bamboozled that he attacked the Roman fortifications, right into a trap prepared by the Roman consul. The Romans killed or captured all the elephants and shattered the Carthaginian army.

Encouraged by the victory, the Romans decided to rebuild a part (fifty ships) of their fleet and concentrate their navy and legions on Lilybaeum, the Carthaginians' last major supply point and fortification in Sicily. Both sides recognized that whoever won here would control the sea to Carthage, and both put their utmost efforts into the struggle. The Romans, as ever masters of the siege, advanced relentlessly through the outer works of the city until it seemed to both them and the enemy that they were on the verge of total victory. Just then, however, a Carthaginian relief force, using favorable winds, broke through the Roman naval blockade and entered the harbor. The Carthaginian commander marshalled his own troops and the reinforcements and attacked the siege works. The Romans had expected that the reinforcements would be employed in an assault on the siege works, and in the subsequent battle, although they suffered heavy casualties, they also inflicted heavy casualties, and they beat back the Carthaginian assault.

The Carthaginian fleet sailed away from Lilybaeum to Drepana (where there was a good harbor). Meanwhile, time passed and the leaders in Carthage were desperate to know what was happening in Lilybaeum, but the way into the city ran through treacherous shallows hard to navigate. Finally, a Carthaginian called "Hannibal the Rhodian" proposed that he would enter the harbor and find out what the situation was. He had a particularly fast ship, in which he sailed close to Lilybaeum, waited out of sight behind an island, from where he figured out how to use landmarks to align his ship for one dash through the Romans into the harbor, and, when the wind was favorable, set sail and entered the harbor safely. On his return trip to Carthage, he rowed out of the harbor and, so confident was he in the speed of his ship, paused to give the Romans a chance to chase him. The Romans refused the bait.

He continued to enter and leave the harbor, to bring encouragement to the inhabitants and to bring news of them to Carthage; he instructed other Carthaginian captains in his method and they, too, were able to escape from the harbor of Lilybaeum and return. Consequently, the Romans tried to fill the harbor mouth. They found it too deep in most places, but in one place they succeeded, and a Carthaginian quadrireme, which attempted the passage at night, grounded on the Roman fill and was captured.

The captured ship was especially well-built and speedy and the Romans repaired it, put an elite crew in it, and, then, as the "Rhodian" left the harbor, the Roman quadrireme started in pursuit. The Carthaginians rowed hard, but the Roman ship was overhauling them and the captain had to turn to fight. As with all such encounters, he was overwhelmed by the Roman legionnaires, his ship was captured, refitted, and used in company with the quadrireme to put an end to blockade-running.

At this point, the defenders took advantage of a violent storm with heavy winds blowing right at the Roman siege works. They launched a raid, set part of the siege works on fire, the wind whipped up the flames, spread them out of control, and destroyed all the Romans' works. But not even the complete destruction of their siege works could stop the Romans. They rebuilt the circuit wall and then an outer wall to protect themselves, so that they would not be interrupted as they starved out the defenders.

In 249, the Romans recruited ten thousand crewmen in Italy for the Roman fleet at Lilybaeum, ferried them across the strait, and marched them across Sicily. They reached Lilybaeum in secret, and the consul, Claudius the "Handsome," decided to attack the Carthaginians in Drepana, their last harbor. He expected that he could take the Carthaginians by surprise, which, in fact, he did, but the Carthaginian commander, Adherbal, reacted quickly, manned his fleet, and advanced to attack.

Claudius's first ships were already entering the harbor, but when he learned—he was bringing up the rear—that the Carthaginians were coming out to fight, he ordered the ships to pull back out of the harbor. In the process, they ran afoul of other Roman ships entering the harbor, and, in the confusion, some ships had their oars shattered, although, nonetheless, they managed to get out of the harbor and form up in the open sea. Adherbal, meanwhile, had led his ships out past the Romans and then formed up with his sterns to open water, while the Romans had the land close behind them. Now the Carthaginians maneuvered, rushing in and ramming the Romans, and backing water before the Romans could respond. The Roman ships were slow and unwieldy and the crews inexperienced. Some foundered on the shore, others were sunk, and others captured. Claudius escaped with thirty ships. The Carthaginians captured ninety-three Roman ships.

A story got around that Claudius had ignored an omen—he had been told that the sacred chickens on board would not eat. "Perhaps they will drink, then," he said and had them thrown overboard. In a later story—this branch of the Claudians was known for its arrogance—his sister, sometime after his death, as she was trying to make her way through the crowded streets of Rome, remarked, "I wish my brother were alive today to take this rabble out and drown it."

Now disaster just followed disaster for the Romans. They put together a supply fleet to send to Lilybaeum, and the consul ordered half of it to go ahead while he collected the rest of his force at Syracuse. The Carthaginians intercepted the fleet and drove it into a small and insufficient harbor, and then they intercepted the rest of the fleet. The Roman commander fled toward shore to protect his ships, but a violent storm blew up, the Carthaginian fleet read the signs and escaped to a secure anchorage, while the full force of the storm struck the Romans and destroyed their fleet so thoroughly that not even wreckage was ever found afterwards.

In 247, the Carthaginians appointed Hamilcar Barca commander in Sicily. He used their temporary superiority at sea to ravage the Italian coast and to seize and hold a mountain stronghold in western Sicily right in the midst of the Romans. By now Hamilcar and the Carthaginians were almost completely bereft of allies in Sicily, but even so, Hamilcar was able to continue his attacks on the Italian coasts and fight multiple skirmishes with the Romans. He followed this strategy from 247–244 in an attempt to wear the Romans down, but the result was more to wear both sides down, to empty their treasuries, and to demoralize their troops.

Finally, the Romans decided that they could only win the war with one more effort at sea. The state treasury was empty, but the Senators and other wealthy citizens spent their own money, forming two hundred small companies, each to pay for the construction of one ship (resulting in a fleet of two hundred quinqueremes). The ship they used as a model was the "Rhodian's" ship, which had out-sailed them so often at Lilybaeum. The new fleet sailed to Lilybaeum to support the siege. The Carthaginian fleet, convinced that the Romans had given up on the sea, had sailed back to Carthage. The Roman commander, Lutatius Catulus, while pressing the sieges of Lilybaeum and Drepana, did not lose sight of his main objective—to fight and defeat the Carthaginian fleet—and exercised his crews daily to bring up their proficiency and their physical condition.

When the Carthaginians learned that a Roman fleet had arrived, they appointed Hanno as commander, manned their fleet, loaded it with grain for Hamilcar, and Hanno set off to Sicily. He intended to unload the grain and receive a force of marines from Hamilcar and then to fight the Romans. The Roman commander was well aware of his plan and intended to intercept him, but on the day Hanno approached the coast, a strong wind was blowing from sea to shore, which would give the Carthaginians a considerable advantage. Nonetheless, when Catulus considered the situation, either to accept the disadvantage of weather conditions and meet a Carthaginian fleet that had insufficient marines and was laden with grain, or to await better weather and thereby give the enemy a chance to prepare for battle, he decided to fight. He removed every extraneous piece of equipment, including the masts and sails, from his ships, and lightened them as much as they could be, to hold an added force of legionnaires.

He intercepted the Carthaginians and formed a line of attack, while they were still under sail. The Carthaginians, when they saw that the Romans intended to fight, stowed their sails and masts, and likewise formed a line. The Romans and Carthaginians now had switched circumstances: The Romans were well trained and experienced in working together, the Carthaginians had never expected battle, and their crews were raw and their ships heavy and slow. The Romans closed with them, sank fifty ships, and captured seventy with their crews, almost ten thousand prisoners. The rest of the Carthaginians raised their sails and escaped.

With this battle (the battle of the Aegates Islands), the Romans finally succeeded in cutting Sicily off from all resupply and reinforcement. The Carthaginians managed to get a message through to Hamilcar to take what measures he saw fit to end the war, as the Carthaginians just simply had no more resources. Hasdrubal negotiated peace terms, which the Romans accepted with some modifications: The Carthaginians would completely evacuate Sicily (which became Rome's first province), would guarantee the freedom of Syracuse, and would pay a large indemnity to reimburse Rome for the costs of the war.

In all, in this greatest of all ancient naval wars, the Romans and Carthaginians fought one battle involving five hundred quinqueremes and another battle with almost seven hundred. The Romans lost a total of seven hundred quinqueremes, including those lost to the storms (more than two hundred thousand men), and the Carthaginians about five hundred quinqueremes. These were the largest fleets ever put together up to this time. Truly this war demonstrated the later Roman dictum that the "victor has not won until the defeated admit its defeat."

Carthage was doubly broke. It had an empty treasury, and it had to pay a huge indemnity to the Romans. Consequently, it could not pay its mercenaries, and the mercenaries attacked Carthage and convinced the African subjects of Carthage to join them. Only the genius of Hamilcar Barca saved Carthage from defeat and destruction. During this war (the War of the Mercenaries), the Romans gave the Carthaginians some assistance and allowed Hiero of Syracuse to help them, but, in the end, through naked self-interest, they took advantage of Carthage's difficulties to annex Sardinia and Corsica.

CHAPTER TWENTY-EIGHT

The First Illyrian War, 229–228 BCE

The Illyrian shore of the Adriatic Sea with its maze of inlets, coves, and natural harbors is a pirate paradise, so long as the power that controls the shore turns a blind eye to their activities. The Illyrian pirates operated ships called *lembi*—an open boat specifically designed for piracy. Crammed with a hundred pirates, the lembi would lie in wait for a merchant and then they would dash out, half the crew rowing furiously to intercept the merchant and the other half ready to board. No one seemed capable of stopping these pirates on the sea, and their ruler, Queen Teuta, sanctioned piracy as a part of government operations—the pirates, for the most part, were free to pursue their occupation, so long as they paid her her share of the booty, and, now and then, acted as the queen's own navy.

By 230 BCE, Queen Teuta had united Illyria. She decided to extend Illyrian control down the whole length of the eastern shore of the Adriatic. She lifted whatever restrictions had been placed on the pirates formerly, and the pirates attacked whomever and wherever they pleased—they operated even in the southern Peloponnesus. The Illyrian army and navy had a string of successes, and the kingdom of Epirus, after a defeat at their hands, left them alone. The pirates soon had eliminated all opposition, but then—catastrophically—they erred: they attacked some Italian ships.

The Italian merchants appealed to the Roman Senate, and the Senate sent a commission, including a young Senator, to Queen Teuta. They read her their list of grievances, which they understood as the first step in a process that would culminate in a declaration of war, unless the queen offered them sufficient satisfaction. But the queen misunderstood the process that had begun against her, considered it a simple presentation of a list of complaints, and responded, haughtily enough to trigger all the Romans' antipathy towards royalty; she declared that she had no policy to injure Romans, but . . .

". . . it is an ancient custom of the land of the Illyrians and of its rulers that the queen does not interfere with the actions of her private citizens in taking plunder on the sea."

To which the young Senator replied,

"Queen Teuta, the Romans, too, have an excellent tradition, which is that the state concerns itself with punishing those who commit private wrongs and with helping those who suffer them. With the gods' help we shall do our utmost, and that very soon, to convince you to reform this ancient custom of your kings."

The queen was furious at this—to her—insolent speech. On the voyage home, pirates intercepted the Roman ship, boarded, and murdered the young Roman. Even so, time passed and the Romans seemed not to be doing anything, so the queen proceeded with her plans. In 229, her fleet and army proceeded down the Adriatic to capture Epidamnus and Corcyra, two crucial trading stops on the route between Greece and Italy.

The attack on Epidamnus failed, and the Illyrians turned to Corcyra. Corcyra appealed to the different Greek leagues, but one had already thrown its fortunes in with the queen, another remained neutral, and a third sent only token help, a few ships, which fought the Illyrians in the traditional method, maneuvering and ramming the Illyrians, only to discover that the Illyrians had lashed their ships together into unsinkable platforms; the rams stuck and the Illyrians boarded and overwhelmed the Greeks. The Greek ships, which had not yet engaged, withdrew and sailed home. The Corcyraeans sued for peace and accepted the Illyrians' terms. The Illyrians then resumed their attack on Epidamnus.

Just then, when Greeks believed that the Illyrians would conquer the whole eastern shore of the Adriatic and beyond—what was there to stop them?—and Epidamnus was in danger of falling to them, a Roman fleet of two hundred ships appeared at Corcyra. The Illyrian commander, Demetrius, realized immediately that the game was up, he surrendered to the Romans, and he made himself useful (and later received more than adequate compensation). The Romans continued their operations against the Illyrians.

One division of twenty thousand men and two thousand cavalry under the command of the first consul advanced up the shore by land and the other under the command of the other consul advanced by sea. The Illyrian soldiers at Epidamnus broke and fled as soon as they heard that the Romans were coming. In one year of campaigning, the Romans split Illyria apart, captured and destroyed numerous pirate vessels, liberated captured Greek cities, and installed Demetrius on the throne. The queen fled to a fort in the interior and in 228 accepted all the Romans' terms and capitulated entirely. For the moment, the Romans had wiped out piracy in the Adriatic.

Roman envoys traveled the Greek world to clarify what they had done and why they had done it—in short, they had no ambitions in Greece beyond the protection of the Greek cities on the Adriatic.

Not long (225 BCE) after the Romans had concluded the Illyrian War, they were forced to deal with an incursion of Gauls into northern Italy. In 224 BCE, the Roman consuls caught the Gauls between their two armies and inflicted a large number of casualties on them. In 223, the Romans again defeated the Gauls and continued operations until the Gauls of northern Italy delivered themselves totally to Roman control. Thus it seemed at that time that the Romans had secured their northern border.

The Romans now were free to address a troublesome situation in Spain.

CHAPTER TWENTY-NINE

A Different Kind of War

The Romans dominated the seas around them, they occupied the islands—Sicily, Sardinia, and Corsica—from which an enemy could launch raids, and they had soundly defeated the Gauls in northern Italy, so they felt secure enough to turn their attention to Carthaginian activities in Spain, where the Carthaginians were attacking a Roman ally.

After the First Punic War and the Romans' seizure of Corsica and Sardinia, Hamilcar Barca had concluded that Rome would never leave Carthage in peace and that Carthage would have no chance in that future war, unless it somehow could match the Romans in manpower and money. He believed the answer lay in Spain, and so Hamilcar and, after his death, his successor, Hasdrubal, campaigned there and were so successful that the Romans sent a delegation to Hasdrubal to complain about his activities and to ascertain his objectives. He deflected their inquiry by asking them, "How else do you expect us to pay off the indemnity we owe you?" His answer satisfied them for the moment, but when Hasdrubal died in 221 BCE, Hamilcar's son, Hannibal, became the leader of the Carthaginian forces and his enmity toward Rome was well known. Indeed, at the age of nine, Hamilcar had taken him into a temple to swear that he would never be a friend of the Romans. In more concrete terms, his father had also taught him that there was not enough room in the western Mediterranean for both Rome and Carthage.

When Roman envoys ordered Hannibal to lift the siege of their ally, Hannibal issued promises and continued to press the siege; Carthage rejected Roman demands to recall him, and the Romans declared war. They had an impeccable strategic plan—one consular army would sail to Spain and engage Hannibal there, the other consular army would invade Africa and besiege Carthage. At this time, on the eve of the war, the Roman legions could draw on a pool of five hundred thousand men.

The Romans were confident, but as the consul, Publius Cornelius, was sailing to Spain, he was surprised to learn that Hannibal had slipped by him on land, crossed the Rhone River, and was on his way to the Alps and Italy. Cornelius decided to return to northern Italy, just himself, and organize a defense along the line of the Po, while the fleet and army under the command of his brother continued on to Spain (which still was occupied by the Carthaginians and would, in any case, be a major theater of war—at the least to prevent Spain resupplying Hannibal). Cornelius skirmished with Hannibal at the Ticinus River; he was wounded, and his life was saved only by the quick action of his son, but, more to the point, he realized that in Hannibal the Romans were facing a totally different kind of enemy.

As Hannibal advanced into Italy, the Carthaginians sent a fleet of twenty quinqueremes and one thousand marines to raid the Italian coast. Storms scattered their fleet, and the Romans captured three ships, interrogated the prisoners, and learned of a Carthaginian plan to seize Lilybaeum in Sicily and attempt to foment an uprising in the island. The Romans alerted their forces in Lilybaeum and set watchtowers along the coast. Consequently, one dawn, when a Carthaginian fleet arrived at Lilybaeum, the Romans were ready and quickly manned their ships. The Carthaginians backed water away from the harbor to allow the Romans to come out into open water, not as a gentlemanly act to ensure a fair fight, but, rather, to give the Carthaginians space to fight a battle of maneuver, in which they hoped to avoid collisions, grappling, and the raven. The Romans, on the other hand, wanted to close, ship-to-ship, grapple, and employ the superiority of the legionnaire. In the battle, the Romans captured seven Carthaginian ships, scattered the rest, and returned to the harbor with damage to only one of their own ships. In this battle, and others, time and again, the Romans demonstrated just how superior they were at sea, but that superiority did not prevent Carthaginian raids on the coast of Italy.

At this moment, while the consul Sempronius was arranging his fleet to defend Sicily and Italy—and preparing his forces to invade Africa—he received the news that Hannibal had crossed the Alps. Immediately, he loaded his army on ships and transported them to northern Italy. When Sempronius arrived at the Po, Cornelius advised him to be cautious, but Sempronius was eager to fight. and he believed that Cornelius's hesitancy was the result of his wounds. When Cornelius realized that Sempronius was not going to listen to him, he continued his interrupted trip to Spain, and there he and his brother fought a series of successful battles against the Carthaginians. (The Romans generally were successful in battle against the Carthaginians, except when the Carthaginians were led by Hannibal.) Sempronius fought his battle at the Trebia River in late 218; he led his army across the icy stream, which debilitated his men, was caught in an ambush, and was defeated, although half his army broke through the Carthaginian center and escaped. The Gauls of northern Italy joined Hannibal en masse. (Sempronius tried to conceal the extent of his defeat by saying that he would have won had it not been for the weather.)

With Hannibal in winter quarters in northern Italy, the Romans prepared to prevent his breaking through into central Italy. They knew of three routes Hannibal could take, and they placed the newly elected consuls with their armies to cover the two most likely routes and a praetor with an army at the third, a seemingly impassable swamp. The impassable swamp proved to be passable, and before the Romans expected him to move, Hannibal traversed it. Flaminius, one of the Roman consuls, caught up to him and followed him. The consul was not supposed to engage him but to keep an eye on him, until his colleague arrived and the two could converge on Hannibal, catch him between them, and annihilate him. Flaminius, however, followed too carelessly, fell into an ambush at Lake Trasimene (217 BCE), was killed himself, and lost his whole army.

The Romans were shaken, and they appointed a dictator, Fabius, to try to contain Hannibal; Fabius believed that Hannibal was a different kind of foe, who would not be defeated by traditional tactics. He dogged Hannibal and tried to limit the damage he could do, but his term expired and his caution was rejected. He was called the "Delayer (*Cunctator*)," at the time a pejorative, but later a title worn with pride—"One man, by delaying, saved the state."

As the Romans reacted to Hannibal on land with disastrous results, at sea they were active, aggressive, and mostly successful. The Roman naval commander had a fleet of 120 warships in Sicily and was given a free hand to raid Carthaginian territory. He plundered the African countryside indiscriminately and mostly without opposition.

In 216, the newly elected consuls were determined to fight one great battle to defeat Hannibal. As Polybius wrote (quoted above), "In general the Romans use force in every situation and they think that they must carry everything out to its conclusion regardless, and, in many cases, they succeed by this tenacity. . . . On land against men . . . they are usually successful in their application of overwhelming force, although they do fail from time to time."

This time they failed. They lost the battle of Cannae, and it was a catastrophe with profound consequences for Rome. (Although the losses in men were no greater than the losses in the sea battles and storms of the First Punic War, the difference was that at Cannae it was the incomparable legions that were defeated and in Italy.) Many places in south Italy went over to Hannibal, the most significant of which was Capua—no other defection infuriated the Romans more, because to them, the Capuans were Roman citizens and, thus, despicable traitors. In the same year, in the north of Italy, a Roman army under the command of the consul-designate, who was supposed to keep an eye on the Gauls and not engage them, was wiped out and the commander's skull turned into a drinking cup. (Polybius, however, also wrote that the Romans "are never so much to be feared as when they themselves have the most to fear," and that time had come.)

The Romans reappointed Fabius the "Delayer" as dictator and accepted his strategy of containment and attrition (which depended on preventing resupply and reinforcements from reaching Hannibal). Hannibal was circum-scribed by his policy of "liberating" Italian cities without making demands on them to furnish troops and even more by his misunderstanding of the Roman system, which he believed to be simply an empire ruled by a power-ful city, like Carthage. Consequently, he had expected, if he were to win some major victories over the Romans, he could detach their "subjects," iso-late Rome, and reduce Rome to just another city in Italy. He did not under-stand that the majority of Italians would remain loyal to Rome and, even in their darkest hour, believe Rome to be their protector against the savage and bloodthirsty barbarian, Hannibal. Against Hannibal the Romans engaged all their formidable organizational abilities to recruit and train new armies; they assigned one army to watch Hannibal, one army to guard Rome, and the others, as they became available, to recover the places that had gone over to him.

In 216, the Roman fleet off Calabria intercepted a ship carrying three Carthaginian envoys. A search of their baggage revealed a proposed agree-ment between Philip V, the king of Macedonia, and Hannibal. One clause read, "You [Philip] will bring aid to us, as necessary and as mutually agreed." Philip agreed to raise a fleet of two hundred ships and cross to Italy with an army. He had already prepared a smaller fleet to transport his troops against other enemies "because of the surprise and speed of an attack by sea." The Senate reacted by ordering more ships to be built and twenty-five of them sent to increase the Adriatic fleet to fifty ships, now under the command of the praetor M. Valerius Laevinius. His instructions were to keep his eyes open and to take action as warranted. (One of the characteristics of the Roman system was to give commanders wide latitude to take action as they saw fit. Thus they were free to react to changing situations, although, of course, their indepen-dence also meant that sometimes, if the commander's judgment was faulty, as recently against the Gauls, the consequences could be unfortunate.)

Hannibal, despite his great successes, sent a series of urgent requests for resupply to the Carthaginian assembly, where one of his political rivals summed up his appeal as, "Hannibal says, 'I have wiped out four Roman armies; I need help.'" The Carthaginians did vote to send Hannibal elephants, money, and more troops, but they failed to act with any sense of urgency. Rais-ing money to prosecute the war was also a problem for the Romans. The Roman fleets at Sicily and Sardinia, while so far holding their own, had run out of money to pay the crews. The Romans appealed to their local allies and the allies responded: the towns in Sardinia donated the necessary amount, and in Sicily, Hiero of Syracuse sent enough money and supplies to support the fleet for six months. But after he died, the men who replaced him decided to abandon the Roman alliance.

The Syracusan leaders, who broke the treaty with the Romans, did so from personal motives and ambitions, rather than any desire to help the

Carthaginians or Hannibal, and they soon found themselves under Roman siege and with scant Carthaginian help. The Romans had to use private subscriptions to raise and man the fleet for the campaign against Syracuse. The Roman commander, Marcellus, had already distinguished himself for his courage in the First Punic War and, in between the Punic wars, had fought a Gallic king, hand-to-hand, killed him, dedicated the Gaul's armor, and received the *spolia opima* (awarded only three times in the history of the Republic). At the beginning of the Second Punic War, he had been put in command of the fleet operating around Sicily. After the battle of Cannae, he had sent part of his force to protect the city of Rome, and with the remainder he had rescued survivors of the battle. By a ruse he inflicted a defeat, albeit a minor defeat, on Hannibal's army and gained enormous prestige because of it.

At Syracuse, Marcellus organized an assault by land and sea, incorporating the latest techniques and equipment of naval siegecraft. Siege by sea had become a specialty, which required dedicated ships, weapons, and personnel— soldiers, for instance, had to accustom themselves to a shifting deck, and artillery men had to adjust their fire to a ship's rise and fall and understand the effect of the constant spray on their machines. Assault from the sea, when pressed with expertise and courage and coordinated with land forces, could overwhelm any target. At Syracuse, the Romans linked eight quinqueremes together and placed siege towers on the decks, along with archers, slingers, and javelin men, for a seaborne assault, and they might have taken Syracuse on their first attempt if they had not been attacking the defenses created by an engineering genius, Archimedes, who, so to speak, wrote the book on buoyancy, ship construction, and its consequent vulnerabilities. (Ships today use Archimedes's calculations.) He understood that a warship, such as a quinquereme, was stable at speed in the open, but in a siege it was tippable. To take advantage of these characteristics, he devised counterbalanced cranes that could hook a ship and overturn it. These cranes were an unpleasant surprise for Marcellus.

Archimedes had also analyzed the mathematics of ballistae and catapults and had had different sizes built, so that they could deliver their projectiles with systematic and accurate fire anywhere within the city's defensive perimeter, night or day, including the harbor. When the Romans' siege-quinqueremes (called "harps" because of their shape) first came within range, Archimedes's catapults fired boulders at them, and if they survived that onslaught and came closer, other catapults fired barrages of light darts. And, finally, if they managed to get near the walls, the counterbalanced cranes swung out over the harbor, seized a ship, and lifted it enough to send it crashing down on top of another ship or dropped a five-hundred-pound boulder on the ships or hooked it and tipped it over.

In addition, Archimedes had prepared the walls with narrow firing-slits to protect the defenders, and, as a consequence, the Romans were unable to clear the walls for a successful assault or even to approach them. The Roman commander, Marcellus, managed to make a jest of the rough treatment of his fleet (as though the siege were a banquet)—"Archimedes turned our ships into ladles, which poured out water, but he dismissed the harps, because they had not been invited." The Carthaginians did send a fleet and an army to Sicily, but the fleet withdrew as soon as it had landed its troops, because it had no chance of defeating the Roman fleet. The army was more successful and managed to convince many Sicilian cities to slaughter their Roman garrisons and defect. The Roman response was equally brutal. The possession of Sicily hinged upon the siege of Syracuse.

The siege (214–212) dragged on and on, and the Roman commander was considering lifting it to attack the Carthaginian forces when a traitor brought him news of a poorly defended section of wall. The Syracusans had grown complacent about the efficacy of their defenses, they relied on Archimedes's devices, and they celebrated their continuing success, got incautiously drunk, fell asleep, and woke up to find that the Romans had slipped over the wall. Marcellus, observing Syracuse from a vantage point, is supposed to have wept because this beautiful city would soon be reduced to ashes, but when he was asked to spare the city, he replied that after three years of siege, just capturing the city was not enough recompense for his troops.

Marcellus released his soldiers to loot, but he did, specifically, order that Archimedes be brought to him alive; unfortunately, the Roman soldiers knew very well who, specifically, they had to blame for the destruction visited upon them, and the first Roman soldier to encounter the mathematician ran him through with his sword. Marcellus sent the looted art work to Rome and was subsequently blamed for turning the thoughts of Romans from war to effete cultural pursuits. (Marcellus was killed in an ambush, presaged by the birth of a baby with the head of an elephant.)

After the fall of Syracuse, the Romans campaigned throughout Sicily and reduced the towns, which had gone over to the Carthaginians. The Roman fleet raided Utica and carried off shiploads of grain and other plunder. The Carthaginians put together two fleets of sixty warships with troops, elephants, and money, one to reinforce their armies in Spain and the other to retake Sardinia, where the Romans were struggling with rebel Sardinians for control of the island. The Romans had defeated a rebel army, but the Carthaginian fleet appeared, disembarked its army, and, as usual, sailed away. (On the return trip to Carthage, it met a Roman fleet and the Carthaginian ships scattered.) The Carthaginian army, combined with the surviving rebels, fought a second battle with the Romans. The Romans won and quashed the rebellion.

In general, in this period of the war, the Romans were holding on, winning here, losing there, and they were determined, as a part of their policy of attrition, not to allow Hannibal to acquire a port and to be resupplied. They sent a fleet of twenty-five ships to defend the coast along the heel of Italy and, specifically, the port city of Tarentum. Some Tarentine traitors, however, who wanted to get rid of the Romans—and who thought that the Carthaginians were going to win the war—let Hannibal through the gates. The Roman commander was drunk and only just managed to escape to the citadel with some Roman troops. (The Roman historian Livy [i.e., Livius] omits his name, but the Greek historian Polybius was not so shy. The commander's name was Livius.) The Romans clung to the citadel, which lay at the end of a narrow peninsula and controlled the harbor. Hannibal erected earthworks to seal the citadel off from the city and protect the city from Roman attack (should the Romans reinforce their garrison by sea).

Since the citadel prevented the Tarentines' ships in the inner harbor from leaving the harbor, Hannibal had the townspeople prepare a city street so that it could handle wagons carrying heavy loads, had the ships transported through the town, and had them launched beyond the citadel, to blockade the Romans and threaten them with starvation.

The Romans [Livy writes] and their prefect, Marcus Livius, pinned all their hopes on the supplies that would be brought from Sicily (now that the Romans had regained control of the island). A fleet of twenty-five ships, only three of them triremes, under the command of Quinctius, a man who had distinguished himself in the war, set out under sail from Rhegium with no expectation of having to fight a battle, until, unexpectedly he ran into a Tarentine fleet about equal in size to his own and commanded by the Tarentine, Democrates. Although Quinctius had not expected a battle, he had put in at Croton and Sybaris, levied oarsman and soldiers, and brought his fleet up to full strength. By chance, just as the enemy came in sight, the wind died and Quinctius had time to stow the sails and prepare the oarsmen and soldiers for the battle.

The fleets crashed into each other especially violently as the Tarentines wanted to break Roman domination of the sea, dash their hopes of resupply, and thus preserve their own freedom, while the Romans fought to retain possession of the citadel, prove that they were the better men, and thereby that they had lost Tarentum not through any lack of courage but because of treachery. Therefore, when the signal was given, both sides charged and struck, prow-to-prow. No one held his ship back, nor did they suffer the enemy to pull away once they had grappled them. The fighters were at such close quarters in hand-to-hand combat that they had to use their swords. The prows were stuck together, while the sterns swung back and forth as the oarsmen continued to row. The ships were packed together so tightly that this sea battle was more like a land battle with lines of infantry pushing against each other and soldiers jumping from ship to ship. Scarcely any missile fell harmlessly into the sea.

The most notable battle, however, was fought between the Roman ship of Quinctius himself and the Tarentine ship of Nico (surnamed Perco).

Nico had his public reasons to hate the Romans (as they hated him), but also personal reasons, because he was one of the ringleaders who had betrayed Tarentum to Hannibal. As Quinctius was fighting and exhorting his troops, Nico transfixed him with a javelin. Quinctius, in full armor, fell headfirst off the prow, the Tarantine leader leaped on to the Roman ship and forced the crew to retreat from the prow and mass in the stern, where they were barely holding out, when suddenly another enemy ship attacked and the Roman ship was overwhelmed and captured. Panic seized the other ships when they saw the fate of their commander's ship, and they fled. Some were taken at sea and some escaped by beaching their ships, although the ships themselves were plundered by the people of Thurii and Metapontum. A few of the supply ships were captured, but most trimmed their sails to the changing winds and escaped out to sea.

Despite their victory, the Tarentine fleet was not strong enough to prevent the Romans from landing supplies and reinforcements and blockading Tarentum from the sea. A Carthaginian fleet sailed to Tarentum to bring supplies, but, embarrassingly, the Carthaginian crews not only ate all the food they had brought, they also consumed the town's supply, which only made the situation worse, while the Roman garrison continued to maintain an ample stockpile of rations.

The Carthaginian fleet, therefore, withdrew up the Adriatic to Corcyra, where it could help Philip. The Romans took advantage of the situation to mass warships and freighters equipped with siege towers and artillery to assault the city. (The Carthaginians at this time had controlled Tarentum for five years.) They found a man willing to betray the city, though, in his case, it was rather due to his separation from the woman he loved than from any affection for the Romans. On the chosen night, the Roman commander had his men shout their war cries all along the walls including the citadel wall, everywhere, that is, except the spot where the traitor had promised the Romans easy and unopposed access. The plan worked perfectly; an elite force found the wall deserted, climbed up, got inside, opened a gate, and admitted the army. The army spread through the city and the defense collapsed. The Romans then looted Tarentum.

CHAPTER THIRTY

The First Macedonian War

In 214 BCE, envoys came from Oricum (on the east coast of the Adriatic, just north of Corcyra) to the praetor Marcus Valerius, whose duty it was to guard Brundisium and the Calabrian coast. Philip had attacked Oricum with a fleet of 120 small boats, but, as this operation did not proceed as quickly as he wished, he brought his army up secretly one night for an all-out assault on the city; since the town had neither walls nor men and weapons, Philip had taken the place. The envoys asked the Romans to save them and defend the coast against their common enemy.

Marcus Valerius detailed a rear guard and then loaded up his army on troop ships and sailed to Oricum. He caught the small Macedonian garrison by surprise and retook the city. Envoys now arrived from Apollonia and informed Valerius that unless the Romans sent help, they would succumb to the assault of the Macedonians and be forced out of the Roman alliance. Valerius transported Q. Naevius Crista, a veteran of the war, and two thousand picked men to the mouth of the river on which Apollonia lay.

After Crista landed—the ships returned to Oricum—he led his men along an unguarded path and slipped into the city during the night, unbeknownst to Philip. Crista then reconnoitered the enemy camp and even identified the tent of the king without being detected. At dawn on the next day he introduced himself to the captain of a unit of young men of Apollonia and inspected them and the defenses of the city. He seemed so confident that he imparted some of his own confidence into the Apollonians and fired their enthusiasm by comparing their aggressive attitude with the lassitude and carelessness of the enemy. Then he led them in a dawn attack on the Macedonians.

His sudden appearance at the enemy's gate terrified them; they panicked and scattered, shouting and screaming; not one of the soldiers grabbed his weapons or thought to resist; and even the king, who had sprung up from his sleep, fled, half-naked, to the river and his ships. The Romans killed or captured about three thousand Macedonians, they plundered the camp, and they turned the machines of war over to the Apollonians, who removed them to their city and used them to bolster their defenses.

When the news of this victory reached Oricum, Marcus Valerius bought his fleet up to the mouth of the river to prevent the king escaping by sea. Philip, as his troops had lost much of their equipment, burned his ships and marched his army back to Macedonia. The Roman fleet went into winter quarters at Oricum.

Over the winter, the Roman commander visited the Aetolians and at one of their assemblies proposed an alliance. He promised the Aetolians that the Romans would help them regain control over their northwestern neighbor, Acarnania, and give them whatever cities the Romans took—that is, the buildings, walls, and land—while the Romans would keep the movable property (including the people). He promised the aid of the Roman fleet, and he pointed out how they had manhandled Philip in the earlier campaign. The Aetolians did not need much persuading, as they had long dreamed of acquiring Acarnania.

The treaty of 212 BCE (ratified in 210) committed the Romans to providing twenty-five quinqueremes, while the Aetolians would prosecute the war on land. Perhaps the Aetolians did not fully grasp the very limited objectives of the Romans, which were to keep Philip too occupied in Greece to cross over to Italy. (A Macedonian had warned them that they would be like the light-armed troops stationed before the phalanx; they would do the fighting and, if they suffered a disaster, the phalanx (i.e., the Romans) would just withdraw unscathed.) When the Roman commander reported on the situation to the Senate, including the addition of allies in the Peloponnesus, he said that the fleet, combined with the Aetolian army, would be a sufficient force to deal with Philip and his legion could be returned to service in Italy.

Then the question of crewing the ships was brought up. The Romans had employed a system under which private individuals had donated the salaries of oarsmen, but now they refused to pay anymore. The Senate was at a loss until one of the consuls proposed that first, before the Senate required other people to take on this duty, Senators themselves should bring their private wealth to the treasury, where it could be used to hire oarsmen before the Senate called upon ordinary people to pay. This simple solution satisfied everyone.

The Aetolian alliance accomplished what the Romans wanted—to distract Philip—but the Aetolian army was no match for the Macedonian army. Their land was plundered, and they were ready to seek peace, when the Romans, in their greatest coup, under the command of Laevinius, took the island of Aegina and sold it to Attalus, the king of Pergamum, who, thus enticed, now brought his fleet into the war. The captive Aeginetans begged the Roman commander to allow them to send out messages to their friends and relatives to ransom them. The consul replied that they should have negotiated with him before they found themselves in this predicament, but in the end, he relented.

While Philip presided over the Nemean games (near Corinth), the Romans raided and ravaged the contiguous lands, before Philip surprised them and drove them back to their ships. The king was immensely proud of this victory, and to exploit it, he led his army into Elis, where he expected—after all, he had driven the Romans off—to be fighting only Greeks; instead, to his horror, he encountered four thousand Roman marines, that is, just about a full legion. He considered retiring, but, concerned that he would be labeled a coward, he led a charge at the Romans. The charge was ill-advised. His horse was killed, he was flung to the ground, and he had to defend himself on foot, until his men could come to his rescue and remove him from the battlefield. After this skirmish, Philip returned to Macedonia to put down an Illyrian invasion, and the Roman fleet sailed to Aegina and went into winter quarters with the Pergamene fleet.

In the next year, while Philip was active on land, the allied fleet attacked the city of Orem on Euboea; King Attalus attacked on the land side, while the Romans launched their attack from the sea. By this time, the Romans had perfected their naval siege techniques with siege towers, catapults, and ballistae on the decks of quinqueremes linked together. Coastal cities, where the inhabitants had thought that the sea protected them, now discovered that the sea rather provided the Romans with an avenue of attack. In four days the allies took this city (not without the connivance of the Macedonian commander). They attempted to take Chalcis, but the currents were so strong and the garrison there so determined that they gave up the attempt. At this point, Attalus was informed of an attack upon his kingdom, and he withdrew from the war to attend to his own affairs. Philip continued to attack the Aetolians on land, and he began a building program to strengthen his fleet against the Romans. He had hoped that the Carthaginians would send a fleet around the Peloponnesus into the Aegean, but the Carthaginian admiral was too afraid of the Romans to attempt it.

In 206, the Aetolians, exhausted and demoralized—and without the acquiescence of the Romans—made a separate peace treaty with Philip. This peace infuriated the Romans who had just sent a new fleet and ten thousand troops to carry on a more active war against Philip. Nonetheless, the Romans made the best of a bad situation and negotiated their own peace with Philip in 205— they settled all questions about Illyria, enlisted the Illyrian king as an ally, kept the critical harbors of Corcyra, Oricum, Apollonia, and Epidamnus, all of which measures would facilitate a resumption of hostilities, if necessary. (The Romans had a particular genius, not so much for waging war as for organizing peace to their own benefit.) Then they got on with the final stages of the war against Hannibal.

Although the Romans could not prevent Carthaginian raids on Sardinia and Italy, neither could the Carthaginians prevent Roman fleets from raiding Carthaginian territory. The Romans could sail from Sicily to Africa, ravage the land, take prisoners, collect booty, and return to Sicily in twelve days. The Carthaginians were wary of meeting them at sea—one fleet scattered in panic the moment it spotted a Roman fleet—and the Romans, in addition to carrying out raids, were also collecting intelligence about conditions in Africa in preparation for an invasion led by the hero of the hour, Publius Scipio.

The young Scipio had earned his reputation in Spain following a catastrophic defeat and the death of his father and uncle. In 211, the Carthaginian generals, who previously had refused to cooperate, suddenly and secretly came together and defeated and killed the Scipio brothers in separate actions. The Romans lost everything they had gained and barely held the line of the Ebro River. When word reached Rome, the young Publius Scipio, who had never held an office with the *imperium* (the authority to command troops), asked the popular assembly to grant him the command in Spain. Scipio had a sterling reputation as a man who could, and did, converse with Jupiter, who had fought bravely against Hannibal twice, and who had crushed at sword point an incipient movement by some young nobles to desert Rome.

He attained the command and upon his arrival in Spain galvanized the demoralized army, led it by sea to the Carthaginian strongpoint and depot of New Carthage (Cartagena), assaulted the depot by land and sea, and took it with the help of an elite force, who waded through a lagoon considered impassable by the defenders. The lagoon seemed to have miraculously drained just for Scipio, appropriately enough, given that his watchword for the operation was "Neptune leads us." After this coup he retrained his army, introduced the Spanish sword, and in two battles defeated the principal Carthaginian armies and drove Hasdrubal, the brother of Hannibal, from Spain. (The Romans combined against Hasdrubal in northern Italy at the Metaurus River, eliminated his army, killed him, and tossed his head into Hannibal's camp—Hannibal is supposed to have said, as he looked upon the face of his brother, "At last I see the end.")

Scipio and his indispensable second-in-command, Laelius, concentrated on the last Carthaginian stronghold in Spain, Gades. Gades was a city past the Strait of Gibraltar on the Atlantic coast just where the strait opened up. The Romans had hoped to take Gades by treachery, but the Carthaginians had discovered the plot and decided to send the conspirators to Carthage. They put them on board a quinquereme, let it take the lead because it was slow, and followed with eight triremes. However, just as it was entering the strait, Laelius spotted it and set out in pursuit with his flagship, also a quinquereme, and seven triremes; he was confident that the enemy quinquereme, already in the currents of the strait, would not be able to turn around and recover its harbor.

Adherbal, the Carthaginian commander, was caught by surprise, could not make up his mind whether to follow his quinquereme or turn on the enemy, and then it was too late—the Romans had come within missile range and were attacking from all sides, although, because of the stiff currents, no one could steer their triremes where they wanted—the currents negated experience and skill. Some ships, in attempting to ram an enemy ship, rammed their own. Ships were spun around, willy-nilly, so that an attacking ship, in position to ram an enemy amidships, suddenly spun and presented its side to the enemy, while a ship about to be rammed spun so it could attack its enemy. As the triremes were carried here and there in the battle, the Roman quinquereme, a heavier, more powerful ship, was able to bull through the currents, and ram and sink two triremes, and smash a tier of oars on a third. At that point, Adherbal raised his sails and fled with the remaining five ships to Africa.

Meanwhile, a Carthaginian admiral, Mago, under instructions from home, raided Italy and seized Genua (Genoa). From there he sailed north to enlist an army of Gauls and Ligurians large enough to challenge the Romans, but the Romans defeated his army, wounded Mago, and forced him to retreat even farther to the north, where he received orders to return to Africa to help defend Carthage from the Roman invasion. He died en route, and some of his ships were captured by the Roman fleet off Sardinia.

By this time (206 BCE), Scipio had returned from Spain to a hero's welcome in Rome, he was elected consul, and he proposed that the Senate authorize him to invade Africa. His political opponents in the Senate pointed out that Hannibal was still in Italy and, perhaps, Scipio should concentrate on defeating him or expelling him before setting off on an African adventure. The Senate compromised. It would allow Scipio to take command of the troops in Sicily, and if a later inspection concluded they were ready, the Senate would approve the invasion. The army passed the test.

Scipio, according to the most modest estimates in our sources, had a force of ten thousand infantry (two legions) and twenty-two hundred cavalry. (Some authors report, however, that when the multitudes of men all shouted at the same time, birds flying overhead dropped from the sky, dead.) Scipio took great pains to ensure the orderly boarding and manning of the fleet. First the commanders and then the crews of the ships boarded and settled themselves; next they loaded the supplies of food and water, rations for forty-five days and bread for fifteen. He assigned the commander, the navigator, and two soldiers to man the gangway to count the supplies, and he questioned every party about the heads of cattle and the amount of feed and water for each. When each ship had forty-five days' water, he ordered the soldiers to board.

Scipio told his navigators to set a course for Emporia (in Africa), where the land was fertile and well watered and the population not at all warlike. Scipio personally commanded the fleet of twenty warships on the right flank; on the left was Laelius. Each warship had one lantern, each freighter two, and the commanders' ships three, so they could all be identified at night. In total, Scipio had forty warships and four hundred freighters. (Twenty quinqueremes and ten quadriremes were built in forty-four days.)

A huge crowd, not only from Lilybaeum but from the whole of Sicily, gathered to watch the fleet depart: a tremendous number of ships, Rome's most famous general, an expedition to force Hannibal to leave Italy and to end the war. Scipio prayed to all the gods and goddesses, who inhabited land and water to grant him victory in Africa. Then he made his offerings, dumped the bodies of the sacrificial animals into the water, and had the trumpeter give the signal to depart. A brisk favorable wind soon carried the fleet out of sight of land.

About midday, the sky grew so dark that the ships could hardly distinguish one another and the fog continued through the night, but the wind strengthened at daybreak and blew the fog away. The navigator told Scipio that he recognized a headland called Mercury and that Africa was close, no more than a couple of miles distant. Scipio ordered the ships to continue, and for a while, they sailed under the same wind, but again a fog came up, and, as they sailed into the night, they became uncertain of their course and location, and Scipio ordered the ships to anchor, to avoid running into each other or crashing on the shore. The following day, when Scipio asked the name of the next headland, his navigator replied, "Beautiful" (*Pulcher*), and Scipio said that he accepted the sign and ordered the fleet to go ashore there. (Scipio was still confident that Neptune led him.)

As soon as they landed, they advanced to a height inland and built their camp. The local inhabitants panicked and filled the roads with refugees—men, women, children, and animals. Carthage was thrown into turmoil as great as if the city itself had been taken, a foreshadowing of what was to come sixty years later. As part of his campaign to blockade Carthage, Scipio lay siege by land and sea to the port city of Utica (which controls the bay in which Carthage lies). During these operations a Roman quinquereme at sea was surprised by three quadriremes. The quadriremes could not outmaneuver the quinquereme, because it was handier than they, and when they tried to close, the crew of the quinquereme used its higher position to hurl javelins down on the quadriremes; boarding was out of the question, because the marines of the quadriremes could not scale the higher ship, and the Romans were well able to defend themselves until they ran out of missiles. At that point they were close enough to their camp on shore to run their ship aground, leap out, and save themselves, although the ship was lost.

Scipio had converted his quinqueremes for the assault on the seaward walls of Utica by adding catapults and towers. He continued the siege, or the appearance of a siege, even as he was drawn away to fight the Carthaginians in the field. In the next two years, Scipio defeated the Carthaginians in three battles, drove them into the city, separated them from Numidia (the source of their

best cavalry), and, after his final victory in the field (before the return of Hannibal), he seized the town of Tunes (which cut Carthage off from its hinterland). As he was securing Tunes, which overlooked Carthage, he saw the
Carthaginian fleet leave harbor, and he assumed, rightly, that it intended to
attack his fleet at Utica. Scipio set out for Utica immediately to prepare his
forces to withstand the Carthaginian attack. (There was not enough time to
refit his warships.)

How [writes Livy] could ships armed with catapults and other such para-
phernalia, ships designed to be used more like parapets from which to scale
the walls, how could such encumbered ships fight more maneuverable and
more appropriately armed enemy ships?

As soon as Scipio arrived, he put his warships, contrary to normal practice, in the rear nearest the shore and placed the merchants in four lines
opposite the enemy, like a wall. To prevent them from becoming scattered
in the tumult of battle, he joined them together with masts and yardarms
thrown from ship to ship and then linked the ships with stout ropes, one
to another, as though woven together in a chain. Planks were laid, as
bridges, so that the soldiers could pass from one merchant to the next.
Under these bridges he left passageways so that scout ships could go out to
attack the enemy and withdraw in safety. Almost a thousand elite soldiers
were placed on the merchants with a stock of missiles sufficient for a long,
drawn-out battle. They completed their preparations and then they awaited
the arrival of the enemy.

If the Carthaginians had moved with dispatch, while the Roman fleet
was in turmoil, they could have completely defeated the Romans, but they
were conscious of the disasters they had suffered on land and no less so by
sea, where they should have been able to have confidence in their greater
strength. Thus, on the crucial day, they wasted time and only directed their
fleet toward the port (which the Africans call Rusucmona) as the sun was
setting. On the next day, as the sun rose, they drew up their ships in the
open sea and waited for the Romans to come out and fight a conventional
sea battle. When, after a considerable delay, they saw no sign of movement by the Romans, they attacked the merchants. The affair was less like
a naval battle and more like a naval siege in which ships assault walls,
because the merchantmen towered above the attackers. The Carthaginians,
from the inferior position of their decks, threw many missiles toward the
higher decks of the Romans without much effect, while the Romans' missiles, launched from above, struck hard and accurately.

Scout ships and other light craft rushed out through the spaces under
the bridges. At first, they had some success, but many of them were sunk
by the heavier warships and the surviving ships were jumbled together
with the enemy and caused the soldiers on the line of merchants to hold
their fire for fear of hitting their own men. The Carthaginians threw barbed

shafts (which the soldiers called harpoons) into the sterns of the merchants. The Romans could neither dislodge the barbs nor break the shafts nor shatter the chains attached to them, and, as the Carthaginians broke the links holding the first line of ships together and towed some off, the Roman soldiers retreated to the second line. The Carthaginians drew off about sixty merchant ships.

Back in their city, the Carthaginians declared a great victory, but it was an empty victory—they had neither weakened Scipio's fleet of warships nor had they managed to lift the siege. With no options left, the Carthaginians recalled Hannibal, and Hannibal, eluding the Roman fleet, landed back in Africa. He and Scipio fought the decisive battle at Zama in 202 BCE. Although Hannibal, with the odds stacked against him, developed a masterful battle plan—in brief, to use mercenaries and Carthaginian troops to wear out the legions, at which point his veterans would enter the fighting and win the battle—Scipio out-thought him, the Roman allied cavalry defeated Hannibal's cavalry, Hannibal's elephants were ineffective, and the legions were just too tough, even for his veterans. Carthage capitulated and the Second Punic War was over (201 BCE). One condition of the treaty was that the five hundred ships of the Carthaginian fleet would be destroyed.

The most important consequence for the rest of the world was the development—perforce—of the Roman army, which now was flexible, able to fight in any direction, able to divide into separate units, which could fight independently, and, more importantly, now commanded by men who had, as it were, been trained by Hannibal. No army in the world was its equal.

Greeks Will Be Free

After the defeat of Carthage, the Romans launched a series of wars: one to exterminate the Gauls north of the Po (Cisalpine Gaul); another to organize southern Gaul (Transalpine Gaul) into a new province (modern Provence) to join Italy with Spain; and a third to pacify Spain. (They also revised their calendar—and hence ours—so that the first month of the year would be January instead of March, to give the newly elected consul time to get to Spain for the start of the campaigning season.) By 133 BCE, the Romans, after waging the most brutal sort of war (including the murder of five thousand men lured to their death by a promise of amnesty), had Spain fairly well under control (although they did not completely pacify it for another hundred years). In addition, at the urging of the elder Cato—*Carthago delenda est* ("Carthage must be destroyed")—the Romans attacked and razed Carthage (Third Punic War, 149–146).

In the east, the peace of Phoenice (which concluded the war with Philip, 205 BCE) had settled affairs—more or less—and allowed Rome to concentrate on Hannibal and Carthage, but it also allowed Philip a free hand in Greece and the Aegean. Philip's rival in the east, Antiochus III (who had brought much of Alexander's eastern empire back under his control) threatened Rome's allies, the Ptolemies, Rhodes, and Pergamum. Philip threatened them no less, but, at first, waged a covert war in the Aegean through his sponsorship of pirates, which gave him a cheap way to raise money to attack his enemies and disavow responsibility. In one case, he fomented a war between Rhodes and some Cretan cities, which were little more than pirate strongholds. Of the three powerful kings in the east, Philip, Antiochus, and Ptolemy, Ptolemy alone understood that the world had changed and the power had shifted to Rome.

Philip built a fleet, paid for by the proceeds from piracy—Philip's agent in the Aegean sacrificed to the divinity *False Oath and Felony*, and another agent, apparently also devoted to the same divinity, destroyed thirteen ships at

Rhodes in an unprovoked attempt to burn the dockyards. The king, in his own person, undertook a campaign in the northern Aegean, which threatened free trade and alarmed the Athenians and the Rhodians; and then, in the Spring of 201, he extended his campaign into the middle Aegean. There he defeated the Rhodians and occupied Miletus, but his aggression alarmed Attalus, the king of Pergamum (and a Roman ally), enough to form an alliance with Rhodes and enter the conflict.

In the summer of 201, Philip attacked Chios. By this time the ins-and-outs of naval siegecraft had been well analyzed, and an expert in such operations had produced a handbook with specific recommendations, one of which was that the besieged should keep a supply of naphtha for burning the enemy's works and also, where available, keep a store of Arabian drugs, mollusc extract, mistletoe juice, salamander blood, and the venom of vipers and asps "to coat the missiles and deal sudden death to those who are wounded and excite fear in those attacking the walls." On the other hand, this expert also recommended that the besieged (and one would hope the attackers as well) "hire the most skilled physicians, those specializing in wounds and the extraction of missiles; they must have suitable instruments and a range of drugs and they must be provided with wax, honey, bandages, and compresses, in order that the wounded soldiers do not die and can soon recover and return to action, confident that they will be well cared for."

King Attalus and his allies, the Rhodians, responded to Philip's attack on Chios (summer of 201). Their approach forced Philip to lift the siege and try to withdraw, but Attalus overtook the Macedonian right wing, and Philip ordered his ships to turn and fight (while he slipped behind some smaller islands in a light craft and took up a concealed position where he could watch the battle). Philip had a fleet of over a hundred ships of all sorts, but only fifty-three decked warships, while Attalus and the Rhodians had sixty-five decked ships, but only a scattering of light craft.

Attalus led the charge. His flagship rammed an "Eight," striking it below the waterline, grappling it, and engaging in deck-to-deck combat, before putting it out of action. Philip's flagship, a "Ten," was rammed by a *trihemiolia* (a single-tiered ship with three men to an oar). The ram stuck fast amidships as the trihemiolia had attacked so violently that the steersman had been unable to check its speed. The "Ten" lost way and could no longer be steered; then two quinqueremes rammed it, one from each side, grappled it, and boarded, and in the fighting killed Philip's admiral and crew.

Two admirals in Attalus's fleet, brothers, commanded separate ships; the one brother attacked an "Eight," prow to prow. The Eight's ram struck his ship above the waterline, since it had a high prow, while his ram struck the "Eight" below the waterline; and then, with both rams stuck fast and the Eight taking on water, he could not break away. The enemy marines boarded his ship and almost took it, but Attalus rushed to the rescue and managed to separate the two ships, which left the whole hostile marine force on board the friendly ship, where they were killed, while Attalus boarded and took the hostile marines' own, abandoned ship.

The other brother had worse luck. He missed his charge on an enemy ship and had the oars of one side of his own ship shattered, rendering him helpless. The enemy boarded; he escaped only by diving into the sea and swimming to a trihemiolia coming to his rescue. Here, on the right wing, the issue of the battle was in doubt.

The Rhodians, meanwhile, had caught Philip's left wing while it was retreating, and engaged it. The Rhodian ships charged and smashed the oars of the last of the fleeing ships, and Philip ordered those in the lead to turn and fight. Both sides formed a battle line. Philip had the advantage in smaller craft and placed them between his decked ships to thwart the Rhodians *diekplous*-tactic. Nonetheless, some of the Rhodian ships, by their superior skill, were able to pass between the enemy ships, smash their oars on the way, and, having rendered them helpless, turn and attack them from the rear. But more Rhodian ships were unable to employ their preferred maneuver, because the smaller craft, stationed between the decked ships, attacked them, smashed their banks of oars, or disabled the steering oars. Nonetheless, the Rhodians, compelled to attack prow on, still had the advantage, because they were so practiced that they would dip their bows at the moment of impact and receive the enemy ram above the waterline while ramming the enemy below. Still, ramming was dangerous; if the ships became stuck, the Macedonian marines had the edge in the exchange of missiles and in hand-to-hand combat.

One Rhodian ship rammed an enemy and sank it, but its own ram broke off, water poured into the Rhodian ship, the ship was rendered immobile, and was grappled and boarded. The Rhodian commander and his marines fought valiantly, until the commander, heavily wounded, fell into the sea in full armor and sank out of sight. Another Rhodian captain led three quinqueremes to the rescue and attacked the attackers. He, in turn, was boarded and was wounded three times in the melee. He stepped back from the combat, so he could have his wounds bound up, and then again plunged into the fight.

As the Macedonian right wing, under orders to get to land and safety, continued to pull away, Philip saw that Attalus was pursuing too vigorously and was getting ahead of his own fleet. Collecting his ships, Philip cut Attalus off and forced him to beach his ship and flee on foot. The Macedonian marines, who were pursuing him, stopped to plunder the royal flagship and thus allowed Attalus to escape. In the aftermath, Philip issued a proclamation that he had won a great victory, and if his display of the accoutrements of Attalus seemed to signify that the Pergamene king had been killed in the fighting, so much the better.

Philip, however, had been roughly handled in the battle. He had lost twenty-four decked ships, including a "Ten," and also three thousand Macedonian marines and six thousand oarsmen. (Two thousand had been captured. The allies had lost five decked ships and 130 men killed.) The Macedonians believed their king's proclamation of victory until they had to collect the corpses of their comrades washed up on shore. This aggressive sea campaign of Attalus and the Rhodians blunted the drive of Philip and inspired his enemies and, in a subsequent action, blockaded him and removed him from action for the winter.

Ironically, Philip's victories were, in the end, self-defeating, because as Philip became more successful, he drew more attention to himself; when the Rhodians and Attalus asked the Romans to intervene, the Romans acquiesced and declared war on the Macedonians (Second Macedonian War, 200–197). For two years, while the Roman commanders on land were trying and failing to bring Philip to battle, the Roman fleet had a series of successes—it relieved Athens, which was under attack by the Macedonians; it captured a significant amount of Philip's war materials at Chalcis; and by its presence won over many Greeks and, more importantly, convinced the Achaean League not to support Philip.

In the next year, the new Roman consul, Flamininus, assumed command and advanced into Phocis. He and his army were all veterans of the Second Punic War—hardened, ruthless, and tenacious. In 197, he defeated Philip in the battle of Cynocephalae. At the Isthmian games in 196, Flamininus announced to the audience that, henceforth, all Greeks would be free. The Greeks cheered so loudly that birds flying overhead dropped dead (the standard by which crowd noise was measured)—an omen for future relations between Greeks and Romans. Greeks neither understood the Romans nor what the Romans really meant by *freedom*. The Roman true intention was that no single entity—neither Philip, who was confined to Macedonia, nor the Aetolians, who had wanted Philip deposed, nor any other power—would pose a threat to Rome. *Libertas* didn't mean that you could do whatever you wanted; it meant that within the Roman system you would receive due process.

Antiochus, the king of the Seleucid empire, like Philip, did not understand just how aggressive and how suspicious the Romans could be. They believed in preventive strikes, they saw themselves as the protectors of the Greeks, and they also were fine calculators of how much profit could be derived from a war. Antiochus understood only that the situation was ripe for exploitation. Taking advantage of Philip's involvement in the war with the Romans, Antiochus, through a combination of naval and land operations, seized much of coastal Asia Minor. He was careful to avoid Rome's allies, Rhodes and Pergamum, although he did campaign dangerously close to the borders of Pergamum, and he committed one huge blunder—he hired, as a mercenary general, the best military mind in the world, Hannibal, the man the Romans most hated and feared. No Roman could doubt that a king who had such an employee was also himself an enemy of Rome.

The Aetolians (who were unhappy with the Roman settlement of the war against Philip) pressed for Antiochus to help them, and Antiochus entered Europe to support his new allies with a fleet of sixty ships and some ten thousand troops. He settled into winter quarters with no sense of urgency and, indeed, treated the expedition as more of a honeymoon excursion with his new bride than a military campaign. The Romans had already reacted to rumors of Antiochus's plans by sending a fleet under the command of a praetor to the Peloponnesus and by enlisting Philip into the war with the promise that he could keep any place he captured. In 191, the Roman consul, Glabrio, began land operations against Antiochus. Antiochus's professions to Greeks that he had come as their liberator failed to convince anyone. He was harassed relentlessly by the Romans, tried to make a stand at Thermopylae, was quickly dislodged, and was chivvied back to Asia.

In 190, the Senate gave the consul, *Lucius* Cornelius Scipio, the command in Greece with instructions to cross into Asia if he felt that it was necessary. (The Senate, not having a particularly high opinion of Lucius, agreed to give him the command only if he would take as an associate his famous brother, *Publius* Cornelius Scipio Africanus.) The Roman fleet had been operating in conjunction with the Pergamenes and had won a victory at Corycus (near Chios), where the enemy fleet had captured two Carthaginian ships (allies of Pergamum). The Roman admiral had ordered his own ship to attack the enemy immediately, and had gotten far out in front of his fleet. His ship was grappled by three enemy ships, at which point, one might say, the Romans had the enemy right where they wanted them. The Roman legionnaires stormed on board the enemy ships, defeated the marines of all three, and captured two. The other ship broke away and fled, while the Roman admiral towed his prizes back to the main fleet.

While their enemies' attention was fixed on this combat, the Pergamene fleet circled around and launched a surprise attack on the flank of the enemy fleet (thus completing a successful *periplous*). After this victory, the Romans went into winter quarters. Their victory, satisfying as it was, did not clear the northern Aegean of Antiochus's naval forces, and the Roman army had to march overland to Asia through Thrace (facilitated by Philip) and circumvent places controlled by Antiochus.

At sea, Antiochus had reinforced his fleet and put Hannibal in charge of one detachment, but the Rhodians prevented Hannibal from joining the rest of the fleet. (One of Hannibal's innovations was to launch pots filled with poisonous serpents onto the decks of the enemy ships.) Antiochus's fleet had eighty-nine ships with two Sevens and three Sixes. The Romans and their allies, the Pergamene fleet and a division of Rhodians, had eighty ships, mainly quinqueremes with some quadriremes and trihemiolias. Antiochus's admiral moved his fleet in secret close to the Romans at Teos, where he could make a surprise attack on them, but the Romans received warning that the enemy's fleet was coming, and they got to sea and met the enemy at Cape Myonnesus.

The enemy's plan was twofold, first to extend the left flank to envelop the Roman fleet and second to advance in two lines to prevent the Romans executing a *diekplous*. The Rhodians covered the Roman flank to prevent the *periplous*, while the Romans just plowed straight ahead into the enemy formation, threw their grapnels, and let their legionnaires board and capture the enemy ships. The Rhodians, meanwhile, out on the flank of the enemy, attacked with rams and fire baskets attached on long poles at the bows of their ships. Their innovation with the fire baskets scattered the enemy, who refused to come anywhere near them, and who, with half their ships captured, fled.

(Fire was seldom decisive in a naval battle because of its inherent danger. However, during the civil wars between Antony, Octavian, Cassius, and Brutus, the naval forces of Cassius attacked a fleet of transport ships carrying Antony's troops. The soldiers on the transports lashed the ships together, so the warships attacking them could not sink them without ramming and running into the danger of being boarded and captured, so they lay off, shot fire arrows into the transports, and set some of them on fire. The ships attached to the burning ships cut loose to avoid the fire and thus made themselves vulnerable again to attacks by the warships.)

The defeat at Myonnesus caused Antiochus to abandon Lysimacheia, which the Romans then used as their main base for their advance into Asia Minor. Then, having gained local control of the Hellespont, the Romans were able to ferry their army across. Antiochus tried to negotiate, but the Romans would have none of it, and the two armies met in December at Magnesia-ad-Sipylum. Although the Romans were outnumbered two to one, they routed Antiochus and then dictated the terms of the treaty (of Apamea, 188): Antiochus was to evacuate Asia Minor, reimburse the Romans for all the costs of the war, and pay an indemnity to Pergamum. Antiochus was also required to hand over Hannibal. (Hannibal committed suicide.) The Greek cities, which had supported Rome, were to be free; those that had not were divided between Pergamum and Rhodes.

In 179, Philip died and his son Perseus became king. He inaugurated his reign by offering himself to the Greeks as a counterweight to Rome. The Romans concluded that his actions were directed against them, and in 172, they assembled a fleet of fifty ships and dispatched two allied legions and cavalry to their staging area in Greece, Apollonia, while envoys traveled throughout Greece, discouraging the allies of Perseus and confirming the loyalty of Rome's allies.

In an initial cavalry skirmish in Thessaly, the Romans were defeated and news of this ran throughout the Greek world, shaking the confidence of some allies. The Roman fleet, meanwhile, conducted more of a plundering campaign than a military operation. With the Greek world unsettled and the war not coming to a speedy end, the Rhodians made the disastrous mistake of offering to mediate between Perseus and the Romans. Hardly had their offer been received in Rome than news arrived that the consul Paulus (a veteran of the Second Punic War) had resoundingly defeated Perseus at the battle of Pydna (168 BCE). In the subsequent peace, the Romans broke the kingdom of Macedonia into four republics and punished Rhodes for its ill-advised— or, to the Romans, *treacherous*—interference by establishing the island of Delos as a free port—an act that devastated the Rhodian economy.

In the aftermath of the victory, the Romans ordered the Achaeans to allow Sparta, Corinth, and Argos to depart the League. The Greeks of the Achaean League had split into two factions, one of which believed that Rome had to be courted and obeyed no matter what, while the other—which prevailed— that the League was the juridical equal of Rome and that it had sole discre- tion over its members, even those members, like Sparta, that had been forcibly enrolled into the League against the expressed wishes of the Roman Senate. And so the Achaeans rejected the Roman command, prepared for war with Sparta, and, instead, found themselves at war with Rome. The Achaeans were soundly defeated in 146, Corinth was razed (and ceased to exist until refounded by Julius Caesar a century later), and all movable goods were shipped to Rome, Macedonia was converted into a Roman province, and its governor was given oversight of Greece. The Romans now considered themselves to be the mas- ters of the Mediterranean world. No authority existed that could resist them, and no action could be taken without their consent. Consequently, they did as they pleased for the advantage of Rome and the profit of individual Romans.

Thirst for Gold

In the west, the wars in Spain continued and the Romans experienced continual difficulty in raising the legions to fight the war. Roman citizens, taken from their farms, returned after multiple deployments to ruins. The Italian allies found themselves increasingly called upon for service in the army without any compensatory increase in wealth or benefits. These different issues intertwined and came to a head in the period 133–90 BCE.

Two brothers, Tribunes of the People, Tiberius and Gaius Gracchus, thought that they had found the answer to Rome's military problems. They proposed that the public land be divided up among army veterans as a sort of pension. They were opposed by the nobility, which had for years considered the public land their own, and, more to the point, the Gracchi disturbed and offended the Senatorial class by circumventing the Senate and going directly to the people to pass their program. At its most fundamental level, their political innovation meant that the Senate could be entirely eliminated from the political process. The result was a generation of violence inside Rome, culminating in the murders of Tiberius and Gaius Gracchus.

Despite their deaths, however, their program went forward. The last king of Pergamum—he was trying to keep himself from being assassinated by a prospective heir—willed his kingdom to the Roman people; the new province of Asia financed the Gracchan reforms and also provided the Romans with an anchor in Asia Minor, from which Rome continued to extend its influence and control in the east, partly by diplomacy but more effectively by military action.

Back in the west, however. the Roman nobility was so mismanaging a minor war—the Jugurthine War—in North Africa that the people elected as consul a "new man," Marius, none of whose ancestors had ever been consul. Unlike most Roman leaders, he entered politics with purely a military background (although to add to his bona fides was his marriage to Julia, the aunt of Julius

Caesar). He had no humanities; he knew no Greek and despised those who did; he was fierce, harsh, obstinate, and consumed with ambition. He rose from obscurity through his courage in battle in Spain, when he came to the notice of Scipio (the second *Africanus*, who destroyed Carthage in 146).

Marius was chosen to lead the army in Africa, because he had promised not to draft Roman citizens. He fulfilled his promise (in a way) by opening the ranks for the first time to citizens without property. His reforms included the standardization of legionary equipment and the reorganization of the legion so that the cohort became the smallest independent unit. His reforms increased the efficiency of the army, but transformed it into a profession, in the sense that the soldiers' sole livelihood now came from military service.

No sooner had Marius concluded the Jugurthine War than he had to fight a coalition of Germanic tribes, which had destroyed a double consular army in Gaul, routed an army in northern Italy, and now threatened Rome itself with a two-pronged advance. Marius exterminated the tribe he faced in Gaul, returned to Italy, and defeated the Germans there. As a general he was unsurpassed, but back in Rome, as a politician, he proved to be a babe in the woods and found himself shut out of the political process.

In 90 BCE, the selfish and shortsighted policy of the Senate toward the Italians led to the Social War, a civil war within Italy, which was ended by the Romans offering citizenship to those communities and individuals who had not joined the opposition and, in the end, by extending Roman citizenship to all free Italians, a step that should have been taken years before.

Meanwhile, in the east, the Romans had become hated, because of their insatiable greed and their contempt for anyone who was not Roman. Mithridates (r. 113–63 BCE), the king of Pontus (a land that stretched along the south shore of the Black Sea and was rich in natural resources and, in particular, in shipbuilding timber) took advantage of the situation. He claimed to be descended from the ancient Persian kings and to be the champion of Greeks and Greek culture. From his new capital, the prosperous port of Sinope, the king built an empire, first comprising most of the lands along the shores of the Black Sea, but as he extended his reach and became more successful and more assertive, he found himself falling under Roman scrutiny.

Mithridates kicked off a quasi-war with Rome by attacking their sometime-ally Rhodes. He had a fleet of three hundred decked ships and one hundred biremes and a large and formidable army. He caught the Romans by surprise and forced them into an immediate response of raising armies from, and relying upon, their local allies. Mithridates's army scattered the allies and forced the Roman commander to run for his life. The Roman fleet, guarding the Bosporus, retreated and gave Mithridates free access to the Aegean. His armies soon controlled almost all of Asia Minor, and as an object lesson on Roman greed, he professed to assuage the thirst for gold of one unfortunate Roman officer by pouring molten gold down his throat.

Word reached Rome of the defeats, and the atrocities, while the Romans were still settling the affairs of the Social War; they appointed Marius's hated rival Sulla to command the war against Mithridates. Sulla was a noble, but descended from an impoverished and disgraced lineage—one of his ancestors had been bounced from the Senate for corruption. Nor was he prepossessing in appearance—his facial complexion, according to an Athenian wit (whose tongue was sharpened, perhaps, because he was then being starved to submission in Sulla's siege of Athens), was a mix of red berries and oatmeal. Sulla repaired his impoverished state by seducing an older and wealthy woman, who bequeathed him her estate. (His step-mother also left him hers for similar reasons.)

Sulla required five months to raise an army and secure the funds for his campaign. Moreover, faced with an all too real chance that Marius, remaining behind, might seize control of Rome, he had to take time to stabilize the situation—as he thought—while, in Asia Minor, Mithridates ordered that all Italians, men, women, and children, be executed and their bodies left in the streets to rot. This massacre was carried out with varying degrees of enthusiasm.

Mithridates's next move, before advancing farther into Asia, was to attack Rhodes, a rival seapower and the last significant Roman ally in Asia Minor, but his fleet was damaged by a storm and outfought by the Rhodians—they held their fleet within their harbor and launched surprise sallies upon individual ships of Mithridates. Nonetheless, Mithridates's forces advanced upon Rhodes with a special, secret weapon, a combination of a tower and bridges, the *sambuca* (transported on two triremes fastened together). The sight of the *sambuca*, advancing toward their walls, frightened the Rhodians up to the moment when it collapsed under its own weight. Thus thwarted, Mithridates abandoned the siege and sailed to Europe, where the Athenians had offered him their fleet and their harbor. He tried to drive the Romans from Greece before Sulla arrived, but he failed. Sulla, upon his arrival, immediately undertook a double siege, one of Athens and one of the Piraeus.

He invested Athens closely enough to interdict all supplies and drive the people to resort to cannibalism. The Piraeus was more difficult because Mithridates's general, Archelaus, could be resupplied by sea. In addition, Sulla had difficulty acquiring timber for his siege engines, and he was cut off from Rome, because, on his departure, Marius had seized the city, set his bodyguard (recruited from slaves) loose to slaughter citizens, murder Sulla's adherents—nobody was safe—and he even rejoiced, while he was at dinner, to have the head of a rival brought to him. Headless bodies were a common sight in the street. Marius couldn't sleep because of constant nightmares; he turned to drink and even drunk could not escape his terrors. So he took to his bed and there, for six days under the delusion that he was commanding an army, shouted orders, gestured for the troops to advance, and uttered war cries. On the seventh day he died and left Rome in the power of his blood-thirsty son.

Mithridates had complete command of the sea. To raise a fleet, Sulla sent his trusted legate, Lucullus, to Egypt and Syria. Lucullus came from a well-known family, though not known for the right reasons—his father had been convicted of extortion and his mother had a certain reputation; Lucullus him-self loved liberal studies, could speak both Greek and Latin equally fluently and composed a historical study in Greek. (Sulla, when he came to write his memoirs, dedicated them to Lucullus, who, he said, could have made a better job of it.)

Lucullus, then, to carry out his commission from Sulla, had to sail on a pirate ship (with an escort of three Rhodian biremes) during the season of winter storms. He sought help first in Crete and then in Cyrene. From Cyrene he escaped a pirate attack and reached Alexandria. There Ptolemy greeted him with honors but refused to help, except to escort him to Cyprus. Along the way, Lucullus collected a few ships and evaded a pirate fleet by the ruse that he was going into winter quarters in Cyprus. Instead, he set out, rowing by day (so the enemy would not spy the sails of his fleet) and sailing by night, until he reached Rhodes. From Rhodes he acquired some more ships and then set out north along the coast.

As Lucullus gathered his fleet, Mithridates sent a large army to force a land battle in Greece while Sulla was occupied with Athens, but, before the army arrived, Sulla learned of a weak point in Athens's defenses and fought his way into the city. He forbade widespread burning, but the result, nonetheless, was a brutal sack and slaughter. In the Piraeus, Archelaus concluded that the siege could not be borne any longer and withdrew, allowing Sulla to enter and burn the shipyards. Archelaus assumed command of Mithridates's army and fought Sulla in Boeotia. In two battles—at Chaeroneia and Orchomenus—Sulla destroyed the enemy armies in a display of tactical brilliance and his legions' prowess.

Sulla now advanced to the Chersonese, where Lucullus, after all his adven-tures, culminating in a single ship-action against the king's flagship, finally joined him with a fleet of eighty ships, so that Sulla had a total force of 150 ships and Lucullus could protect the Roman crossing into Asia. Sulla offered terms to Mithridates: the king must turn over part of his fleet to Sulla, aban-don his conquests, and pay an indemnity. Another Roman general had landed in Asia Minor and rampaged through it, at one point almost cornering Mith-ridates, and so (in 85 BCE) Mithridates met with Sulla and agreed to his terms. Sulla left Lucullus in the Aegean to deal with the places that had supported Marius, while he returned to Italy with a fleet of over a thousand ships to face his enemies.

Mithridates retained his throne, but ambitious Romans had seen the defi-ciencies of his army and the amount of available plunder, and they were waiting for the first opportunity; for the moment, however, Sulla had to get his own house in order. He returned to Italy, won a brutal civil war, and pro-scribed hundreds of Romans, who could be put to death without trial. Sulla reorganized the Roman constitution, in brief, to prevent any other *Sulla* from arising, and then, having accomplished what he wished, he married a beau-tiful young woman and retired to the country to enjoy his new bride. He did not last out the year.

Unfortunately, Sulla's two main lieutenants, and successors, Crassus and Pompey, followed his example rather than his precepts. They saw all too well that the path to wealth, prestige, and political power lay through military com-mand. Thus, in the late seventies, Pompey and Crassus competed for com-mand, prestige, and the spoils arising from the civil war.

Pompey was an unusual individual. His father was so hated that when he died, Romans pulled his corpse off the funeral bier and pummeled it, but it seemed that as much as his father was hated, so much was the son loved. He was temperate, well-spoken, tactful, generous, and good looking, although a courtesan he favored (though not so much that he did not pass her off to a friend) said that after a bout of love she always bore the marks of his teeth.

Crassus, too, was temperate (although some said it was because of his par-simony and not his character). He was so well known for his avarice that when he was accused of intimacies with a Vestal Virgin, he was able to con-vince a court that he was interested in her property, not her body.

Crassus had such enormous wealth, that he dedicated a tenth of his prop-erty to Hercules, invited the whole population of Rome to a feast, and gave the citizens enough money to support them for three months (and still have millions left). But, even so, even as the victor over Spartacus, he was unpop-ular in Rome, and thus he employed a front man, a young, popular Roman—Julius Caesar.

Meanwhile, in the east, the Romans kept pressing Mithridates with mixed results until, finally, in 74 BCE, Lucullus was given the command. Lucullus had a good Roman road to facilitate the movement of his troops against Pon-tus and a fleet under the command of a praetor, ostensibly to fight the pirates of Cilicia, but really to fight Mithridates. The king prepared for the war with Lucullus by increasing his fleet to a total of four hundred ships of all types including 150 warships. He made an alliance with the Cilician pirates, and he enlisted some Roman commanders from the losers in the civil war. In the spring of 73 BCE, Mithridates attacked the Roman fleet at Chalcedon and defeated it, which gave him absolute command of the sea, and he used it to advance on Cyzicus (on the Black Sea).

A small Roman force inside Cyzicus inspired the townspeople to resist, and a swimmer with Lucullus's army paddled through Mithridates's fleet on an inflated skin—they thought he was some sort of sea monster—and brought the news that Lucullus was coming. Therefore, despite facing a vigorous assault by land and sea, the Roman garrison held out until Lucullus arrived with five legions, numerically inferior to Mithridates but in fighting ability far superior. Lucullus inflicted heavy losses—the women of a neighboring town became wealthy by stripping the enemy dead—and forced Mithridates to withdraw to Nicomedia. The king, with his superiority in ships, was able to withdraw safely.

In the next year, the Roman fleet—recruited from Rome's Asian allies—defeated the Pontic fleet. Lucullus had been sleeping in the precinct of Aphrodite, and he dreamed that she appeared to him and asked him, "Why are you sleeping, Lion. The fawns are near." He woke and, while he was pondering the significance of the dream, a messenger informed him that thirteen of Mithridates's quinqueremes were at sea nearby. Lucullus set out and captured them and then attacked the rest of the enemy ships, which were drawn up close to each other on shore. When, on his first attempt, Lucullus attacked from the sea, he was driven back by the massed fire of javelins and other missiles, so he landed his legionnaires, the legionnaires circled around by land behind the enemy ships, and forced them to launch and go out to sea, where Lucullus's fleet defeated them. He drove Mithridates out of the Bosporus and pursued him along the south shore of the Black Sea, while a second Roman fleet eliminated Mithridates's Aegean fleet.

Even without those defeats Mithridates had found that seapower was a limited advantage when a Roman army was already on the ground. Lucullus completely outmaneuvered the king and destroyed the bulk of his army during an ill-disciplined retreat in 71 BCE. Mithridates fled for refuge to the king of Greater Armenia, while Lucullus systematically reduced Pontus (but angered his army by not allowing them to "systematically plunder"). The Armenian king combined a scanty knowledge of Rome with a heightened opinion of his own power and refused to hand over Mithridates. Lucullus invaded Armenia in 69 BCE. The Armenian king uttered a jest about the size of Lucullus's forces, "If they have come as ambassadors, they are too many; if as an army, too few." He soon rued those words.

PART 7

The Roman Empire

Illustration 21. Liberna from the column of Trajan. (Drawing by Pamela M. Bradford)

I Shall Crucify You

While Mithridates was on the run, he lost control of the pirates of the eastern Mediterranean and let loose a scourge on the sea unparalleled in the ancient world except for the earlier massive raids of the sea peoples and the later Germanic raids on the Roman empire. These pirates "farmed the sea," sometimes in fragile little boats designed only to bring their crews alongside a merchantman and sometimes in fleets of triremes, with which they not only attacked ships but also towns and temples and festivals; sometimes they struck quickly and sometimes they laid siege to walled cities. On one occasion, they formed a fleet of four hundred ships and occupied and systematically looted the free port of Delos. They held captives for ransom, and they sold captives into slavery. They raided Italy. And on one occasion, they captured the young Julius Caesar, who had slipped out of Rome to avoid political awkwardness. (He was the nephew of Marius and he had barely escaped the proscriptions of Sulla.)

The pirates, whose base was in "shaggy Cilicia" and who (as the Romans said) preferred "to commit a crime rather than be a victim," demanded the paltry sum of twenty talents (i.e., today several hundred thousand dollars), until Caesar told them that he was not just one more young Roman noble but a person of stature and that he was worth at least fifty talents. He dispatched friends to raise the money, while he lived with the pirates in their lair, keeping two servants to tend to him and a friend for company.

For over a month he stayed with the pirates—"as bloodthirsty a crew as ever lived"—exercised with them, recited his own poetry to them, and called them ignorant savages when they did not show their appreciation. If he wanted a nap, he ordered them to be quiet. In short, he acted as though he were their boss. They particularly liked his sense of humor and laughed when he declared that once he was free, he was going to come back and crucify the whole lot of them. When the ransom was paid and he was free, he commandeered some ships, captured the whole gang, and then, on his own authority, had them all crucified. But since Caesar prided himself on his mercy, after he had them nailed to the crosses, he had their throats cut so they would not suffer. (Caesar recovered the fifty talents and kept them.)

The Romans, when they chose, could suppress any single nest of pirates. For instance, the inhabitants of the Balearic Islands kept a watch on the sea from their cliffs and attacked the merchant ships passing by—they thought the sea rather belched merchants forth as a kind of natural function. As soon as they saw a ship, the men would paddle rafts out and unloose a barrage of slung stones until the ship surrendered, and then they would plunder it. (They were especially adept with the sling because in their youth their mothers had insisted that they hit a designated target before they could eat supper.)

The Romans finally got fed up and sent some warships. The natives mistook them for merchants, and they rushed out on their rafts and slung their stones, but the Romans defended themselves with their shields and threw back javelins. The natives howled in dismay, fled back to shore, and hid, in vain, because the Romans landed, hunted them down, and put an end, once and for all, to the pirates of the Balearic Islands.

Another, and larger, hotbed of piracy was Crete, which had always had a reputation, stretching back to Homer, of being a nest of pirates. The Roman Senate appointed Marcus Antonius (father of the famous Marc Antony) to suppress the pirates of Crete, and he, in typical Roman fashion, used his command to enrich himself.

"He was so supremely confident of victory that he transported more chains than weapons and he paid the price for his arrogance: the enemy captured many of his ships and celebrated a kind of triumph by rowing into their harbors with their prisoners hanging from the yardarms."

Marcus Antonius, in his arrogance and avarice, was not atypical. The Roman Senate usually answered requests for aid by appointing commanders and commands for specific targets for a limited period of time. The Romans expected their allies to furnish the ships and the crews and also to pay for everything, including a substantial profit for the Roman commander. This ad-hoc system did not work well against pirates, because suppressing one pocket of pirates only created opportunities for all the other pirates.

By 75 BCE, the coasts of Italy were declared unsafe. Two Roman praetors and their lictors were captured by pirates, towns and temples were sacked, Roman ladies were kidnapped and held for ransom, the port city of Ostia was raided, and a consular fleet was burned. When the pirates captured someone who told them that he was a Roman citizen, they pretended to be afraid, and they would promise to deliver the captive from their ship immediately and then throw him overboard. Trade stopped.

One of the most corrupt and incompetent, but not untypical, Roman officials was the governor of the province of Sicily, Verres. As he said—and he lived by it—a governor had to acquire three fortunes: one to bribe the Senate to obtain the appointment, one to bribe the jury to acquit him of extortion, and one to live on. Verres knew all the tricks for obtaining money: order a city to build a warship, to furnish a crew, to pay a year's expenses, and hire a captain or, instead, just pay a lesser amount directly to the governor.

Verres appointed his mistress's husband, Cleomenes, to command his fleet.

When Cleomenes got word that pirates had put in at a nearby harbor, he called upon the garrison of the closest city for soldiers and oarsmen, but Verres had sold them exemptions, so, at this point, Cleomenes had the mast raised, the sails hoisted, the anchor cables cut, and then he issued his order—*run for your lives!* When Cleomenes saw that the pirates were coming after him, he ordered his ship to beach, jumped overboard, and fled back to Syracuse. The other captains beached their ships and ran after him. The pirate chief, Heracleo, burned the ships.

Verres had fallen asleep with Cleomenes's wife—Cleomenes had slunk home and was hiding there—and no one was allowed to wake the sleeping governor, even though the whole city had gathered at the headquarters. The noise of the crowd finally penetrated to the bedchamber and Verres came forth. The crowd demanded to know where he had been and what he had been doing, and was on the verge of riot when cooler heads prevailed upon them to arm themselves and prepare to defend themselves from the pirates.

For one night only the pirates delayed at the scene of the fleet's destruction, and then with smoke still rising from our ships, they pointed their bows toward Syracuse. Perhaps they had heard that there was no more beautiful sight than the walls and harbor of Syracuse and they decided, if they ever wanted to see them, they had better see them now while Verres was governor or they never would have the chance again.

Without any trepidation they decided to enter the harbor itself. Yes, the harbor itself—if you are unfamiliar with Syracuse this means into the city itself because the city rings the harbor and the sea flows into the heart of the city—and so, Verres, while you were governor, Heracleo and his four tiny ships sailed right up to the marketplace and they sailed in a triumphal procession so close that their oars splashed spray in the face of the governor.

Cicero recounts this as only one small episode in a string of many shameful episodes. Yes, Verres was several measures more corrupt than most Roman officials, but, just the same, Roman governors considered that the provinces were theirs to be exploited as they willed. (Perhaps, however, the reader might reconsider Chapter 23: Dionysius and ask whether the Sicilians were better off being killed and enslaved under their own leaders or robbed blind under the Romans.)

Alongside Roman corruption and greed, there existed also that particular Roman mix of efficiency and ruthlessness. After Marcus Antonius had failed to put an end to Cretan piracy, the Romans in 69 BCE sent another commander, Metellus. The Cretan leaders had mustered a defensive force of twenty-four thousand skilled archers. It proved to be totally ineffective. One by one, Metellus put the Cretan cities under siege, and one by one, over the course of three years, he took them and sacked them. When he attacked a harbor city, he choked off the harbor entrance, constructed a siege wall, assaulted the city, broke in, and massacred the population. Many of the inhabitants committed suicide rather than fall into Roman hands. Crete was thoroughly subdued, but it was just one place; and no matter how thoroughly subdued one place was, pirates thrived in many other places. Cicero summed up the situation for the Roman people.

Did anyone take to the sea who did not run the risk of death or slavery? The merchant had to choose either the risks of a dangerous voyage in storms during which the pirates could not operate or the risks in good weather of traversing pirate-infested waters. We were faced with a war that was ancient, widespread, and shameful. What province was free of pirates? What ship-borne cargo was safe? Did your fleet offer any protection? How many islands, do you think, are deserted? How many of your allies' cities abandoned or captured by pirates? And I do not need to talk of events in foreign countries.

It has long been the custom of Romans to fight their wars far from home, and to fight on behalf of their allies, not to defend their own houses. I say to you that during these years you could not reach your allies by sea, since your army dared not sail the seas from Brundisium except in the depths of winter. How many envoys came to you from foreign nations, to ask help for their captives, when Roman legates themselves had to be ransomed? Could I say that the sea was safe for trade when a praetor's twelve axes were pirate booty? Should I talk of those illustrious cities Cnidus, Colophon, or Samos, and many more captured by pirates, when you know that your own port city fell to pirates? A praetor on an inspection tour of Caieta, your most famous and prosperous port, was seized by pirates; in Misenum pirates captured the children of the men who previously had waged war against them. Or should I even mention the misfortune and devastation of Ostia, when you were all eyewitnesses to the capture and destruction of a fleet under the command of the consul elected by you, the Roman people?

Finally, the Roman Senate appointed their most distinguished and efficient general, Pompey the Great (Gnaeus Pompeius Magnus), to a three-year command with the *greater imperium*—that is, the command over all other commanders—and the province of the Mediterranean Sea and all contiguous waters and all the coast up to twenty-five miles inland. Pompey had the power to call upon all kings, dynasts, peoples, and cities for aid; he could levy troops and appoint his own subordinate commanders—he created a staff of twenty-five legates with the *lesser imperium*—and could call upon the treasury for whatever sum of money he required, and he could have as many ships as he wanted.

In the end, Pompey raised a force of 120,000 men, four thousand cavalry, and 270 ships. He divided the Mediterranean into thirteen different zones of operation, each with ships and men and commanded by one of his legates. They were to keep the pirates occupied, so each area's pirates would be forced to defend themselves in their home waters and not go to the aid of any other pirates. Pompey himself with the main fleet sailed from zone to zone, drove the pirates before him until he had cornered them, and then he destroyed them. Pompey showed himself to be a master of that particular Roman trait: the ability to marshal and organize resources.

"What an incredible man! [Cicero wrote.] What heaven-sent courage and ability! In a short time he caused the sun to shine upon the republic again! You, who, just a brief moment before, saw an enemy fleet at the mouth of the Tiber, now do not even hear rumors of a pirate in the ocean outside our sea. And this was accomplished so quickly that I think it is worth describing, even though you yourselves are witnesses to it. For what merchant or trader ever visited so many places so quickly or made so many voyages as Gnaeus Pompey and his fleet? He sailed to Sicily, although the sailing season had not yet begun; he visited Africa, he brought his fleet to Sardinia; and he secured these three granaries of the republic with powerful garrisons and a fleet. He returned to Italy he secured Spain and Gaul (across the Alps) with troops and ships. [*All this in forty days.*]

"He dispatched ships into the Adriatic and to Greece and he recognized the vital importance of the two seas around Italy and he appointed for them the greatest fleets and the bravest soldiers and then he himself set out from Brundisium. . . .

"Pompey himself came to Cilicia with many different specialized troops and siege devices because he expected different tactical situations and sieges would be required in inaccessible strong points. But in fact, he needed none of them, because his fame and his preparations stunned the pirates [*who had planned to cooperate against him*]. They hoped if they did not force him to fight, that he would be lenient. First the fortresses of Cragus and Anticragus surrendered and then the Cilicians of the mountains and their neighbors; they handed over a mass of weapons, some still being manufactured, and ships in dry dock and on the water, and bronze and iron fittings for them, and sailcloth, and lumber of different kinds, and mobs of captives, some held for ransom, some put to hard labor.

"Pompey burned the lumber, towed out the ships, and freed the captives to return to their own homes. (Many of them returned home only to discover that they had been declared dead and a funeral had been held for them.)"

In no more than four months, Pompey cleared the Mediterranean of pirates. He captured almost four hundred ships; took 120 cities, forts, and places of refuge; and killed about ten thousand pirates. He put a violent end to piracy, but he also tried to deal with its root cause, poverty, and settled former pirates on land of their own, though, to avoid temptation, inland and away from the sea.

When Pompey was finished with the pirates, he was assigned the command against Mithridates, who had returned to Pontus and defeated the Roman forces there. In a swift campaign, Pompey forced Mithridates to flee from Pontus and seek sanctuary in the kingdom of his son, who, a chip off the old block, usurped his father's power and drove him to suicide. Pompey built upon this success by persuading the king of Armenia to become a friend and ally of the Roman people. Pompey then organized the east into Roman provinces.

And so the only threat remaining for the Romans were the Romans themselves.

Three Million Killed, Enslaved, Pacified

When Pompey returned to Rome, he, Caesar, and Crassus negotiated an illegal and secret agreement (the triumvirate) to further the political ambitions of each. The big winner was Caesar. He had used Crassus's money to become popular with the people of Rome, but even after he had run through the money—at one point he was thirteen hundred talents in debt—he remained popular because of his easy, sympathetic manner and his approachability. But he was very conscious of his personal appearance and exceedingly vain about his receding hair, which led Cicero to say of him, "When I see that he has coiffed his hair with so much attention, and notice him massage his head with one finger, I cannot think that this man would ever intend so great a crime as the subversion of the Roman republic." Sulla, however, had predicted that Caesar would be another Marius. Caesar was ambitious.

In one sense, however, the triumvirate had already subverted the republic as, through its machinations, Caesar became consul and, after his year in office, was assigned a province commensurate with his ambitions, Transalpine Gaul (the ancient *Provincia* and modern Provence), from which he launched his conquest of "long-haired" Gaul. In his first year, 58 BCE, he defeated the Helvetians and the German king Ariovistus. His campaign against the Helvetians was justified by the necessity to defend his province, his campaign against Ariovistus was defensible as a response to a request from Rome's Gallic allies, but then he wintered his forces in Gaul and thereby delivered a statement about his true intentions. In the next year, he campaigned against the Belgae, who had "conspired" against Rome by fighting for their own independence.

In the third year, Caesar subjugated the Veneti, a people whose land lay opposite Britain and who relied upon their geography and their fleet to preserve their independence. They were used to the treacherous currents of the channel, they had regular trade with Britain, and they controlled all the usable harbors. They built their towns on peninsulas, which thwarted attacks by land or sea. If the attacker came by land, the high tide surged across the landward approach and washed away the siege works. If the attacker came by sea, the low tide stranded his ships. And if somehow the attacker overcame these obstacles and seemed to be about to force his way into the town, the Veneti would board their ships and sail away to another town.

Caesar met the challenge. He quickly realized that until he had eliminated the Veneti fleet—about two hundred ships—he could not hope to subdue the people. Therefore, he ordered his Gallic allies to furnish ships, and he had more constructed on the Loire River; he drew his crews from the Province (i.e., principally from Massilia). The difficulty lay in the differing nature of the Roman and Veneti ships. The Roman ships were the standard Mediterranean trireme or quinquereme, which depended upon ramming and boarding to defeat an enemy, but the Veneti ships were built of oak for the rough Atlantic waters. They could withstand ramming, and they were so high that the Romans could not easily grapple them nor overwhelm them with missiles, while, from their higher decks, they could rain missiles down on the Romans. In addition, the Veneti ships had a low draught, which enabled them to negotiate the shallows in a way the Romans could not. As the Veneti depended on sail and the Romans on the oar, the Romans had an advantage in speed and maneuver in gentle seas, but when the seas rose, the Veneti were in their element.

The Romans, however, had noticed one characteristic of the enemy ships, learned in unsuccessful skirmishes with the Veneti—the yardarms holding the sails were attached to the main mast with ropes. The Romans adapted their mural hooks, and as they closed with the enemy ships, they caught the ropes with the mural hooks and then rowed rapidly away, pulling the ropes taut and cutting them. In one great battle the Romans snagged and cut the ropes, the yardarms fell, the Veneti ships were unable to fight, and then, when they tried to flee, a calm descended on the water and the Romans were able to surround each enemy ship, grapple it, and board from all directions. They destroyed the whole of the Veneti fleet, and the Veneti, having no reinforcements and no refuge without their ships, surrendered. Caesar executed the leaders and sold the rest of the population into slavery.

In the fourth year, he undertook to seal off Gaul from any outside interference. He built a bridge across the Rhine, punished the Germans (who had aided the Gauls), returned to Gaul, and decided to cross into Britain, even though the summer was ending and with it the campaigning season. He confesses to total ignorance of Britain—how large the island was, what tribes inhabited it, or what harbors there were. He gathered the meager intelligence he could from the traders who sailed to Britain, and he found that they knew little more than he did. Consequently, he sent a warship to reconnoiter the coast opposite modern Calais.

Caesar collected eighty transports—enough, he estimated, to carry two legions across the channel—and an additional eighteen for the cavalry. He had a fleet of warships, though he did not expect resistance at sea. He seized upon the opportunity of a break in the weather to cross the channel, setting out at midnight and arriving off the coast at about eight or nine in the morning of August 26, 55 BCE. His arrival was no surprise to the Britons, and he found the cliffs lined with enemy, who, from the heights, could rain spears onto the beach below. Finally, in the early afternoon, he discovered a suitable landing spot. The Britons, however, sent their cavalry and chariots to follow his ships, so that he could not land unopposed.

Caesar was aware that he was expecting his men to do something for which they were not trained and from ships that were not designed for shallow waters or for landing troops.

"Our soldiers were frightened, because they were in an unfamiliar place, with their hands full, weighed down by the very heavy burden of their arms. And, all at the same time, they were supposed to leap from the ships, get their footing in the surf, and fight the enemy, who stood either on dry land or slightly out in the water, had their limbs free, knew the terrain, and were boldly throwing spears and urging on their horses. Our soldiers were completely inexperienced with this sort of fighting and did not show the same alacrity and zeal which they were accustomed to display in battles on land."

Caesar maneuvered his warships where they could bring fire on the Britons and support his men. The missiles drove the Britons back from the beach, but the soldiers still hesitated. Then the standard-bearer of the Tenth Legion called upon the gods for help and addressed his fellow soldiers,

"Jump, soldiers," he said, "unless you want to hand our eagle over to the enemy. I, for sure, am going to fulfill my duty to the republic and to our commander," and he jumped into the water.

The legionnaires followed, and men on the other ships, seeing them advancing to the shore, also jumped into the water. They did not have an easy time of it. The enemy massed wherever they saw the Romans struggling and surrounded them. Caesar ordered small boats to be manned by soldiers and to go to the assistance of any group in trouble. The Roman soldiers could not keep any order and marshaled at whatever standard was closest to them. Finally, however, they drove the enemy back. This was the moment at which the cavalry should have disembarked and pursued the enemy, but the winds had prevented the cavalry from taking part in the landing. Caesar remarks that his famous luck deserted him here, but rather he exhibits the typical Roman expectation that he should be able to control even the wind and the waves.

Still, the Briton chieftains' first encounter with the Roman army was such a shock to them that they sued for peace and blamed the common people for their resistance. The cavalry still had to be transported across the channel, but, as they drew in sight of the shore, a storm blew up which drove them all the way back to Gaul. The Romans were unused to the tides and channel storms. The fleet in harbor, some drawn up on shore, some at anchor, were blasted by the wind and the high tide. A number of ships were wrecked, and others lost their rigging.

The soldiers were overcome with fear because the ships were supposed to take them back to winter quarters in Gaul, and they had not amassed a supply of grain. Moreover, they suspected that the Britons, seeing that the Romans were in difficulties, were planning to attack them. Caesar gathered as much grain as he could from the surrounding areas, and he cannibalized twelve ships for the material to repair the rest. Then, when the Britons forced him to fight, he routed them, and around the 24th of September (the autumnal equinox when he learned that the channel was particularly stormy), he embarked his troops and returned to Gaul.

During the winter, he had his troops construct six hundred transport ships and some twenty warships. Caesar gave them general specifications for the new ships: the ships were to be lower in the water to facilitate the landing of troops, and slightly broader to accommodate the supplies including horses and pack animals, and he required that they have both sails and oars for speed. He estimated the distance they had to cross at about twenty-five miles, and when the weather seemed favorable, he set out with four legions and a force of cavalry. All went well until they were in sight of Britain, and then a storm and the tidal flow carried them far off course. The warships were able to row against the tide, but the transport required the soldiers on board to join the rowers and put their backs into the oars.

The landing was unopposed, not because the Britons did not want to resist, but because the size of the fleet scared them off. Caesar chose a broad sandy beach for his fleet, but, nonetheless, could not beach all his ships. And after a few days, a storm arose and broke the anchor cables of some of the ships and dashed them against each other so that most of the ships were damaged and about forty ships were lost. Caesar ordered the ships repaired, he sent a message to the troops in Gaul to construct more ships, and for ten days he worked his troops night and day to expand the size of his camp so that he could bring all the ships within the fortifications.

Caesar spent most of the summer, from July to September, reducing British resistance, although he had no intention of conquering Briton or wintering there. He accepted hostages to ensure the Britons' good behavior (not to aid the Gauls) and arranged an annual tribute. When he had accomplished his objectives, he intended to transport his army back to Gaul in two stages, but, once again, the weather was against him. Some of his transport was wrecked, more driven off course, and he had to pack his troops into the remaining boats. He waited for a period of calm and then set out to Gaul, which he reached without incident. He writes that in the whole operation of two years he did not lose a single boat loaded with soldiers. He *was* lucky.

In the next three years, he completed the conquest of Gaul. (His conquest was totally successful—Gaul as Gaul was gone and in its place was a Roman province, which increased in prosperity through the years until it became a second Italy. The conquest of Britain waited until the emperor Claudius.) In 53 BCE, while Caesar was still in Gaul, Crassus led a campaign into Parthia, which culminated in his death, decapitation, and the destruction of his army. (His head was used by the Parthians as a prop in Euripides's play *The Bacchae*.) The triumvirate was dead, the Senate turned to Pompey and ordered Caesar to dismiss his army and return to Rome; instead, he marched his army across the Rubicon River (the boundary of his province), invaded Italy, and occupied Rome. Villagers were surprised by the discipline of Caesar's legions and, perhaps, also by their marching songs—

"Men, lock up your wives, because here we come, following our bald lecher."

At the beginning, the most pressing military issues of the civil war between Pompey and Caesar were who could raise the most troops and who could move those troops the fastest. Caesar held the central position in Italy, but Pompey had sizable forces in northern Greece and Spain. He also held North Africa, and he was contending for control of Sicily, Sardinia, and Corsica. Pompey had crossed the Adriatic to Greece and, in the process, had cleared the Italian coast of transport vessels, so that Caesar could not follow. Caesar, therefore, determined, while a fleet was being gathered and constructed, to eliminate Pompey's army in Spain.

To block the easy transport of troops from Italy to Spain, Pompey's adherents convinced the Massiliotes to close the city and harbor to Caesar. Caesar tried to persuade the leaders of Massilia to side with him, but they replied that as the Romans were divided into two camps and both Caesar and Pompey had done service to Massilia, they could not decide which side to join, so they would remain neutral and not allow either side to use their harbor. In fact, however, they intended to back Pompey—they thought he would win—and they were delaying, while they prepared their city to withstand a siege.

The city sent out its small fleet under a Pompeian commander to intercept any transport vessels they could and bring them into harbor, where they were either cannibalized to repair other ships or brought into service. If they contained grain, it was added to the city's stock. Meanwhile, Caesar sent three legions to begin the siege of Massilia, and he had twelve warships constructed. (The construction took thirty days from felling the trees to launching the ships.) With Massilia safely under siege, Caesar began operations in Spain to deal with the Pompeian forces there. The Pompeian leaders planned to detain Caesar, until Pompey, using his command of the sea, could transport his army to Spain, catch Caesar between the two forces, and eliminate him. But Pompey did not come and it was the Pompeian army in Spain that was eliminated.

As the campaign in Spain proceeded, the Massiliotes attempted to break the siege by attacking Caesar's fleet. They had faster, more maneuverable ships, crewed with experienced sailors and Gallic volunteers to do the ship-to-ship fighting, and, in addition, the commander had brought a personal contingent, recruited by himself—his shepherds. Caesar's ships were slower—they had been built with green timber—and the helmsmen and sailors were drawn from merchant ships, had no experience with warships, and did not even know the terminology of the parts of the ship. However, Caesar had drawn volunteers from his legions to board and fight when an enemy ship was grappled.

Pompey had sent a small fleet. When it arrived, it joined up with the Massiliotes and set out to do battle.

"When the battle was joined, the Massiliotes showed no lack of courage; indeed, they remembered the precepts given a little bit before by their commanders and they fought with the certainty that upon this battle lay the fate of their city."

The issue was whether the speed and better handling of the Massiliotes' fleet would overcome the slower Caesarian ships with their advantage in marines. The smaller vessels attempted to surround the ships of Caesar, but as the battle became more circumscribed and the Caesarian ships were able to grapple the enemy and the legionnaires were able to board—in some cases even when they were caught between two enemy ships and had to divide their boarding parties—the battle shifted to Caesar. They captured five ships, and the rest of the enemy fleet fled to the safety of the harbor. It was a battle much like the battles between the Carthaginians and the Romans in the First Punic War, where the fleet with the superior boarding parties won. The Pompeian commander, when he saw the battle was lost, disengaged his fleet and sailed away. The Massiliotes, without any possibility of resupply, and seeing the siege works advancing, decided to surrender.

After capturing Massilia and eliminating the Pompeian army in Spain, Caesar crossed into Greece, defeated Pompey himself at Pharsalus, and pursued him to Egypt (where he was given Pompey's head, as the Egyptians had acted on the precept "The dead don't bite"). During the civil war, the fleets provided transportation but little else (except at Massilia). Caesar was forced to fight his opponents in Egypt, Africa, and Spain before reaching an uneasy settlement in Rome. His next objective was the invasion of Parthia, but before he could leave Rome, he was assassinated (on the Ides of March, 44 BCE).

In Caesar's wars he used ships to conquer the Veneti, to cross to Britain, to close the siege around Massilia, and to transport his troops to Egypt, Africa, and Spain (again). Pompey is said to have regretted not contesting the

Adriatic more aggressively. In sum, however, the naval action was secondary, and the great decisions were made on land. In the next phase of the civil wars, however, the son of Pompey the Great, Sextus Pompeius, relied completely upon seapower to insert himself into the contest for the prize of the Roman empire.

Son of a God

In his will, Julius Caesar adopted his nineteen-year-old grandnephew Octavian and bequeathed him his estate. Octavian's family advised him to reject the legacy, because if he went to Rome to accept it, he would be killed.

Octavian, however, was an extraordinary individual, who knew his own capabilities, despite his enemies' dismissal of him. He was, Antony said, the descendant of bakers, rope-makers, and usurers. Cassius called him "a little piece of your mother's dough, kneaded into some shape or other by a usurer, whose hands were stained with money." Cicero, too, misjudged him and thought that he could use this naïve young man for his own purposes and then get rid of him. (Cicero wound up with his tongue cut out, nailed to a door, and admonished. "There. Wag no more.")

Octavian, by relying on his adoptive name, C. Julius Caesar (*Octavianus*), borrowed enormous amounts of money, secured the loyalty of Caesar's veterans, and outmaneuvered allies and opponents, until he and Antony were left at the top. (They divided the Roman world between them, Antony in the east with its wealth and, also, with the Egyptian queen, Cleopatra, and Octavian in the west with the city of Rome, the rebel Sextus Pompeius, and multitudes of veterans who demanded land and an end to their service. (He gave them the land, which he confiscated from Antony's supporters.)

Octavian, for all his abilities, including great courage but little military experience, was in a perilous position. Antony had a fleet and an army, and his prestige was high among Caesar's veterans. Octavian could not necessarily depend upon his own troops to fight Antony, although, conversely, Antony could not be sure that his own troops would fight the adoptive Julius Caesar. But Antony had an ally, Sextus Pompeius (son of Pompey the Great). Sextus Pompeius had raised a sizable fleet, manned by whomever he could recruit, including slaves, and funded by pirate raids on Italy. He held Sicily, Sardinia, and Corsica and, with the tacit approval of Antony, interdicted grain on its way to Rome, which caused a famine in the city (in 39 BCE). Antony and Octavian came to the brink of war, but the news that Sextus Pompeius had been checked in his attacks on Italian towns and the uncertainty about the loyalty of their own soldiers convinced the two men to come to an accord. Antony ordered Sextus Pompeius to cease his attacks on shipping and invited him to a conference to settle all issues.

Sextus Pompeius arrived in a *hexeres*, ready to fight if necessary. Nor did the other two trust him or each other—they met on three platforms anchored just off the coast, Pompeius on his platform, close enough to converse, but far enough away for his personal security. He believed that he had been invited to the conference to be promoted to triumvir. He hadn't, but Antony mollified him with the promise that he would look after his interests; and then Antony and Octavian divided the empire in two, down the middle of the Adriatic, except that Antony was allowed to recruit troops in Italy. They reached an agreement and solidified it by marriage alliances and a round of feasts, during which Sextus joked, "I live in the district of Hull."

Sextus Pompeius's most aggressive general, Menodorus (a freed slave who had command of Sardinia and Corsica), advised Pompeius that this was the perfect moment to eliminate Antony and Octavian. Pompeius is supposed to have remarked, in a classic sloughing off of responsibility, "I wish that you had done this without asking me." Pompeius departed the conference with the feeling that he had been outmaneuvered and wronged. Consequently, he allowed his adherents to commit piracies, he maintained his blockade of Rome, and he undertook a new program of shipbuilding.

Menecrates, another freedman and a captain in Pompeius's navy, hated his rival Menodorus (and wanted to take his place) and filled Pompeius's ear with calumnies against him. Menodorus learned of this, feared that he would be assassinated, and offered to surrender to Octavian with his fleet, three legions, and the islands of Sardinia and Corsica. Octavian accepted the offer and, with this addition to his strength, prepared naval forces on both coasts of Italy and then set sail to converge on Sicily. Pompeius decided to engage Octavian personally and sent a separate fleet under the command of Menecrates to deal with Menodorus.

The battle of the two lieutenants took place off Cumae. Menodorus (now Octavian's man) brought his fleet out from the harbor and formed a crescent as close to the shore as he could to prevent a *diekplous*. Menecrates (Sextus's man) advanced, and the fleet of Menodorus backed water. At that moment the two commanders caught sight of each other and charged with no thought of the rest of their fleets. The two ships smashed into each other, Menodorus stove in the prow of his enemy, and Menecrates smashed the oars on one side of Menodorus's ship. They grappled each other (for they now were unable to maneuver), and their crews threw javelins, shot arrows, slung stones, and then lowered their boarding bridges.

Menodorus's ship was the higher, his missiles were more effective, and his marines boarded Menecrates's ship. The dead and wounded were lying all about. Menodorus was hit in the arm by a javelin, and Menecrates's thigh was transfixed by a barbed iron point, which could not be cut off or extracted. He could fight no longer, but he continued to command his ship until resistance collapsed; then he threw himself into the sea and drowned. Menodorus towed his enemy's ship into harbor in triumph. Despite Menodorus's spectacular personal victory, Sextus's fleet had gotten the best of the battle and destroyed and burned many ships, and, yet, despite its triumph, because of the death of Menecrates, it retreated to Sicily as though it had been defeated.

Meanwhile, Octavian refused to engage the fleet of Pompeius, because he expected Menodorus's fleet to join him. His inaction caused the loss of many of his ships, his crews fled to the shore, and Octavian spent an uncomfortable and ignominious night on a mountainside. Nonetheless, the next day Octavian gathered his fleet and waited for the weather to clear so he could engage Sextus. Instead, a storm arose and shattered his fleet against the rocks. Octavian was so angry about the storm that, on the divine level, he refused to include the statue of Neptune in the parade of gods (although, after Actium, he forgave him). On the practical level, he created a sheltered harbor where he could train his oarsmen over the winter. An epigram made the rounds in Rome:

His fleets defeated twice,
He is trying his luck at dice.

At the beginning of spring 36 BCE, Antony and Octavian renewed the triumvirate, and Antony gave Octavian 120 ships in exchange for a number of legionnaires. Octavian, then, with newly constructed ships and, more importantly, after appointing the incomparable Agrippa as commander of his second fleet—by this time Menodorus had re-ratted to Sextus—he prepared to attack Pompeius. In preparation, he performed the customary naval sacrifices.

"The altars are built along the shore and the crowd of sailors take their position around them, ship by ship, in the most profound silence. The priests stand by the sea and make their sacrifices, and the commanders carry the sacrifices around the fleet in skiffs three times, and they pray that these sacrificial victims will suffer any bad omens, instead of the fleet. They divide the victims and cast part into the sea and part they place on the altars and burn them, and the people pray. This is how the Romans purify a fleet."

Octavian's plan was to converge on Sicily from three directions: Lepidus (the third and almost forgotten triumvir) from Africa, Octavian from Puteoli, and Agrippa with the third fleet from Tarentum. Octavian set out, after praying to the divinity, *Calm Seas*, to attack Pompeius, who had concentrated his main fleet at Messana. Despite Octavian's prayer, a violent storm arose and

Octavian was struck by its full force. Some of his ships were lost at sea, others were wrecked in harbor, and he was so shaken that he considered postponing his campaign until the next sailing season.

At this point he probably agreed with his friend Horace that "the man who entrusts himself to the sea must be made of sterner stuff than mere flesh and blood, or he would never plunge into the winds that howl from every direction and twist into deadly gales. In vain has a prudent god divided the land from the inhospitable sea—in vain, because foolish men still take to ships."

Pompeius, for his part, boasted that he was the "son of Neptune" and put on a blue cloak in honor of his "father." Octavian replied, "I will defeat him even if Neptune *is* helping him." Pompeius soon learned that Octavian was repairing his ships and building new ones and getting ready to renew the campaign. Pompeius sent his lieutenant, Menodorus, to reconnoiter, and Menodorus was so impressed with Octavian's preparations that he deserted back to him.

As Octavian's forces bore down on Sicily in two divisions, the division under the command of Agrippa met the Pompeian fleet under the command of Pompeius's officer, Papias, at Mylae. Agrippa's ships were larger and higher, Papias's lighter and more maneuverable. Papias tried to maneuver to shatter oars, and then ram and retreat, while Agrippa tried to close, throw missiles down on the enemy, ram them, and grapple them. When Agrippa succeeded and boarders crossed to Papias's ships, their crews jumped overboard. Small boats picked up the swimmers.

Agrippa charged the flagship of Papias, rammed it so violently that men on the towers fell off, and water poured into the lower tiers of oarsmen. Papias was able to transfer to another ship, but he had had enough. He led the flight to whatever shelter his ships could find. As night came on, Agrippa reluctantly withdrew. Papias lost thirty ships, Agrippa five, but both sides suffered considerable damage. Pompeius encouraged his men by telling them that they had not fought so much against ships as against "walls."

Once again, Octavian was taken by surprise and defeated at sea. Once again, he scrambled to bring his forces back together, aided this time by Antony's decision to remove his support from Pompeius—he was preparing to invade Parthia—so that Octavian and his brilliant lieutenant, Agrippa, could concentrate on Sextus with all their forces and finally defeat him at the battle of Naulochus.

Sextus's fleet had more ships but of a lesser size. His admiral tried to prevent an enemy *periplous* by fixing one flank on the coast and to prevent a *diekplous* by crowding his ships together. Agrippa spread his larger ships out, flanked the enemy, and used an innovation, the *harpax*—a grapnel with several hooks and an iron shaft so that it could be fired by a catapult. Both sides used fire arrows initially, but as the ships closed, they refrained because of the danger of confusing friend and foe, though it was more of a problem for the Pompeians, because Agrippa had foreseen this possibility and had painted all his towers the same color. The sea was filled with wreckage, corpses, and sailors struggling to survive. Agrippa's ships grappled Sextus's ships, pulled them close, and boarded. Almost all the enemy ships were destroyed. Sextus escaped to Egypt, where Antony had him executed. Agrippa lost three ships in the battle.

Subsequently, in a masterful propaganda campaign, Octavian convinced the Roman people and, more importantly, the soldiers that Antony had become the creature of a foreign queen and had willed Rome to his children by her. In 32 BCE, Antony brought his army and navy west to meet Octavian. Antony commanded a force of one hundred thousand men and a fleet of five hundred warships and three hundred transports. Cleopatra had a personal fleet of two hundred ships. Antony wintered in Patrae, his main forces wintered at Actium, and the rest were scattered in the harbors of the Adriatic and south to Taenarum, the central peninsula of the Peloponnesus. Octavian had an army of some eighty thousand and a fleet smaller than Antony's both in numbers and ship size.

Antony hoped to intercept and—if he could—destroy Octavian's fleet, but Octavian's capable general, Agrippa, struck before Antony was ready and seized Methone and the other harbors as far north as Corcyra, while Octavian managed to cross with his army just north of Corcyra, advance to Actium, and assume a superior position. As Octavian held his position and Antony concentrated his troops against him, Agrippa attacked by sea and took Leucas, Patrae, and Corinth, effectively putting Antony under siege. As Antony's supplies failed and his position deteriorated, his allies fell away from him, and some of his troops deserted.

In the end, Antony did not have the forces to win a land battle, and so he had to try his luck at sea. His fleet had been effectively reduced to 200–250 ships—he had more ships, and larger ships (some Tens and Sevens), but not the crews to man them—and Octavian had four hundred ships. On September 2, 31 BCE, Antony put to sea. He had his treasury and his sails stored on board—a sign that he was ready to flee as much as fight. According to one author, Antony's ships were so large that the sea groaned beneath their weight. Cleopatra had a fleet of about sixty ships, many of them large. Antony loaded as many soldiers and archers as he could, both to fight as marines, but also, just in case, to be preserved for the future. He abandoned the rest of his forces. Octavian and Agrippa had two great advantages: first, they themselves had led fleets in battle (while Antony had not); and second, their crews had fought together before and knew what to expect.

A much-scarred veteran of Antony was supposed to have said to him, as he was on his way to board the flagship, "O Commander, why do you so little value my wounds and my sword, that you put your hopes in these wretched pieces of wood? Let Egyptians and Phoenicians fight at sea; give us the land on which to stand to defeat the enemy or die."

Antony brought his fleet out into the open sea, but formed an arc in front of his harbor with the intention of bringing Octavian to him in his superior position and transforming the sea battle into a kind of land battle with his large ships as redoubts equipped with towers and catapults. Octavian would have none of it, however, and the situation worked against Antony, because Octavian did not have to fight, while Antony was all too aware that his situation would continue to deteriorate if he did not fight. Finally, Antony ordered his fleet to advance.

As the two fleets closed, Antony's fleet lost cohesion and Octavian signaled the attack. Agrippa's plan was to outflank Antony. Antony depended upon his largest ships, which were almost forts on the water, to repel boarders and overwhelm the smaller ships with their armaments, but Octavian's smaller, more maneuverable ships attacked from all directions. According to one source, Octavian depended mostly on his *liburnae*.

"They fought the sea battle in different ways. The ships of Octavian were smaller and faster and they would dart forward to ram the enemy. This was fine if they sank their target, but, otherwise, they would withdraw before they had to fight hand-to-hand, and then, again, they would attack suddenly, either the same vessel or another, or even another, so that their attacks would always be unexpected, for they were afraid of the might of the enemy and of close-quarter combat: so they tried to inflict some damage or throw the enemy into confusion and then escape. The enemy would fire off masses of stones and arrows and in close range fighting would try to grapple the other ship. If they succeeded, they were sure to win, but if they missed, they themselves would be damaged and sunk, or else become vulnerable to further attacks."

As the battle went on, gaps opened between the three divisions of Antony's fleet. Cleopatra, seeing the gaps, had her ships raise sail and escape. When Antony saw her fleeing, he abandoned the rest of his fleet to its fate and followed her. Octavian, rather than risking his men in close fighting against a defeated enemy, resorted to fire.

"Octavian's ships would surround an enemy ship and would shoot burning arrows, throw spears with pots of fire, and hurl larger containers of fire from their ballistae. The enemy tried to fend off the individual weapons, but some penetrated and set the ship timbers and pitch on fire."

The enemy crews used their drinking water at first, and then tried to smother the fires with their cloaks and even the bodies of the slain, to no avail. Some were overcome by the smoke, others were burned to death, while all this time they suffered from a rain of javelins, arrows, and stones. In the end, the survivors threw themselves on the mercy of Octavian. The battle went so late that Octavian had to spend the night on board his flagship.

In the sense that Antony had rescued as much of his army as he could, he had succeeded, but he lost the campaign and could now only await Octavian's invasion of Egypt. When the invasion came, it came in coordinated attacks from west and east. Antony retreated, his fleet surrendered to Octavian, and in the end, with no way out—Octavian declined his invitation to a personal duel—Antony committed suicide, Cleopatra committed suicide, and Octavian was sole master of the Roman Empire.

He faced herculean tasks—to bring the vast number of soldiers and sailors (from some seven hundred ships) under control, to find land and money to satisfy them upon discharge, to balance the expense of the empire with the income of the empire—he settled upon twenty-eight legions, reduced by a disaster in Germany to twenty-five, with an enlisted service of sixteen years on active duty and four years in reserve. He enunciated certain maxims that illustrate his personality:

> Hasten slowly; the cautious general is better than the bold; and the possible gain must be greater than the possible loss. Men who risk great resources to obtain small victories are like a fisherman who uses a golden hook, when the hook is worth many times more than any fish might be.

Octavian also had to figure out how to rule. Caesar had been assassinated, because he had seemed to be flirting with the idea of making himself king. Octavian, in form, rejected such a title. (He would not even allow his grandchildren to call him Dominus ("Lord" or "Master"). He once told a petitioner, "You act as though you were offering a treat to an elephant." He boasted, "I restored the Republic" and, in form, he did. His Rome still had a Senate and two consuls, praetors, tribunes, and quaestors. Octavian had only two powers: the greater imperium (supreme command of the armies) and the tribunician power (making him sacrosanct, thus justifying a bodyguard). The Senate voted him the title Augustus (and renamed a month in his honor).

He established two main fleets, each with its own commander and chain of command, one at Misenum (the *classis Misenensis*) to patrol the western Mediterranean from the bay of Naples westward, the other at Ravenna (*classis Ravennate*), the eastern Mediterranean from the head of the Adriatic eastward. The main fleet, the *classis Misenensis*, maintained subsidiary bases in the western Mediterranean and was the special fleet of the emperors, to provide transportation for them (and to spread the awning at the Coliseum). The whole fleet required fifteen to twenty thousand men, drawn from the (noncitizen) provinces, to crew about one hundred ships, triremes, a few quinqueremes, and some lighter ships, the *liburna*.

The *liburna* became the principal ship of the Romans. Developed from the Illyrian *lembi*, an open boat with about fifty oarsmen, designed for a quick spurt of speed followed by boarding, the Romans redesigned the ship as a bireme with fifty or sixty oarsmen and a ram. The ships could operate at sea or on the riverine borders of the empire, the Rhine and the Danube. The advantages of this ship in a time when Rome did not face major naval powers were twofold: they were fast and they did not require a large crew. In short, they sufficed for the job. The Rhine fleet, for instance, in exploring the North Sea coast at the end of the first century BCE, met and defeated a fleet manned by a German tribe, the Bructeri.

The Romans established patrol boats along the Rhine (*classis Germanica*), the English Channel (*classis Britannica*), the Danube (*classis Pannonica* and *classis Moesica*), the Black Sea (*classis Pontica*), Egypt (*classis Alexandrina*), Syria (*classis Syriaca*), and north Africa (*classis Mauretania*). The Roman navy kept the Mediterranean clear of pirates, and did not face a major foe, for more than two hundred years.

The Long Peace

By the time of the emperor Claudius (41–54 CE), the term of service in the fleet was set at twenty-six years, after which the sailors were granted Roman citizenship.

Caesar had invaded Britain with limited objectives; Augustus planned to invade but was diverted by greater priorities; Gaius (Caligula) made an abortive attempt that ended with his order to the invading army, "Gather seashells"; and the conquest was left to Claudius in 43 CE. He had a force of four legions, which, with auxiliaries, numbered some forty thousand men and overwhelmed the Britons, while Claudius himself, despite all his physical infirmities, won the *spolia opima* (awarded to a Roman commander who kills the enemy commander in single combat).

Under the Julio-Claudians (Augustus—Tiberius—Gaius—Claudius—Nero), 31 BCE–68 CE 68, the system of government was regularized, the powers of the emperor were defined by grants of the imperium and the tribunician power, a bureaucracy was created to oversee the provinces, and the forces to defend the empire were marshaled and defined. The emperors established a naval base in the Black Sea at the port of Chersonesus, which projected Roman power and protection throughout the Black Sea area until the fourth century.

The civil wars of 68–69—which began when Nero's plan to sooth the dissident spirits of the rebellious troops by serenading them evaporated under the harsh light of reality—culminated in the victory of Vespasian. His dynasty, the Flavian dynasty (69–96), stabilized the empire, created new sources of revenue—Vespasian put a tax on urine—and established the dual domination of the military over the civilian and the imperial over the Senatorial. The Flavian emperor was addressed as *dominus et deus* ("master and god").

The century-and-a-half of the early empire was the period of the *pax Romana,* a time without major naval campaigns or battles. In particular, the

Romans had complete control of the Mediterranean (*mare nostrum*—"our sea"). In the 40s, the Rhine fleet beat back, pursued, and punished a German tribe that had raided the Belgic coast. The Rhine fleet was also involved in suppressing—not without some travail—a German disturbance in 69–70. In 83 CE, German sailors in the Roman fleet off the British coast commandeered three ships, fled up the west coast, over the top of the British Isles, and down across the North Sea—the first Germans to do so. They crashed on the rocks of the German shore, where their attempt to escape Roman control ended with the local Germans executing some of them on the spot and selling the rest of them into slavery.

German ships had a distinctive design . . . "in that both bow and stern are the same and the ship can go in either direction. They neither use sails nor oars in regular rows on the sides, but they can be changed (like some river-boats) as their heading might dictate."

The crew numbered no more than fifty men, a sufficient number for a quick single-ship smash and grab, or, for larger operations, the Germans could combine into a more formidable force, a fleet of a dozen ships, say, and six hundred men. Mostly, however, the Roman fleets patrolled the Rhine and the Danube and tried to interdict small raiding parties. The raiding parties chose the time and place to cross, which made intercepting them an almost impossible task, and the Romans depended more on receiving news that a raiding party had crossed and then intercepting it on its return. (This practice led to repeated accusations—for four centuries—that Roman ships were only interested in confiscating the loot and not in stopping the raiders.)

The last of the Flavians, the emperor Domitian, was assassinated, and the Senate chose one of its own members, Nerva, to be emperor. His reign (96–98) initiated the period of the "five good emperors" (96–180 CE). He adopted the commander of the Danube army, Trajan, and Trajan became emperor at a time when the Danube fleet had been unable to stop raids by the Dacians. Trajan solved the Dacian problem once and for all by conquering Dacia (modern Romania). To celebrate his victory, he commissioned a column that depicts the ships he used in his campaign.

His river transport-vessels could be paddled, rowed, or towed, and were also employed as the base of boat bridges. They appear to be the main supply carriers—at least, for the first stockpiling of stores, equipment, and horses. The crews wear sleeveless tunics. The barrel, not the amphora, is the basic commodities container. The boats were about forty-eight feet in length. It is clear that the transports depicted on the column were also the type used in the boat bridges.

The *liburna*, as depicted, appears to be a two-tiered bireme. It is open, without a deck. The ram has an upturn. The upturn could be an artistic embellishment, but at some point, the ram was lifted and transformed into a "spur."

The ship "is constructed from cypress and pine, larch and fir, grown in groves or forest. Bronze nails are more practical than iron, although they are a bit more expensive, because they last longer, for iron nails are susceptible to rust through time and moisture and thus there is a net gain. Bronze nails are more durable and so, just as, when building a house, you want the best materials, when building a ship, you also want the best materials, because a defective ship is much more dangerous than a defective house."

Decline and Fall

The period of the decline and fall of the Roman Empire has its moments of great sea battles and expeditions, upon which hinged the fate of sections, at least, of the empire. Unfortunately, the extant sources are scarce, scattered, and spotty, and they do not describe naval battles. As the author of a tactical manual written in the later fourth century states,

"[As for] naval war, little needs to be said, because the seas are peaceful and our battles with the barbarians are fought on land and, should there be some emergency, the Roman people already have a fleet prepared. In short, no one dares to make war on the empire or its people, because they know that they would be swiftly punished."

Actium is the last battle of the ancient world described in any detail.

The Romans continued their naval domination through the reigns of the five good emperors (96–180 CE: Nerva—Trajan—Hadrian—Antoninus Pius—Marcus Aurelius), but in the latter part of the second century, the destruction of towns and villas and the building of fortifications along the British coast bear witness to increased German raids. Commodus, who succeeded his father, Marcus Aurelius, did little to defend the empire's borders and was murdered (not for that reason). The ultimate victor of the ensuing civil war was Severus (whose famous advice to his sons was, "Keep the soldiers happy and to hell with the rest"). Severus stabilized the empire and restored security to the British coasts. His son, Caracalla, succeeded him (after murdering his brother as he sought refuge in the lap of their mother). His one notable achievement was a decree making all the free inhabitants of the Roman Empire Roman citizens. His murder in 217 by his Praetorian Prefect (who discovered that he was marked for death because of a horoscope predicting his imperial destiny) ushered in a chaotic seventy years.

In 238, the defense line, the *limites*, of the empire broke under the onslaught of multiple invasions by various German tribes. Germans crossed the Rhine; Goths occupied the northern rim of the Black Sea, entered Dacia, and raided across the Danube; and, on the eastern frontier, the new Persian power invaded Roman territory.

In 254, a Germanic tribe, the Borani, convinced a Black Sea vassal king— how could he say *no?*—to lend them his fleet. In the next two years, they and the Goths advanced together on land and sea and sacked the cities of Pityus, Trapezus, Chalcedon, Nicomedia, Nicaea, and Prusa. In 267, bands of Goths devastated a helpless Asia Minor and then sailed into the Aegean, burned the temple of Artemis of Ephesus, and torched Ilium. If they did face resistance, they just re-embarked and looked for a different victim.

In 268, Germanic tribes led by the Heruli, a seafaring people, collected a huge fleet at the mouth of the Dniester (variously estimated at five hundred to two thousand ships) and a land army of 320,000 (!) men. They ravaged Byzantium and Chrysopolis and moved at will through Greece as far south as Sparta. The imperial fleet fought them first, but did not stop them, in the Propontis, where many of the enemy ships were wrecked, and eventually drove their fleet from the Aegean, but only after Greece had been ravaged. On land the Roman emperor and his generals defeated the Goths and proved the superiority of Roman arms (enhanced by famine, plague, and a little targeted bribery), but the Goths' hunger for land and booty was only momentarily assuaged when the Romans abandoned Dacia to them. (The Goths, who had terrorized so many, all too soon would be terrorized themselves by a new and unexpected enemy, the Huns.)

In the west, however, the Romans faced an even more serious threat than the Goths. The German tribes along the North Sea coast had coalesced into two great confederations, the Franks and the Saxons. During the reigns of the emperors Gallienus (253–268) and Postumus, the Franks plundered their way through Gaul; crossed the Pyrenees into Spain, where they secured a fleet; and raided North Africa. (There is also a story that, during this time, a large number of Franks who had been resettled along the Black Sea commandeered a fleet and plundered the Mediterranean from one end to the other, before sailing up the Atlantic back to their homes.) Increased raids caused the Romans to fortify British coastal towns and to establish a system of watchtowers and massive fortifications along what came to be known as the "Saxon Shore." (It is disputed whether the term denoted a shore defended against the Saxons or a shore occupied by the Saxons.) The massive nature of the fortifications suggests that the defenders had been left on their own.

A series of "soldier-emperors" stabilized the borders and defeated the Germans, although rival Roman armies proclaimed rival emperors, so succession and imperial stability remained a problem until the death of the emperors, Carus and his sons Numerian and Carinus. The army was summoned to a meeting at which the praetorian prefect Aper addressed the troops in the expectation that they would acclaim him emperor. As he spoke, a general named Diocles, who was sitting behind him, remembered an old prediction that he, Diocles, would become emperor when he killed the "wild boar," and, further, it occurred to him that the name "Aper" meant "wild boar," so he drew a dagger, stabbed Aper to death, and was proclaimed emperor by the army assembly. (He adopted the more dignified name of Diocletian.)

In the twenty years (285–305) Diocletian was emperor, he established a tetrarchy with two senior emperors, the Augusti, and two subordinate emperors, the Caesars, each with his own court and army. Under this system the emperors reestablished control over the empire. To defend Britain, Diocletian's co-Augustus, Maximian, appointed Carausius, a talented general, to command the Britannic Fleet—the Rhine fleet had been wiped out—and curb the attacks of the Saxons and Franks. Carausius waged an aggressive campaign, but still, the best he could do was to intercept the raiders on their voyages home, and the inevitable rumors reached Maximian that his general was more interested in confiscating the booty of the raiders than in destroying them. Maximian decided to execute him, but Carausius got wind of his intention, rebelled, and claimed imperial honors for himself, and he also lay claim to the territories of Britain and Gaul. He attempted to fit himself into the tetrarchy by issuing coinage declaring the two Augusti his "brothers," but they were not convinced, and he proceeded to recruit Saxons and Franks into his fleet and to encourage Saxon raids on Roman territory to divert his opponents. Carausius defeated Maximian's first naval expedition.

The Augusti bided their time until they were again strong enough to strike, and then Maximian ordered his Caesar, Constantius Chlorus (the father of Constantine the Great), to assume the command of Gaul and Britain. In 293, Constantius blockaded the port city of Gesoriacum (modern Boulogne), the main stronghold of Carausius in Gaul; he closed the harbor with a mole, which prevented Carausius from supplying or reinforcing the city, and he captured the city just before an unusually high tide broke the mole and opened the harbor again. By capturing Gesoriacum, Constantius wrested control of Gaul from the hands of Carausius and shook confidence in him—Carausius's right-hand man, Allectus, murdered him and took his place.

Constantius spent two years preparing for his attack on Allectus. When Constantius was ready, Maximian brought an army to watch the Germans across the Rhine (and cover the absence of Constantius). Constantius divided his fleet into two divisions, one led by himself and one led by his Praetorian Prefect, Asclepiodotus, and, when their arrangements were complete, they set out across the channel. Allectus was proud of his fleet—he issued coins under the names of his flagships, *Virtus* and *Laetitia*—and he intended to meet the invaders at sea and stop them there, but his plan was foiled when a heavy fog caused him to miss the invading fleet. Asclepiodotus landed, burned his ships to remove any thoughts his troops might have of retreat, an act that, apparently, inspired them, because they routed the enemy army and killed Allectus. Allectus's Frankish mercenaries, no less undaunted, regrouped and marched toward London to sack it, but Constantius, sailing up the Thames, reached London in the nick of time.

Diocletian, satisfied that he had restored the empire, retired in 305 and insisted that his co-Augustus, Maximian, retire as well. He did, and the succession proceeded as planned, but soon the new Augusti, their Caesars, and the sons of the Augusti fell to squabbling, the squabbling degenerated into civil war, and the son of Constantius Chlorus, Constantine, emerged as the ultimate victor (which he attributed to a vision of the Chi-Rho and a voice proclaiming, "In this sign you shall conquer"). After Constantine, with one exception, all the succeeding emperors were Christian.

Against his last opponent, Licinius, whom he characterized as a "serpent uncoiling," he could only reduce his position in Byzantium by defeating Licinius's Hellespontine fleet (which he did, although detailed accounts do not survive). Constantine reunited the empire, but his death introduced a new period of civil war culminating in the accession of the pagan Julian (361–363). Julian invaded Mesopotamia and died there, and an army council selected two new Christian emperors to divide and rule the empire. During this unsettled period, massive and coordinated raids on Britain effectively removed it from Roman control and by the end of the fourth century, the Romans had conceded the North Sea to the Saxons.

By this time the nature of naval warfare had changed, at least as the Romans conducted it. In a battle on open waters, three main weapons were employed: the *asser,* a long, thick pole on which an iron blade was fixed, both to kill enemy sailors and to grapple their ships; the *falx,* a long pole with a sickle-like blade, with which to cut the enemy's rigging; and the *bipennis,* a double-bladed ax with which to cut enemy cables and disable the ship's ability to steer. Rams and ramming seem to have disappeared.

In 378, the emperor of the east lost a disastrous battle at Adrianopolis to the Goths (driven into the empire by the Huns). The empire never fully recovered from this defeat. The army increasingly accepted German recruits, and in 410, the Gothic king Alaric sacked Rome. Germanic tribes overwhelmed the western empire, and Vandals crossed the sea to North Africa and captured Carthage. The last Roman emperor of the west was deposed in 476. The eastern empire, however, which came to be known as the Byzantine empire, survived and prospered for centuries. The Byzantines modified the *liburna* into a decked *dromon,* and with these ships, for a time in the sixth century, reasserted Roman domination over the Mediterranean.

Conclusion

The warship powered by oars dominated the Mediterranean for more than one thousand years after the fall of the Western Empire.

With the fall of Rome, sea trade almost vanished from the western Mediterranean. Constantinople became the capital of the truncated empire, maintained a fleet, and used it to transport troops to the west in costly and, ultimately, futile efforts to reunite the empire. The fleet, then, became vital to the protection of Constantinople from a growing Arab threat. In the mid-seventh century, Arabs advanced across North Africa by land and attacked Sicily by sea, defeated the Byzantine navy, and lay siege to Constantinople. The Byzantine fleet turned to a new super-weapon—Greek fire (a substance like napalm)—delivered directly through tubes or catapulted in jars. For a time, the Byzantine fleet, armed with Greek fire, was the master of the Aegean.

During the seventh to thirteenth centuries, as the power of Islam grew and the power of Byzantium faded, the Muslim fleet was the dominant force in the Mediterranean, while in northwest Europe in the eighth to tenth centuries, Viking longships raided Britain and France, looted monasteries and towns, and, eventually, settled in the British Isles, Normandy, and Russia. (Normandy and Russia derive their names from the Vikings—the "Northmen" and the "Rus.") As the Viking presence grew, Viking fleets fought other Viking fleets, largely by crashing together, linking themselves ship-to-ship, and fighting hand-to-hand.

The Viking longships were replaced by the *cog*, a ninety-foot, double-ended, decked ship with a single mast and square sail, and an after- and forecastle, on which units of archers could fire down on other ships. Its chief advantage, beyond its defensive capabilities, was that it could carry cargo. It was used in the Mediterranean during the Crusades (1095–1272).

Beginning in the early eleventh century, the Italian cities of Genoa, Pisa, and Venice developed navies to protect their trade networks. To secure trade routes, they had to fight Arabs, Normans, and each other. Venice fought a series of wars with Genoa through the thirteenth and fourteenth centuries, which culminated in Venice gaining control of the eastern Mediterranean. These wars were fought with galleys propelled by oars (although they also carried sails); they traded archery fire and boarded. The galley evolved into the *galleasse*, which had a cannon mounted in the bow. (Before the introduction of cannon, any of the Christian or Muslim fleets would have been chopped into mincemeat by an Athenian trireme fleet.)

As the struggle for the control of the Mediterranean went on, England and France were fighting a series of sea battles to determine who would dominate the channel. On August 24, 1217, in the battle of Dover, both fleets depended entirely upon sail. The English, with the wind behind them, threw quicklime into the air to blind the French, attacked with archers, and then boarded. In the mid-fourteenth century (during the Hundred Years' War), the English defeated the French decisively and dominated the northern seas. Up to the late fifteenth and early sixteenth centuries, naval tactics had changed little—victory depended upon archery and boarding, and battles were fought in coastal waters—but in the mid-fifteenth century, ships were designed with three masts to use the wind more efficiently, and they were armed with cannon.

While the English and French were fighting in the north, in 1453, in a combined assault by land and sea, the Ottoman Turks broke through the walls of Constantinople with cannon fire and finally and forever put an end to the last remnants of the Roman empire. Throughout the Mediterranean the muscle-powered galleys of the Barbary pirates were decisive. (The pirates also developed ships that could attack merchants in the Atlantic Ocean.) A galley might be 150 feet in length and have four hundred slaves at the oars. Christian and Muslim fleets raided each other's territory, with the Muslim fleets having the edge, until the decisive battle of Lepanto in 1571. The Christian fleet comprised 206 galleys, the Muslim fleet about the same. The Muslims tried to close and board; the Christians fended them off and used firearms to break up the boarding parties. The use of firearms was crucial to the Christian fleet's victory.

In the sixteenth century, the development of the nation-state and global exploration changed the dynamic of power. Small states, rich with ocean trade, could afford to build fleets. The fleets consisted of carracks (which evolved from the caravel, the ship Columbus sailed to the New World), a weatherly oceangoing vessel of varying size with two to four masts (which could be rigged for six sails), armed with bombards. Although the Barbary pirates would continue to prey on shipping in the western Mediterranean for more than two centuries after Lepanto, nonetheless, in the 1600s, the oared galley gave way to warships powered exclusively by sail and armed with light cannon.

The caravel evolved into the galleon, a longer and narrower ship without a forecastle (which caught the wind), and armed with anti-ship cannon. The galleon transformed naval battle tactics from closing and boarding to exchanges of gunfire. By the time of the Spanish Armada (1588), the English had eliminated the necessity for masses of soldiers on board in favor of long-range guns and maneuver. Ships had gunports, improved and dependable gunpowder, and were designed to deliver a broadside. In 1637, HMS *Sovereign of the Sea* was launched—it had three decks and one hundred cannon. For two centuries it was the prototype for the ship-of-the-line.

In the mid-seventeenth century, the Dutch and the English fought the first war conducted only at sea. After the conclusion of the Dutch war, England and France entered a period of warfare by land and sea that lasted centuries and was fought by ships-of-the-line. England gained a measure of ascendancy, during which it acquired Canada but lost the American colonies, when a French fleet gained local superiority off the coast of Yorktown for a brief period (Chesapeake Bay, September 1781). The English, perforce, became masters of combined operations with the primary objective of dominance at sea, culminating in their operations in the Napoleonic Wars. During those wars, they pretty much eliminated the French fleet and were able to raid French territory at will, but on land they could not defeat the French without continental allies.

While ships-of-the-line ruled the Atlantic, the Russians and Swedes fought for control of the Baltic in modified galleys. In the second battle of Svenskund (1790), the Swedes won a victory with the last use of galleys. Forty years later, the battle of Navarino (October 20, 1827—in which an allied fleet of English, French, and Russians destroyed an Ottoman fleet—was the last great battle fought exclusively by wooden ships under sail. The destruction of the Ottoman fleet led to Greek independence from Turkey.

Through the mid-nineteenth century, wooden ships were reinforced with steel plates down to the waterline ("ironclads"), and the United States produced a true steel ship, the *Monitor*. The first major encounter of ironclads was the battle (March 8/9, 1862) between the *Monitor* and the *Merrimac* in the American Civil War. The *Merrimac* was a wooden ship protected by iron plates and armed with conventional gunports, while the *Monitor* was a steel ship with a revolving turret.

Herman Melville wrote a poem about the encounter—

The ringing of those plates on plates
Still ringeth round the world.
War yet shall be, but warriors
Are now but operatives.

The battle of the *Monitor* and the *Merrimac* inaugurated a period ending with the exclusive deployment of steel ships powered by steam engines, but so long as fleets contained ironclads, which were vulnerable below the water line, ships still employed rams. In the Adriatic, Italy and Austria fought the first battle between fleets of ironclads—although wooden ships were also present—the battle of Lissa in July 1866. The Austrian admiral (outnumbered and outgunned) ordered his fleet of black-painted ships to ram "anything grey." The Austrian ship *Ferdinand Max* rammed and sank the Italian flagship, *Re d'Italia*. This success led to a period when ramming was considered a viable tactic and warships were built with rams (effective only so long as the enemy armor ended at the waterline). Navies employed ramming for several decades afterwards (and have employed it occasionally since then, principally by surface ships against U-boats in World War I and II).

With the introduction of the aircraft carrier, fleets fought battles without ever sighting each other. In one sense, however, even with the technological changes of gunpowder, the sail, steel, steam, and aircraft, while transforming tactics, did not change the overall strategic objective. The objective, still, was to facilitate invasion or to prevent invasion, or to protect trade or interdict trade. The destruction of the Spanish Armada was tactically different from the defeat of the sea peoples millennia before, but the strategic objectives were the same: to move an invasion force by water or, conversely, to prevent an invasion force from landing.

Today, for the first time, a ship armed with nuclear weapons could devastate an enemy country and negate the necessity of an invasion.

Notes

Introduction: The Blue on the Map

. . . they delighted in tales of Odysseus,—*Odyssey* I 1–5.
". . . life to poverty-stricken men."—Hesiod *Works and Days* 686–7.
. . . to his advantage by looting the countryside).—*Odyssey* III 153–185, 276–301.
". . . and he was terrified."—*Odyssey* V 291–298.
". . . churned the sea now here, now there."—*Odyssey* V 313–330.
. . . would be dashed to pieces.—*Odyssey* V 366ff—a close paraphrase.

Chapter One: The First to Risk Their Lives upon the Water

. . . and to numerous other Aegean islands.—Johnstone, pp. 55–56 (specifically Thessaly, Cyprus, Knossos, Chios, Skyros, and the Argolid), discussion of types of boats, pp. 56–62.
. . . closing in on a swimming reindeer.)—Paine, p. 12.
". . . with no boasting or exaggeration."—*The Napata Stela (Gebel Barkal Stele)*; Nicolas Grimal, *A History of Ancient Egypt,* New York, 1988, p. 216.

Chapter Two: The Minoans and the First "Thalassocracy"

"King Minos," who in the *Odyssey*—*Odyssey* XIX 177–181.
. . . come from Crete to teach them navigation.—Wachsmann, pp. 83–85.
. . . invaded Crete, and sacked Cnossus.—Plutarch *Theseus* 15–20.
The fifth-century Athenian historian Thucydides,—Thucydides I 4.
. . . *ship* of Theseus, if, in fact, it ever did?—Plutarch *Theseus* 23.
advancing upon an unsuspecting town.—Wachsmann, pp. 88–89.
. . . and small boats were still paddled—Illustration, Rethemiotakis, Chapter 13, pp. 106–107.

". . . and the screams of those being killed."—*Iliad* IV 450–451.

. . . ravage the lands of the eastern Mediterranean).—Wachsmann, pp. 130–137.

. . . seem to rule out Greeks).—*Cambridge Ancient History* II 2 (3rd ed.), p. 366.

. . . massive movement of people by sea.—CAH II 2 (3rd ed.), pp. 366–367.

Chapter Three: The Collapse of Civilization

. . . Phocis, and Thessaly—were sacked.—CAH II 2 (3rd ed.), pp. 352–353.

". . . as others love other employments."—*Odyssey* XIV 185–320.

. . . as he was to raid and plunder),—*Odyssey* IX 107ff.

". . . to do harm to strangers?"—*Odyssey* IX 231ff; (*Black Flag* p. 6).

. . . destined to work as slaves).—*Odyssey* XIV 259–271.

". . . a great breaker cast me upon the shore . . ."—*Odyssey* XIV 300–315.

Chapter Four: The Assault on Egypt

". . . forward toward Egypt."—CAH II part 2 (3rd ed.), p. 371.

. . . hands, spread across the surface of the water.)—Wachsmann, pp. 167ff., 317ff;
Larson, pp. 277–278.

". . . provisions from the treasuries and granaries every year"—CAH II 2 (3rd ed.),
p. 377.

"because we were afraid."—*Periplus of Hanno the Navigator* 14.

Chapter Five: Greek Colonization in the East

". . . in the front ranks of the battle."—*Iliad* XII 310–328 (Author's translation
from *With Arrow, Sword, and Spear,* pp. xvii–xviii).

. . . According to tradition,—Every polis had a foundation story. These stories
were a combination of memory, legend, and speculation with a good portion
of invention. Nonetheless, the validity of any particular story or episode in the
foundation story does not contradict the basic fact that a colony was planted
and a polis formed.

". . . hospitable wine with just enough water. . . ."—Alcaeus in Athenaeus X
430a-b.

". . . nine-foot tall Babylonian you killed."—Alcaeus in Murray et al. (ed.), p. 168,
n. 134 (slight paraphrase).

. . . express their poisonous resentment).—Herodotus I 146.

". . . on my spear I lean to drink."—Murray et al., p. 154, n. 103. Critias (88B 44
D.-K. *ap.* Aelian *VH* 10.13) writes that we would not know that Archilochus
was lecherous, licentious, arrogant, adulterous, and poverty-stricken if he had
not told us these things himself.

. . . adopted the name "Sheep-Wolf" (*Oeolycus*—it works better in Greek).—
   Herodotus IV 148–149.
. . . Rhodes, according to the *Iliad*,—*Iliad* II 653–670.
. . . colony in the western Delta at Naucratis;—Strabo XVI 801–802.
". . . bronze men came from the sea."—Herodotus II 152.
"Telephos, the son of Ialysos, was here!"—Meiggs and Lewis, p. 12, n. 7: literally
   "Telephos carved me."
"I can buy another just as good."—Murray et al., p. 154, n. 104.
. . . to kill Greeks and eat them.—Strabo VII 298.

Chapter Six: How to Build a Boat in the Eighth Century BCE

Odyssey V 234–264.

Chapter Seven: Greek Colonization in the West

. . . locations, such as described in the *Odyssey*:—*Odyssey* IX 116ff.
. . . allies, which had a modest sea empire—Strabo X 446–449.
. . . left his mark in just about every polis there.—Diodorus V 1–10 *passim*.
. . . "eating themselves to death.")—Aristotle *HA* III 17.
. . . not bound by the oath, to expel the Sicels.—Diodorus V 5.1.
. . . in Sicily, Syracuse. Corinth (according to Thucydides—Thucydides I 13.
. . . fought a sea battle in 664.)—Thucydides I 13.4; Herodotus III 48.
. . . made offerings to him as a hero,—Herodotus V 41–48.

Chapter Eight: A Typical Foundation Story

This account reflects what the founders and the colonists believed was the story
of their founding.
. . . narrated by Herodotus and augmented by an inscription).—Herodotus IV
   150ff; Meiggs and Lewis, #5, 21–51.
". . . divide the farmland into lots."—*Odyssey* VI 7–11.
. . . cure-all much sought after in Greece.—Pindar *Pythians* IV 4–8, 59–63,
   5.85–95.

Chapter Nine: Ramming

. . . an indecisive war in the early seventh century—Herodotus V 82–88.
". . . personally, I don't believe it.")—Herodotus V 86.
". . . armor in the temple of Athena."—Alcaeus in Strabo *Geography* on Sigeum.
. . . awarded the island to the Athenians.—Plutarch *Solon* 10; *Iliad* II 556–557.

". . . first offers you hospitality."—Herodotus VI 34.

. . . ever had to work again.—Herodotus IV 152.

. . . defeated by the new Persian king, Cyrus;—Herodotus I 53.

. . . ties of friendship with the Gauls.—Plutarch *Solon* 2.

. . . he would give them a day.—Herodotus I 164.

". . . because they were so homesick."—Herodotus I 165.

". . . their rams were knocked askew."—Herodotus I 166.1–2.

. . . the normal fate of captured pirates.—Papalas, 1–28.

Chapter Ten: The Trireme

. . . first to design and build triremes, according to Thucydides—Thucydides I 13.2.

. . . dates to about 550—the author, Hipponax of Ephesus,—Mulroy, p. 117.

. . . something like "a bowstring on a bow.")—Welsh, p. 115.

. . . which required an oak keel.—Theophrastos *HP* V 7.1–3.

. . . unseaworthy and would not have insured it.—Welsh, p. 114.

. . . to maintain the requisite skills.—Thucydides I 142.9.

. . . to the poor than to train the crews).—Plutarch *Pericles* 11.

. . . escaping gas, like frogs croaking: *brekekekexkoaxkoax.*—Aristophanes *Frogs* 209ff.

". . . you must not have eyes either."—Plutarch *Pericles* 8.

. . . suggested by a few bits of ancient evidence.—Welsh, pp. 60f.

. . . Based on the performance of the *Olympias*—Welsh, p. 205.

Chapter Eleven: Polycrates, King, Tyrant, Pirate

. . . left their weapons at home.—Polyaenus I 23.2.

. . . and dedicated it to Delian Apollo.—Thucydides I 14.

". . . never taken anything in the first place."—Herodotus III 39.

. . . he collected a large library,—Athenaeus I 3a.

. . . bred pedigreed dogs,—Athenaeus XII 540c-f.

. . . kept the poor citizens employed, occupied, and content.—Aristotle *Politics* 1313b 24.

. . . and to provide a steady platform for archers.—Plutarch *Pericles* 26.

. . . the Samians were "deep-lettered.")—Plutarch *Pericles* 26.

. . . a temple that, Herodotus wrote, was the biggest he knew.—Herodotus III 60.

. . . as a meeting place of aristocrats).—Athenaeus XIII 602d.

. . . a more congenial place in Greater Greece was Pythagoras.—Strabo XIV 1.16.

. . . long ode of praise for his mighty patron),—Athenaeus XII 540c-f, XIII 599c, XV 673d.

". . . I drained a pint of wine"—Apuleius *Flor.* 15.51, 54; Athenaeus 10.427ab.
". . . I brought it to you as a gift."—Herodotus III 42.
". . . a friend pulled down by a tragic fate."—Herodotus III 43.
". . . be wary of the wooden enemy and the red herald."—Herodotus III 57.
. . . and the rain—"Zeus washing him."—Herodotus III 120–125; Even the execution of Polycrates and the sack of Samos by the Persians did not end the depredations of the Samians: Meiggs and Lewis, p. 30 (#16).

Chapter Twelve: Darius and the Greeks

. . . Cambyses, died of a "self-inflicted wound"—Herodotus III 64.
". . . no compulsion to rush to battle with you."—Herodotus IV 127.2.
. . . learn what the "wrath of a king is,"—Meiggs and Lewis, p. 20 (#12).
. . . only been able to find one—Parmenion.—Plutarch *Moralia* ("Sayings of Kings and Commanders") 177C–179D, 10; (*Philip*, p. 53).)
"Daddy, get away from this bad man!"—Herodotus V 51.
". . . easier to persuade 30,000 men than one."—Herodotus V 97.
". . . those once small have become great."—Herodotus 1.5.

Chapter Thirteen: The First Naval Assault on Athens

"to get their own earth and water,"—Herodotus VII 133.
". . . you will not save the Argives,"—Herodotus VI 76.
. . . stories of their derring-do sixty years later.—Aristophanes *Acharnians passim.*

Chapter Fourteen: "Flee to the Ends of the Earth"

". . . insignificant city into a world power."—Plutarch *Themistocles* 2.
"the worst criminal of all the politicians."—Meiggs and Lewis #21.
. . . steady hoplites to "sea-tossed sailors."—Plato *Laws* IV 706.
. . . Sparta would fall. He told the Athenians,—Herodotus VII 140.
. . . "Aristides the brother of Datis."—Meiggs and Lewis #21.

Chapter Fifteen: "Pray to the Winds"

. . . enhanced the potency of the gesture.—Herodotus VII 179.
. . . some Persian ships had once been wrecked there),—Herodotus VII 188.
. . . divine advice "to pray to the winds."—Herodotus VII 178.
. . . able to turn in time to meet the new attack?—Herodotus VIII 9ff.
. . . and the dead had been burned.—Plutarch *Themistocles* 8.

Chapter Sixteen: "Brave Sons of Greece, Advance!"

". . . Come over to us! . . ."—Herodotus VIII 22.
". . . Athena, Nike, and Poseidon the Protector."—Meiggs and Lewis #23.
An eyewitness account (of a sort) exists—Aeschylus *Persians* 353–432.
. . . who was able to interview veterans of Salamis).—Herodotus VIII 83–92.
"'Cowards, how far do you want to retreat?'"—Herodotus VIII 84.
. . . picked it up, and brought it to Xerxes.—Plutarch *Themistocles* 14.
". . . and shrieks together filled the open sea until night hid the scene."—Aeschylus
   Persians 425–427.
. . . Themistocles, according to one version,—Plutarch *Themistocles* 16.
. . . wrote some verses about Themistocles,—Plutarch *Themistocles* 21.
. . . they plucked its leaves and cut off its branches.—*Ibid.* 18.
. . . Athenian executioners cast out the bodies of the executed.—*Ibid.* 22.

Chapter Seventeen: "Lead the Army"

". . . the world's bravest infantry and cavalry."—Plutarch *Aristeides* 10.1.
. . . and still have something left over.—Plutarch *Cimon* 9.
". . . they saved all Greece from slavery."—Murray et al., p. 214 (Simonides).
. . . forced them to turn and fight.—Plutarch *Cimon* 12–13.

Chapter Eighteen: Yoke Mates

"like a pair of oxen under one yoke,"—Plutarch *Cimon* 16.10.
the Athenians called them "The Legs"—Plutarch *Cimon* 13.6.
. . . Themistocles had proposed that the Athenians burn the allied Greek fleet.—
   Plutarch *Themistocles* 19.
. . . from a tribe that had three to four thousand men of military age.—Meiggs
   and Lewis, pp. 73–76, #33.
"As far as I am concerned, you can live forever."—Plutarch *Pericles* 17. He also is
   supposed to have said on his deathbed that his greatest accomplishment was
   that no one went into mourning because of him.
. . . which may better reflect the opinion of the man on the street:—Aristophanes
   Acharnians 514–531.
. . . Pericles had a personal grievance toward Megara—Plutarch *Pericles* 29.
"Might not the decree be turned with its face to the wall?"—Plutarch *Pericles* 30.
. . . an "old-fashioned" battle, Thucydides writes) is described in detail by him,—
   Thucydides I 49.

Chapter Nineteen: "A Bad Day for Greece"

"This will be a bad day for Greece."—Thucydides II 12.
Aegina the "eyesore of the Piraeus."—Plutarch *Pericles* 8.

. . . pursued the rest, and captured twelve.—Thucydides II 83ff.

. . . the Athenians' "reckless audacity"—Thucydides II 89.6.

. . . a surprise attack on the Piraeus, the main port of Athens.—Thucydides II 93ff.

. . . and the common people, but he wrote,—[Xenophon] *AthPol* II 2–6.

. . . the Athenian assembly loved it.—Plutarch *Nicias* 9.

. . . Athenians to kill them all now.—Thucydides III 39–40.

. . . the "very best enemies the Athenians could have had"—Thucydides IV 55.

". . . when we capture their soldiers?"—Thucydides IV 21.

. . . people spoke again . . . loudly, "Sail! Sail!"—Thucydides IV 28.

. . . spoke "pretty well for a Spartan," Thucydides writes—Thucydides IV 84.

Chapter Twenty: The Strong Do What They Want

. . . "thought one thing and said another,"—Herodotus IX 54.

. . . intellectual circles of Socrates.—Plutarch *Alcibiades* 1.

In the meantime, the Athenians in 416—Thucydides V 84–114.

"prophecies and oracles, which destroy people."—Thucydides V 103.

. . . Melos, and, by Alcibiades's decree,—Plutarch *Alcibiades* 22.

Nicias spoke against the expedition.—Thucydides VI 9.3.

. . . anything else "the commanders thought necessary."—Thucydides VI 26.

And so the fleet was prepared and it was magnificent.—Thucydides VI 30–31.

". . . flutes, bosuns, tootlings and whistlings."—Aristophanes *Acharnians* 545–555.

. . . one of the most famous courtesans in the Greek world.—Plutarch *Nicias* 15.

. . . between a black [guilty] and a white [innocent] token.—Plutarch *Alcibiades* 22.

. . . and close the siege works around Syracuse.—Thucydides VI 103.

Chapter Twenty-One: "Thrice Nine Days"

". . . defeat them and drive them from your land."—Thucydides VII 5.

"God knows, you Athenians are not easy to command."—Thucydides VII 12–14.

As Aeschylus says (in Aristophanes's *Frogs*),—Aristophanes *Frogs* 1073–1075.

. . . six hundred Lacedaemonian (but not Spartiate) hoplites. Gylippus—Description of battle: Thucydides VII 22–26.

. . . Corinthians erected a trophy, because (as Thucydides wrote—Thucydides VII 34.7.

In Sicily—Thucydides VII 36ff.

The Syracusans were jubilant,—Thucydides VII 42f.

". . . hope, that deceiver of men,"—Thucydides had written. Thucydides V 103.

". . . and they withdrew for that reason."—Thucydides VII 48.4.

As Nicias dithered—and he was famous for his dithering—Aristophanes *Birds* 638–39.

. . . magnificent fleet and Athens's chances in the war.—Nicias is the poster boy for politicians denying science.

. . . into the Great Harbor with seventy-six ships,—Thucydides VII 52ff.

. . . low in spirits [Thucydides wrote—Thucydides VII 55.

. . . Nicias decided to encourage them with a speech.—Thucydides VII 61.

". . . their weight would unbalance the ship."—Thucydides VII 62.2.

". . . know our ways, you are admired throughout Greece."—Thucydides VII 63.3.

. . . Gylippus, for his part, also addressed the crews of the Syracusan ships—Thucydides VII 65f.

. . . while the Syracusans and their allies . . . —Thucydides VII 70–71.

Their bodies were displayed by the city gate.—Plutarch *Nicias* 28.

Chapter Twenty-Two: Athens at Bay

. . . wanted his sons to be kings in Sparta.—Plutarch *Alcibiades* 23.

. . . although they were outnumbered by twenty ships, prepared to fight.—Diodorus XIII 45.8–46.

. . . Mindaros got safely away to Abydos.—Thucydides ends here and Xenophon *Hellenica* begins.

". . . on the sea, on land, and in their fortifications,"—Xenophon *Hellenica* I i 14–15.

"The Athenians—Diodorus XIII 50.2–51.

". . . soldiers starving, we don't know what to do."—Xenophon *Hellenica* I i 23.

. . . in a blunt and realistic appraisal.—Diodorus XIII 4–6.

". . . sail it past the Athenians at Samos."—Xenophon *Hellenica* I vi 2–3.

". . . your dalliance with the sea"—Xenophon *Hellenica* I vi 15 (the actual expression is blunt and vulgar).

. . . *your power is your fleet, nothing else matters*—*Frogs* 1464–1467; Plutarch *Alcibiades* 15: Athenian youths took an oath to consider crops of wheat and barley and the grape and olive as their borders.

Chapter Twenty-Three: Hanging by a Thread

. . . Plato's monster who ate his own children,—Plato *Republic* X 614ff.

. . . if he had some spare time, Dionysius said, "Never."—Plutarch *Moralia* ("Sayings of Kings and Commanders") 176A.

. . . twenty-four feet wide, and nine feet above the waterline.—Pitassi, p. 39.

". . . I have gotten everything there is."—Plutarch *Moralia* ("Sayings of Kings and Commanders") 175 E 5.

". . . were defeated piecemeal by the Carthaginians."—Diodorus XIV 59–60.

". . . the fear of a quick death lose us a long reign?"—Plutarch *Moralia* ("Sayings of Kings and Commanders") 175 D 2.

. . . led a concerted attack by land and sea.—Diodorus XIV 72–74.

". . . as just as a slave as he can as a free man."—Plutarch *Dion* 5.

". . . such a method." Dionysius paid him.—Plutarch *Moralia* ("Sayings of Kings and Commanders") 175 F 8.

He was so excited, he dropped dead.—Diodorus XV 74.1–4.

Chapter Twenty-Four: Conon the Athenian

"now they would be free."—Xenophon *Hellenica* II ii 23.

". . . could give an order and it would be carried out."—Xenophon *Hellenica* III i 5.

. . . on the verge of victory, he yelled, "I see the man himself,"—Xenophon *Anabasis* I 8.

. . . driven out by "10,000 golden archers," he said—Plutarch *Agesilaus* 15.

. . . under the command of the Spartan admiral, Pisander.—Diodorus IV 83 (my translation).

. . . fought a battle with the Spartans at Naxos—Diodorus XV 34.

The Spartan commander, Pollis,—Polyaenus III 11.2.

"waged peace as though it were war."—Demosthenes 18.166 (*Philip II of Macedon*, p. 104).

. . . deserted for service as mercenaries in other navies.—Demosthenes 50.14–16.

Chapter Twenty-Five: Giant Men, Giant Ships

. . . he should keep his ships beached.—Arrian I 18.

The siege of Tyre—Diodorus Siculus, Book XVII 40–46.

. . . *Alexander would not send a friend to certain death.*—Arrian *Indica* 20.8

. . . appeared to be "shoveling the water."—Arrian *Indica* 27.5.

. . . *because they ate fish*—Arrian *Indica* 29.9.

. . . figured out how to fight a sea battle on land—Diodorus XVIII 72.

". . . from the deck and there were two kubernetai."—Jacoby, #434 (Memnon) 1 8.4–5.

. . . the first Ptolemy had a "Forty" built.—Casson, *Ancient Mariners*, p. 130.

. . . ship-based siege equipment in besieging port cities.—*The Age of Titans*, pp. 127–128.

Eventually Antigonus had to accept that he had lost the east.—Diodorus XIX 80–6, 93, Justin XV 1.6-9, Plutarch *Demetrius* 5–6.

. . . its shipbuilding supplies and shipyards. In 306 BCE—Diodorus XX 49–52.

. . . led the prayers to the gods, and the crews repeated them.—Diodorus XX 50.6.

". . . their sizes matter as much as courage."—Diodorus XX 51.

. . . he had lost the battle and he sailed away.—Diodorus XX 52.

. . . according to legend, stood astride the Rhodian harbor entrance.—Diodorus XIX 58.2.

. . . someone had purposefully suppressed the history of this period.—Pausanias I 6.1.

Chapter Twenty-Six: Rowing on Land

. . . Romans sent three Senators to Delphi in a small warship.—Livy V 28.

". . . wash this garment clean with your blood."—Cassius Dio IX 5–8.

. . . Timoleon, to restore the situation.—Plutarch *Timoleon passim.*

"general and protector of the peace."—Diodorus XIX 9.4.

". . . not even let you wash your hands in the sea"—Cassius Dio XI 8.

. . . the "raven" (in Greek, the *korax*).—Polybius I 22.

. . . the whole length of the enemy ship.—Polybius I 23.

". . . as though the Roman ships were a herd of cattle."—Polybius I 23.3.

. . . to celebrate a triumph for a naval victory.—Broughton, 1.205.

Chapter Twenty-Seven: Sacred Chickens

. . . no position to contest the Roman landing.—Polybius I 26–28.

Polybius described—Polybius I 37.

"a thing not easily believed."—Polybius I 38.6.

The Carthaginians captured ninety-three Roman ships.—Polybius I 49–51.

. . . and had them thrown overboard.—Polybius I 50; Florus I xviii 29.

". . . take this rabble out and drown it."—Aulus Gellius *AN* X 6.2.

. . . the Carthaginians raised their sails and escaped.—Polybius I 60–61.

". . . until the defeated admit its defeat."—Ennius (Vahlen) A497.

Chapter Twenty-Eight: The First Illyrian War, 229–228 BCE

". . . private citizens in taking plunder on the sea."—*Black Flag*, p. 36 to Polybius II 8.

Chapter Twenty-Nine: A Different Kind of War

"One man, by delaying, saved the state."—Ennius (Vahlen) A370.

". . . although they do fail from time to time."—Polybius I 37.

". . . when they themselves have the most to fear,"—Polybius III 79.

". . . aid to us, as necessary and as mutually agreed."—Polybius VII 9.11.

"because of the surprise and speed of an attack by sea."—Polybius V 2.

. . . keep his eyes open and to take action as warranted.—Livy XXIV 40.
"'I have wiped out four Roman armies; I need help.'"—Livy XXIII 13.
. . . only three times in the history of the Republic).—Plutarch *Marcellus* 2, 7.
(Ships today use Archimedes calculations.—Horst Nowacki, "Archimedes and
 Ship Design." pp. 77–112, in Rorres.
. . . hooked it and tipped it over.—Polybius VIII 5(7).9, VIII 5–7 (6–8) for a full
 discussion of the Roman machines and Archimedes's counter-devices.
". . . harps, because they had not been invited."—Polybius VIII 6(8).6.
. . . Romans from war to effete cultural pursuits.—Plutarch *Marcellus* 21.
. . . birth of a baby with the head of an elephant.—Plutarch *Marcellus* 28.
The commander's name was Livius.)—Livy XXV 10; Polybius VIII 29.
"The Romans [Livy writes—Livy XXVI 39.

Chapter Thirty: The First Macedonian War

. . . defend the coast against their common enemy.—Livy XXIV 40.
. . . phalanx (i.e., the Romans) would just withdraw unscathed.—Polybius X
 25.
. . . in this predicament, but in the end, he relented.—Polybius IX 42.
. . . went into winter quarters with the Pergamene fleet.—Livy XXVIII 5–8.
. . . watchword for the operation was "Neptune leads us."—Livy XXVI 45.
. . . as he looked upon the face of his brother, "At last I see the end."—Livy XXVII
 51.
. . . the last Carthaginian stronghold in Spain, Gades.—Livy XXVIII 30.
The army passed the test.—Livy XXVIII 45.
. . . bay in which Carthage lies). During these operations—Livy XXX 25.
"How [writes Livy—Livy XXX 10.

Chapter Thirty-One: Greeks Will Be Free

. . . sacrificed to the divinity *False Oath and Felony*—Polybius XVIII 54.10;
 Diodorus XXVIII 1; Walbank, *Philip V,* p.100.
. . . unprovoked attempt to burn the dockyards.—Polyaenus V 17.2.
". . . excite fear in those attacking the walls."—Philo Mechanicus B53.
". . . confident that they will be well cared for."—*Ibid.* C72.
. . . responded to Philip's attack on Chios (summer of 201).—Polybius XVI 2.9,
 10.1, 15.
. . . more of a honeymoon excursion with his new bride than a military
 campaign.—Florus I xxiv 8–9.
. . . they got to sea and met the enemy at Cape Myonnesus.—Livy XXXVII 29–30;
 Appian *Syrian Wars* XI 27.
. . . vulnerable again to attacks by the warships.—Appian *Civil Wars* IV 115–116.

Chapter Thirty-Two: Thirst for Gold

. . . Scipio (the second *Africanus*, who destroyed Carthage in 146).—Plutarch *Marius* 3.2-3.

. . . been bounced from the Senate for corruption.—Plutarch *Sulla* 1.1.

. . . was a mix of red berries and oatmeal.—Plutarch *Sulla* 2.1.

(His stepmother also left him hers for similar reasons.)—Plutarch *Sulla* 2.4.

. . . with varying degrees of enthusiasm.—Appian *Mithridatic Wars* XII 23.

. . . drive the people to resort to cannibalism.—Appian *Mithridatic Wars* XII 38.

. . . left Rome in the power of his bloodthirsty son.—Plutarch *Marius* 43.3-45.6.

. . . could have made a better job of it.)—Plutarch *Lucullus* 1–2.

. . . set out north along the coast.—Plutarch *Lucullus* 2–3.

. . . single ship-action against the king's flagship,—Plutarch *Lucullus* 3.

. . . to the country to enjoy his new bride.—Plutarch *Sulla* 35.3-5. He did not last out the year.

. . . she always bore the marks of his teeth.—Plutarch *Pompey* 1–2.

. . . was interested in her property, not her body.—Plutarch *Crassus* 1.

. . . for three months (and still have millions left).—Plutarch *Crassus* 2.2.

. . . thought he was some sort of sea monster—Florus I xl 16.

. . . became wealthy by stripping the enemy dead—Plutarch *Lucullus* 11.

". . . The fawns are near."—Plutarch *Lucullus* 12.

". . . if, as an army, too few."—Plutarch *Lucullus* 27.

Chapter Thirty-Three: I Shall Crucify You

These pirates "farmed the sea,"—Appian *Mithridatic Wars*, XIV; (*Black Flag*, p. 43).

"to commit a crime rather than be a victim,"—Appian *Mithridatic Wars*, XIV 92; (*Black Flag*, p. 43).

"as bloodthirsty a crew as ever lived"—Plutarch *Caesar* 2.2 (*Black Flag*, p. 43–4).

. . . to the pirates of the Balearic Islands.—Florus I 42 (iii 7).

". . . prisoners hanging from the yardarms."—Florus I 42 (iii 7) *Cretan War*; (*Black Flag*, p. 44).

. . . mistress's husband, Cleomenes, to command his fleet.—Cicero *Verrines I* 86–90, *II Verrines V passim;* (*Black Flag*, pp. 45–47).

. . . summed up the situation for the Roman people.—Cicero *de imperio Cn. Pompeii oratio* 31–33; (*Black Flag*, p. 48).

"What an incredible man! [Cicero wrote.]—Cicero *de imperio* 33–35; (*Black Flag*, pp. 50–51).

Chapter Thirty-Four: Three Million Killed, Enslaved, Pacified

. . . at one point he was thirteen hundred talents in debt—Plutarch *Caesar* 5.4.

". . . the subversion of the Roman republic."—Plutarch *Caesar* 4.

. . . predicted that Caesar would be another Marius.—Plutarch *Caesar* 1.1.

In the third year, Caesar subjugated the Veneti—*Bellum Gallicum* III 11–16.

. . . and decided to cross into Britain—*Bellum Gallicum* IV 20–37, v 1–2, 5–23.

. . . called upon the gods for help and addressed his fellow soldiers—*Bellum Gallicum* IV 24 2–4, 25.3.

". . . here we come, following our bald lecher."—Suetonius *Twelve Caesars: Caesar* 51.

. . . to close the city and harbor to Caesar.—*Bellum Civile* I 34–36.

. . . to break the siege by attacking Caesar's fleet.—*Bellum Civile* I 56–59.

". . . upon this battle lay the fate of their city."—*Bellum Civile* II 6.

. . . acted on the precept "The dead don't bite").—Plutarch *Pompey* 57.

Chapter Thirty-Five: Son of a God

". . . whose hands were stained with money."—Suetonius *Twelve Caesars: Augustus* 4.

. . . funded by pirate raids on Italy.—Florus II xviii 2–3.

. . . to be promoted to triumvir.—Appian *Civil Wars* V 71.

. . . Antony was allowed to recruit troops in Italy.—Appian *Civil Wars* V 56–65.

"I live in the district of Hull."—Florus II xviii 4. He made a play on the word *carina*, which is both the bottom of the ship and a district in Rome (where his father had lived).

"I wish that you had done this without asking me."—Appian *Civil Wars* V 73.

. . . command of Menecrates to deal with Menodorus.—Appian *Civil Wars* V 81.

. . . towed his enemy's ship into harbor in triumph.—Appian *Civil Wars* V 82–3.

. . . where he could train his oarsmen over the winter.—Suetonius *The Twelve Caesars: Augustus* 16.

He is trying his luck at dice.—Suetonius *The Twelve Caesars: Augustus* 68.

. . . Octavian set out, after praying to the divinity, *Calm Seas*,—Appian *Civil Wars* V 98.

". . . because foolish men still take to ships."—Horace *Odes* I 4.

"I will defeat him even if Neptune is helping him."—Suetonius *The Twelve Caesars: Augustus* 16.

. . . they had not fought so much against ships as against "walls."—Appian *Civil Wars* V 108.

Agrippa lost three ships in the battle.—Pitassi, p. 120; Appian *Civil Wars* V 121–122, 144.

On September 2, 31 BCE, Antony put to sea.—Cassius Dio L 31–35; Velleius Paterculus II 85; Plutarch *Antony* 65–66.

. . . the sea groaned beneath their weight.—Florus II xxi 5.

". . . give us the land on which to stand to defeat the enemy or die."—Plutarch *Antony* 64.3.

According to one source, Octavian depended mostly on his *liburnae.*—Vegetius
   Epitoma Rei Militaris 33, 37.
". . . damaged and sunk, or else become vulnerable to further attacks."—Cassius
   Dio L 32.2-4.
". . . and set the ship timbers and pitch on fire."—Cassius Dio L 34.2.
. . . Octavian had to spend the night on board his flagship.—Suetonius *The Twelve
   Caesars: Augustus* 17.
. . . *hook is worth many times more than any fish might be.*—Suetonius *The Twelve
   Caesars: Augustus* 25.
". . . offering a treat to an elephant."—Suetonius *The Twelve Caesars: Augustus* 53.
He established two main fleets,—Pitassi, pp. 45–49.
The *liburna*—Appian *Illyrian Wars* III; Livy XXIV 35.

Chapter Thirty-Six: The Long Peace

. . . the conquest was left to Claudius in 43 CE.—Cassius Dio LX 19–22; Suetonius *Gaius* 46.
. . . protection throughout the Black Sea area until the fourth century.—Pitassi,
   p. 103.
". . . (like some riverboats) as their heading might dictate."—Tacitus *Germania* 44.
The boats were about forty-eight feet in length.—Pitassi, p. 41.
". . . much more dangerous than a defective house."—Vegetius IV 33.1–2.

Chapter Thirty-Seven: Decline and Fall

. . . *they do not describe naval battles.*—A. N. Sherwin-White notes in his review of
   Starr, *The Roman Imperial Navy*, *The Journal of Roman Studies*, Vol. 33 (1943),
   p. 112, "The evidence is such that a naval history of the Roman imperial fleets
   cannot be written."
. . . *tactical manual, written in the later fourth century, states,*—Vegetius IV 31.1–3:
   "Precepts of Naval Warfare."
. . . Saxons or a shore occupied by the Saxons.)—Cotterill, pp. 227–39.
. . . coinage declaring the two Augusti his "brothers,"—Aurelius Victor *Caes.*
   XXXIX 39.
Carausius defeated Maximian's first naval expedition.—Cotterill, pp. 229–239:
   One theory about the Saxon Shore is that the fortifications were built by Carausius to defend against Maximian and Constantius. *Notitia Dignitatum* (ca. 400
   CE) in the "Register of the Dignitaries, both civil and military, in the Districts
   of the West," lists a "Count of the Saxon Shore."
. . . high tide broke the mole and opened the harbor again.—*Paneg.* VIII (v) 6–7.
. . . issued coins under the names of his flagships, *Virtus* and *Laetitia*—CAH XII
   p. 333.

. . . Romans had conceded the North Sea to the Saxons.—Haywood, Chapters 1–2.

Rams and ramming seem to have disappeared.—Vegetius *Epitoma Rei Militaris* IV 46.

Conclusion

Herman Melville wrote a poem—Goodwin, Chapter 16, p. 437.

Classical Sources Cited and/or Translated (by the Author)

Aeschylus *Persians* 353–432. 425–427.

Alcaeus in Strabo *Geography* on "Sigeum;" in Athenaeus X 430a-b; n. 134 (Gilbert Murray et al. (ed.), *The Oxford Book of Greek Verse*, Oxford, 1966, p. 168).

Appian *Civil Wars* IV 115–116, V 56–65, 71, 73, 81–83, 98, 108, 121–122, 144; *Illyrian Wars* III; *Mithridatic Wars*, XII 23, 38, XIV 92; *Syrian Wars* XI 27.

Apuleius *Florilegium* 15.51, 54.

Archilochus (Gilbert Murray et al. (ed.), *The Oxford Book of Greek Verse*, Oxford, 1966, p. 154, n. 103, 104).

Aristophanes *Acharnians* 514–531, 545–555, *Birds* 638–639, *Frogs* 209FF, 1073–1075, 1464–1467.

Aristotle *History of the Animals* III 17, *Politics* 1313b 24.

Arrian I 18; *Indica* 20.8, 27.5, 29.9.

Athenaeus I 3a, X 427ab, XII 540c-f, XIII 599c, 602d, XV 673d.

Aurelius Victor *Caesares* XXXIX 39.

Cassius Dio IX 5–8, XI 8, L 31–35 (32.2–4, 34.2), LX 19–22.

Cicero *de imperio* 31–35; *Verrines* I 86–90, II *Verrines* V *passim*.

Critias (88B 44 D.-K. *ap.* Aelian *Varia Historia* 10.13).

Demosthenes 18.166, 50.14–16.

Diodorus IV 83, V 1–10 *passim* (5.1), XIII 4–6, 45.8–46, 50.2–51, XIV 59–60, 72–74, XV 34, 74.1–4, XVII 40–46, XVIII 72, XIX 9.4, 58.2, 80–86, 93, XX 49–52, XXVIII 1.

Ennius (Vahlen) A370, A497.

Florus I iii 7, xviii 29, xxiv 8–9, xl 16, II xviii 2–4, xxi 5.

Aulus Gellius *Attic Nights* X 6.2

Hanno the Navigator *Periplus* 14.

Herodotus 1.5, 53, 164, 166.1–2, 165, II 152, III 39, 42–43, 48, 57, 60, 64, 120–125, IV 127.2, 148–151, V 41–48, 51, 82–8, 97, VI 34, 76, VII 133, 140, 178–179, 188, VIII 9ff, 22, 83–92, IX 54.

Hesiod *Works and Days* 686–687.

Hipponax of Ephesus (David Mulroy, *Early Greek Lyric*, p. 117, fr 45 Diehl[3] in Tzetzes).

Homer *Iliad* II 556–557, 653–670, IV 450–451, XII 310–328, *Odyssey* I 1–5,
    III 153–185, 276–301, V 234–264, 291–298, 313–330, 366ff, VI 7–11,
    IX 107ff, 116ff, 231ff, XIV 185–320, XIX 177–181.
Horace *Odes* I 4.
Julius Caesar *Bellum Gallicum* III 11–16, IV 20–37, V 1–2, 5–23; *Bellum Civile*
    I 34–36, 56–59, II 6.
Justin XV 1.6–9.
Livy V 28, XXIII 13, XXIV 35, 40, XXV 10, XXVI 39, 45, XXVII 51, XXVIII 5–8,
    30, 45, XXVIII, XXX 10, 25, XXXVII 29–30.
Memnon F1 8.4–5 (Jacoby, Felix. *Die Fragmente der Griechischen Historiker*. Part
    3B. #434).
Panegyrics VIII (v) 6–7.
Pausanias I 6.1.
Philo Mechanicus B53, C72.
Plato *Laws* IV 706, *Republic* X 614ff.
Pindar *Pythians* IV 4–8, 59–63, 5.85–95.
Plutarch *Agesilaus* 15, *Alcibiades* 1, 15, 22–23, *Antony* 64.3, 65–66, *Aristeides*
    10.1, *Caesar* 1.1, 2.2, 4, 5.4, *Cimon* 9, 12–13, 16.10, *Crassus* 1, 2.2. *Deme-
    trius* 5–6, *Dion* 5, *Lucullus* 1–3, 11–12, 27, *Marcellus* 2, 7, 21, 28, *Marius*
    3.2–3, 43.3–45.6, *Nicias* 9, 15, 28, *Pericles* 8, 11, 17, 26, 29–30, *Pompey*
    1–2, 57, *Solon* 2, 10, *Sulla* 1–2, 35.3–5, *Themistocles* 2, 8, 14, 16, 18, 19, 21,
    22, *Theseus* 15–20, 23, *Timoleon passim*, *Moralia* ("Sayings of Kings and
    Commanders") 175 D 2, E 5, F 8, 176A, 177C–179D, 10.
Polyaenus I 23.2, III 11.2, V 17.2.
Polybius I 22–23, 26–28, 37, 38.6, 49–51, 60–61, II 8, III 79, V 2, VII 9.11, VIII
    5–9, 29, IX 42, X 25, XVI 2.9, 10.1, 15, XVIII 54.10.
Simonides (*The Oxford Book of Greek Verse* 214).
Strabo VII 298, X 446–449, XIV 1.16, XVI 801–802.
Suetonius *The Twelve Caesars: Caesar* 51, *Augustus* 4, 16, 17, 25, 53, 68, *Gaius* 46.
Tacitus *Germania* 44.
Theophrastos *History of Plants* V 7.1–3.
Thucydides I 4, 13.2–4, 14, 49, II 12, 83ff, 89.6, 93ff, III 39–40, IV 21, 28, 55,
    84, V 84–114, VI 9.3, 26, 30–31, 103, VII 5, 12–14, 22–26, 34.7, 36ff, 42f,
    48.4, 52ff, 55, 61, 62.2, 63.3, 65f, 70–71.
Vegetius Epitoma Rei Militaris IV 31.1–3, 33.1–2, 37, 46.
Velleius Paterculus II 85.
Xenophon Anabasis I 8, Hellenica I i 14–15, 23, vi 2–3, 15, II ii 23, III i 5.
[Xenophon] *Athenaion Politeia* II 2–6 (= "The Old Oligarch").

Inscriptions

##5, 7, 12, 16, 21, 23, and 33 (Meiggs, Russell and David Lewis (eds.), *A Selection
    of Greek Historical Inscriptions to the End of the Fifth Century*, Oxford, 1969).

Bibliography

Ahlberg, Gudrun. *Fighting on Land and Sea in Greek Geometric Art.* Stockholm, 1971.

Antonelli, L. *I Greci oltre Gibilterra.* Roma, 1997.

Ashburner, Walter, ed. *The Rhodian Sea-Law.* Oxford, 1909 (2010).

Aubet, M. E. *The Phoenicians and the West: Politics, Colonies, and Trade.* Cambridge, 2001.

Bass, G. *A History of Seafaring Based on Underwater Archaeology.* London, 1972.

Bèrard, J. *La Colonisation Grecque de l'Italie Méridionale et de la Sicile dans l'antiquité.* Paris, 1957.

Bèrard, J. *L'Expansion et la Colonisation grecque jusqu'aux guerre médiques.* Paris, 1960.

Biddlestone, Robert et al. *Odysseus Unbound: The Search for Homer's Ithaca.* Cambridge, 2005.

Bradford, Alfred S. *With Arrow, Sword, and Spear: A History of Warfare in the Ancient World.* Westport, CT, 2001.

Bradford, Alfred S. *Flying the Black Flag: A Brief History of Piracy.* Westport, CT, 2007.

Bradford, Alfred S. *War: Antiquity and Its Legacy.* London, 2014.

Broughton, T. R. S. *The Magistrates of the Roman Republic.* 2 volumes. Cleveland, Ohio, 1968.

Burn, Barbara et al., eds. *From the Land of the Labyrinth: Minoan Crete, 3000–1100 B. C.* New York, 2008.

Burstein, Stanley M., trans./ed. *Agatharchides of Cnidus.* London, 1989.

Cambridge Ancient History. Volume II Part 2, 3rd ed. Cambridge, 1975.

Cargill, Jack. *The Second Athenian League.* London, 1981.

Carpenter, R. *Beyond the Pillars of Heracles: The Classical World Seen through the Eyes of Its Discoveries.* New York, 1966.

Carty, Aideen. *Polycrates, Tyrant of Samos: New Light on Archaic Greece.* Stuttgart, 2015.

Casson, Lionel. *The Ancient Mariners,* 2nd ed. Princeton, 1991.

Casson, Lionel. *Ships and Seamanship in the Ancient World.* Baltimore, 1995.

Clerc, M. *Massilia, Histoire de Marseille dans l'antiquité.* Marseille, 1927.

Descoeudres, J.-P., ed. *Greek Colonists and Native Populations.* Oxford, 1990.

Dickinson, Oliver. *The Aegean Bronze Age.* Cambridge, 1994.

Dickinson, Oliver. *The Aegean from Bronze Age to Iron Age.* New York, 2006.

Dougherty, Carol. *The Poetics of Colonization: From City to Text in Archaic Greece.* Oxford, 1993.

Doumas, Christos G. *Thera: Pompeii of the Ancient Aegean.* London, 1983.

Dunbabin, T. J. *The Western Greeks: The History of Sicily and South Italy from the Foundation of the Greek Colonies to 480 BC.* Oxford, 1948.

Evans, James. *The History and Practice of Ancient Astronomy.* Oxford, 1998.

Fields, Nic. *Ancient Greek Warship, 500–322 BC.* Oxford, 2007.

Frost, Honor. *Under the Mediterranean.* Eaglewood Cliffs, NJ, 1963.

Gabrielsen, Vincent. *Financing the Athenian Fleet: Public Taxation and Social Relations.* Baltimore, 1994.

Garlan, Yvon. *Guerre et économie en Grèce ancienne.* Paris, 1999.

Garland, Robert. *The Piraeus from the Fifth to the First Century B. C.* London, 1987.

Garnsey, Peter et al., eds. *Trade in the Ancient Economy.* Berkeley, 1983.

Giulmartin, John Francis. *Gunpowder and Galleys: Changing Technology and Mediterranean Warfare at Sea in the 16th Century.* Cambridge, 2003.

Goodwin, Doris Kearns. *Team of Rivals.* New York, 2006.

Grimal, Nicolas. *A History of Ancient Egypt.* New York, 1988.

Hale, John R. *Lords of the Sea: The Epic Story of the Athenian Navy and the Birth of Democracy.* New York, 2009.

Hattendorf, John B., ed. *The Oxford Encyclopedia of Maritime History.* 4 vols. Oxford, 2007.

Haywood, John. *Dark Age Naval Power: Frankish and Anglo-Saxon Seafaring Activity.* Norfolk, UK, 1999.

Heikell, Rod and Lucinda. *Greek Waters Pilot,* 12th ed. Cambridgeshire, England, 2014.

Heller-Roazen, Daniel. *The Enemy of All: Piracy and the Law of Nations.* Brooklyn, 2009.

Holst, Sanford. *Phoenician Secrets: Exploring the Ancient Mediterranean.* Los Angeles, 2011.

Horden, P., and N. Purcell. *The Corrupting Sea: A Study of Mediterranean History.* Oxford, 2000.

Horne, Charles F. *The Tel-el-Amarna Letters (1400 B.C.).* Whitefish, Montana, 2010 (print on demand).

Jacoby, Felix. *Die Fragmente der Griechischen Historiker.* Part 3B. Leiden, 1950.

Johnstone, Paul. *The Sea-craft of Prehistory,* 2nd ed. (Seán McGrail). New York, 1988.

Konstam, Angus. *Byzantine Warship vs. Arab Warship, 7th-11th Centuries.* Oxford, 2015.

Köster, August. *Das Antike Seewesen.* Berlin, 1923.

Krings, Véronique. *Carthage et les Grecs c. 580–480 av. J.-C.: Les Texts et histoire.* Leidon, 1998.

Larson, Erik. *Dead Wake: The Last Crossing of the Lusitania.* New York, 2015.

Mac Sweeney, Naoíse. *Foundation Myths and Politics in Ancient Ionia.* Cambridge, 2013.

Malkin, Irad. *Religion and Colonization in Ancient Greece.* Boston, 1987.

Malkin, Irad. *The Returns of Odysseus: Colonization and Ethnicity.* Berkeley, CA, 1998.

Malkin, Irad. *A Small Greek World: Networks in the Ancient Mediterranean.* Oxford, 2011.

Mark, Samuel. *Homeric Seafaring.* College Station, TX, 2005.

Meiggs, Russell. *The Athenian Empire.* Oxford, 1972.

Meiggs, Russell. *Trees and Timber in the Ancient Mediterranean World.* Oxford, 1982.

Meiggs, Russell, and David Lewis. *A Selection of Greek Historical Inscriptions to the End of the Fifth Century B.C.* Oxford, 1969.

Mellersh, H. E. L. *The Destruction of Knossos: The Rise and Fall of Minoan Crete.* New York, 1970.

Miller, Molly. *The Thalassocracies.* New York, 1971.

Monderson, Frederick. *Medinet Habu: Mortuary Temple of Rameses III.* Bloomington, IN, 2009.

Morrison, J. S. *Greek and Roman Oared Warships, 399–30 B.C.* Oxford, 1996.

Mulroy, David. *Early Greek Lyric Poetry.* Ann Arbor, MI, 1992.

Murray, Gilbert et al., eds. *The Oxford Book of Greek Verse.* Oxford, 1966.

Murray, W. M. *The Age of Titans: The Rise and Fall of the Great Hellenistic Navies.* Oxford, 2012.

Nelson, H. H. et al. *Medinet Habu I: Earlier Historical Records of Ramses III.* Chicago, 1930.

Ormerud, H. A. *Piracy in the Ancient World.* New York, 1987 (reprint of 1920's edition).

Paine, Lincoln. *The Sea and Civilization: A Maritime History of the World.* New York, 2013.

Papalas, Anthony J. "The Battle of Alalia." *Syllecta Classica* 24 (2013), 1–28.

Philo Mechanicus. *On Sieges.* (David Whitehead, ed.). Stuttgart, 2016.

Pitassi, Michael. *The Roman Navy: Ships, Men, and Warfare 350 BC–AD 475.* Barnsley, South Yorkshire, 2012.

Podlecki, A. J. *The Life of Themistocles.* Montreal, 1975.

Polignac, F. De. *La naissance de la cité grecque.* Paris, 1984.

Prinz, F. Gründungsmythen und Sagenchronologie (Zetemata), Munich, 1979.

Rankov, Boris, ed. *Trireme Olympias: The Final Report.* Oxford, 2012.

Reed, C. M. *Maritime Traders in the Ancient Greek World.* Cambridge, 2003.

Rethemiotakis, Giorgos. *From the Land of the Labyrinth: Essays.* New York, 2008.

Roberts, W. and J. Sweetman, eds. *New Interpretations in Naval History.* Annapolis, MD, 1991.

Rodgers, William Ledyard. *Greek and Roman Naval Warfare: A Study of Strategy, Tactics, and Ship Design from Salamis (480 B.C.) to Actium (31 B.C.).* Annapolis, MD, 1937 (reprint 1963).

Rorres, Chris, ed. *Archimedes in the 21st Century: Proceedings of a World Conference at the Courant Institute of Mathematical Sciences.* Cham, Switzerland, 2017.

Roseman, Christina Horst. *Pytheas of Massalia: On the Ocean.* Chicago, 1994.

Rougé, Jean (trans. Susan Frazer). *Ships and Fleets of the Ancient Mediterranean.* Middletown, CT, 1981.

Rufus Festus Avienus. *Descriptio Orbis Terrae, Ora Maritima, et Carmina Minora.* Paris, 1825.

Shelmerdine, Cynthia W. *The Cambridge Companion to the Aegean Bronze Age.* Cambridge, 2008.

Shipley, Graham. *History of Samos.* Oxford, 1987.

Sidebottom, Harry. *Ancient Warfare: A Very Short Introduction.* Oxford, 2004.

Silburn, Percy Arthur. *The Evolution of Sea-Power.* New York, 1912.

Southworth, John van Duyn. *The Ancient Fleets: The Story of Naval Warfare Under Oars, 2600 B. C.–1597 A. D.* New York, 1968.

Starr, Chester G. *The Influence of Sea Power on Ancient History.* Oxford, 1989.

Starr, Chester G. *The Roman Imperial Navy: 31 B.C. A.D. 324,* 2nd ed. Cambridge, 1960 (reissue of 1941 edition).

Steinby, Christa. *Rome versus Carthage: The War at Sea.* Barnsley, South Yorkshire, Great Britain, 2014.

Thiel, J. *Eudoxus of Cyzicus.* Groningen, 1966.

Thiel, J. *A History of Roman Sea-Power Before the Second Punic War.* Amsterdam, 1954.

Thiel, J. *Studies on the History of Roman Sea-Power in Republican Times.* Amsterdam, 1946.

Thomson, George. *Studies in Ancient Greek Society: The Prehistoric Aegean.* New York, 1965.

Thubron, Colin. *The Ancient Mariners.* Chicago, 1981.

Tsetskhladze, G. R., ed. *Greek Colonization: An Account of Greek Colonies and Other Settlements Overseas.* Leiden, 2006.

Wachsmann, Shelley. *Seagoing Ships and Seamanship in the Bronze Age Levant.* College Station, Texas, 1998.

Walbank, F. W. *Philip V.* Cambridge, 2013 (reissue of 1939 essay).

Wallinga, H. T. *Ships and Sea-Power before the Great Persian War: The Ancestry of the Ancient Trireme.* Leiden, 1993.

Wallinga, H. T. *Xerxes' Greek Adventure: The Naval Perspective.* Leiden, 2005.

Welsh, Frank. *Building the Trireme.* London, 1988.

Whitehead, David. *Philo Mechanicus: On Sieges.* Stuttgart, 2016.

Wood, Adrian K. *Warships of the Ancient World, 3000–500 BC.* Oxford, 2012.

Yasur-Landau, Assaf. *The Philistines and Aegean Migrations at the End of the Late Bronze Age.* Cambridge, 2010.

Index

Achaean League, 178, 181
Achaeans, 7, 8, 27, 181
Actium, battle of, 206, 208, 215
Adherbal, 153, 171
Adrianopolis, battle of, 218
Adriatic fleet, 162
Adriatic Sea, 18, 123, 143, 156–167,
    195, 201, 203, 208, 210, 221
Aegates Islands, battle of, 155
Aegina, Aeginetans, 31, 45, 54, 60,
    68, 70, 80, 85, 95, 127, 128, 168,
    169
Aegospotami, battle of, 113
Aeolians, 16
Aeschines, 130
Aeschylus, 69, 72, 76, 99, 112, 113
Aetolians, 168, 169, 178, 179
Africa, 3, 18, 28, 29, 145, 149, 151,
    152, 159, 160, 170–174, 182,
    183, 195, 201, 202, 206, 211,
    216, 218, 219
Agamemnon, 7
Agathocles, 144, 145, 149
Agesilaus, 126
Agis, 91, 93, 100, 107
Agrigentum, battle of, 146
Agrippa, M. Vipsanius, 206–209
Ahura Mazda, 49
Ajax, 32, 92
Akawasha, 8
Alalia, battle of, 33–35

Alaric, 218
Alcaeus, 32, 33
Alcibiades, 92–96, 102, 107–111
Alexander IV, 134
Alexander the Great, 119, 130–139,
    175
Alexandria, xv, 26, 185
Alexandros, 73
Allectus, 217, 218
Amasis, 43, 44
Ameinocles, 36
Amorgos, battle of, 135
Amphipolis, battle of, 81, 90–92,
    130
Amurru, 12
Amyntas, 50
Anacreon, 43
Antigonus the One-Eyed, 135
Antiochus III, 175
Antipater, 134, 135
Antoninus Pius, 215
Antony, Marc (M. Antonius), 180,
    192, 204–210
Aper, 217
Apollo, 24, 25, 28, 29, 50, 56,
    61–63
Apollonia, 167, 169, 180
Appius (Claudius), 145, 146
Arados, 50
Arcadia, 55
Archelaus, 184, 185

archers, 13, 39, 42, 43, 68, 80, 82,
    95, 100, 101, 103, 108, 109, 121,
    126, 132, 135, 163, 194, 208,
    219, 220
Archias, 26, 27
Archidamus, 74, 84
Archilochus, xv, 19, 32
Archimedes, 163, 164
Arginusae, battle of, 112
Argos, Argolid, xvi, 10, 41, 54, 55, 81,
    93, 181
Ariadne, 5
Ariamnes, 71
Ariovistus, 197
Aristagoras, 51, 52
Aristides, 62, 71, 80
aristocrat, aristocracy, 16, 18, 25, 26,
    32, 37, 41, 92, 94
Aristophanes, 38, 43, 81, 99, 112
Artabazus, 73
Artaphernes, 51, 55
Artaxerxes, 76, 125, 126
Artemis, 56, 63, 66, 92
Artemisia, 69–71
Artemisium, battle of, 62–70
Arthur Evans, 5, 6
Arzawa, 12
Asclepiodotus, 217
Aspasia, 81
Aspis, 150, 151
Assyria, Assyrians, 15, 17
Athenian empire, 79, 90, 93, 125
Athens, Athenian, xv, 5, 6, 9, 17, 31,
    32, 36, 38, 39, 41–43, 49–114,
    123–130, 134, 135, 137, 178,
    184, 185, 220
Athos, Mount, 53, 60, 108
Attalus, 168, 169, 176–178
Augusti, 217, 218
Augustus, 210, 212. *See also* Octavian

Babylon, Babylonian, 17, 18, 33, 59,
    126, 134
Balearic Islands, 192
ballistae, 137, 163, 169, 209

battering rams, 119, 133
Battos, 29, 30
"Beautiful" Promontory, 172
Belgae, 197
bireme, xv, 7, 34, 34, 42, 115, 119,
    146, 183, 185, 210, 213
blockade, 81, 128, 152, 165, 172, 205
boarding, 66, 71, 114, 115, 118, 122,
    136, 171, 172, 202, 205, 210, 220
Boeotia, Boeotians, 9, 16, 32, 74, 126,
    130, 185
Boeotian League, 128
booty, 10, 11, 28, 42, 43, 94, 110, 111,
    147, 151, 156, 157, 164, 170, 177,
    185, 187, 192, 194, 213, 216, 217
Borani, 216
Brasidas, 85, 89–92
Britain, Britons, 7, 15, 198–202, 212,
    217–219
Britannic Fleet, 217
Bronze Age, 10
Bructeri, 211
Brundisium, 167, 194, 195
Byblos, 15, 50
Byzantine navy, 219
Byzantium, 19, 75, 127, 135, 139, 218,
    219

Cadmeian victory, 34
Caesar, C. Julius, 181, 183, 186, 191,
    192, 197–202, 204, 210, 212
Caesars (imperial title), 217, 218
Callicratidas, 111, 112
Calm Sea the god, 206
Calypso, 23
Cambyses, 18, 43, 44, 49
Cannae, 161, 163
canoes, 3
Cape Myonnesus, battle of, 180
Cape Sepias, 64
captives, 14, 15, 64, 65, 110, 191, 194,
    195
Capua, 161
Caracalla, 215
Carausius, 217

caravel, 220
Carchemish, 12
Caria, Carians, 6, 17, 18, 44, 52
Carinus, 216
carracks, 220
Cartagena, 170
Carus, 216
Carystus, 56, 65
Cassius Longinus, C., 180, 204
Catana, Catania, 26, 95, 96
catapults, 119, 121, 132, 136–138,
    163, 169, 172, 173, 209
Cato, M. Porcius, 175
Catulus, Q. Lutatius, 154
Chabrias, 128, 129
Chaeronea, battles of, 130, 185
Chalcedon, 19, 127, 135, 186, 216
Chalcidian League, 128
Chalcidice, 18, 73, 90
Chalcis, 18, 19, 25, 27, 169, 178
Chaldaeans, 18
chariot-warriors, 7
Chersonese, 32, 49, 50, 52, 53, 111,
    185, 212
China, 7
Chios, 17, 19, 33, 34, 49, 75, 81, 95,
    106, 107, 176, 179
Christian, 218, 220
Cicero, M. Tullius, 193–197, 204
Cilicia, 9, 12, 53, 66, 186, 191, 195
Cimon, 58, 75, 76, 79
Circle Fort, 96, 100
circumnavigation of Africa, 15
"Cisalpine" Gaul, 175
classis Alexandrina, 211
classis Britannica, 211
classis Germanica, 211
classis Mauretania, 211
classis Pannonica, 211
classis Pontica, 211
classis Syriaca, 211
Claudius the Handsome, 153
Claudius the emperor, 201, 212
Cleomenes I, 28, 51, 54, 55
Cleomenes the Sicilian, 193

Cleon, 88–92
Cleopatra, 204, 208–210
Cnidus, battle of, 126
Cnossos, 5
cog, 219
colonization, 15, 18, 24–30, 32, 34,
    42, 81
Colossus of Rhodes, 138
Commodus, 215
Conon, 111–113, 125–127
Constantine the Great, 217, 218
Constantinople, 219, 220
Constantius Chlorus, 217, 218
Corcyra, 26, 81–83, 95, 129, 157, 166,
    167, 169, 208
Corinth, 19, 26, 63, 81–83, 93, 96,
    106, 107, 126, 169, 181, 208
Cornelius, Scipio, L., 179
Cornelius, Scipio, P. (the father of
    Africanus), 160, 170
Cornelius, Scipio Aemilianus, P.
    (Africanus II), 183
Cornelius Scipio Africanus, P.,
    170–174, 179
Corsica, 8, 33, 34, 155, 159, 201, 204,
    205
Corycus, battle of, 179
courage, 11, 16, 64, 104, 109, 122,
    137, 144, 163, 165, 183, 195,
    202, 204
Crassus, M. Licinius, 186, 197,
    201
Crete, Cretan, xvi, 3, 5–13, 17, 18, 42,
    45, 185, 192, 194
Crista, Q. Naevius, 167
Cyclades, 6, 25, 51
Cyclops, 10, 19, 25
Cynocephalae, battle of, 178
Cynossema, battle of, 107, 108
Cyprus, 3, 7–9, 12, 13, 18, 52, 53,
    80, 126, 127, 132, 137, 138,
    185
Cyrene, 29, 30, 185
Cyrus the Great, 33, 34, 41, 43, 50
Cyrus the Younger, 111, 112, 125

Cythera, 90, 92, 126
Cyzicus, battle of, 186

Dacia, Dacians, 213, 216
Damocles, 119
Danube, 49, 50, 59, 210, 211, 213, 216
Danube fleet, 213
Darius, the son of Xerxes, 76
Darius III, 131, 133
Darius the Great, 49–55, 58, 59
Dark Age, 15, 16
Datis, 55, 62
Decelea, 96, 107, 111
Delian League, 79
Delos, 32, 42, 56, 73, 74, 79, 181, 191
Delphi, 24, 28–33, 44, 50, 55, 61, 64, 81, 143
Demaratus, 55
Demeter, 25, 62
Demetrius the Besieger, 136–139
Demetrius the Illyrian, 157
democracy, democracies, 53, 87, 89, 94, 102, 105, 107, 113, 125, 137, 144
Democrates, 165
demons, 56, 61
Demosthenes the general, 89, 90, 99, 100, 101, 102, 105
Demosthenes the orator, 130
Denyen, 12
Dicaearchia, 42
dictator, 161
diekplous, 65, 86, 180, 205, 207
Diocles, 217
Diocletian, 217, 218
Dionysius, 119–124, 132, 144, 193
Dionysus, xv, 25
dodecapolis, 17
dolphins (instrument of war), 101
Domitian, 213
Dorians, 10, 15, 16, 17, 98
Dorieus, 28
dream, 45, 56, 112, 139, 187
Drepana, 152–154

dromon, 218
Duilius, C., 147, 148

earthquake, 7, 79
Ebro River, 170
Egesta, 93, 95
Egypt, Egyptians, xvi, 4, 5, 7–15, 18, 33, 43, 44, 53, 59, 67, 80, 126, 133–136, 138, 185, 202, 204, 208, 209, 211
elephants, 4, 139, 144, 146, 151, 152, 162, 164, 174
Eleusinian mysteries, 111
Emporia, 33, 171
England, English, 36, 86, 220, 221
English Channel, 64, 211
Epidamnus, 157, 169
Epipolae Plain, 96
Epirus, 144, 156
Erechtheid casualty list, 80
Eretria, Eretrians, 18, 19, 25, 27, 52, 53, 55, 56
Eryx, 28, 120, 121
Etesian Wind, xvi
Etruscans, 34, 35, 143
Euarchos, 26
Euboea, xvi, 9, 18, 52, 56, 63, 65–67, 107, 130, 169
Euripides, 112, 201
Euripus, 64, 65, 68
Eurybiades, 63–65, 68, 72
Eurymedon River, battle of, 76
Eurymedon the General, 99, 102

Fabius Cunctator, Q. Maximus Verrucosus, 161
Fall of Miletus, The, 53
fire arrows, 180, 207
fire baskets, 180
fire ship, 102
fire signal, 64
First Messenian War, 27
"five good emperors," 213, 215
Flamininus, T. Quinctius, 178
Flaminius, C., 161

Flavian dynasty, 212
fleets, 26, 28, 31, 66, 67, 99, 111, 132, 136, 155, 162, 164, 165, 170, 191, 195, 202, 205, 206, 208–210, 213, 219–222
fog, 172, 217
Founder, foundation, 26, 29, 30, 32, 33, 92
frame-first construction, 4
Franks, 216, 217

Gades, 170
galleasse, 220
galleon, 220
galley, 220
Gallienus, 216
Gaugamela, battle of, 133
Gaul, Gauls, 18, 28, 33, 143, 158–163, 171, 175, 183, 195–201, 216, 217
Gedrosian Desert, 133
Germans, 183, 198, 213, 216–218
Gesoriacum (modern Boulogne), siege of, 217
Glabrio, M. Atilius, 179
gods, goddesses, xvi, 4, 5, 11, 23, 25, 26, 45, 49, 50, 54, 61, 66, 137, 207, 212
"golden archers," 125, 126
Golden Fleece, xv
Goths, 216, 218
Gracchus, C. Sempronius, 182
Gracchus, Ti. Sempronius, 182
Granicus River, battle of, 131
grapnels, grappling, 14, 103, 108, 109, 147, 180, 198, 202, 207, 209, 218
Great Harbor, 96, 98, 99, 102, 104, 120, 122
greater imperium, 194, 210
Greek fire, 219
Greek League, 73
Gulf of Corinth, 26, 85, 86, 92, 126
Gulf of Pagasae, 65
Gulf of Tarentum, 143
Gylippus, 97, 100

Hadrian, 215
Hamilcar Barca, 154, 155, 159
Hannibal, 159–180
Hannibal (Carthaginian commander) 147, 148
Hannibal the Rhodian, 152
Hanno, 154
Harpagos, 34, 41
Harpalus, 60
harpax, 207
harps, 163, 164
Hasdrubal (Hamilcar's successor), 155, 159
Hasdrubal (Hannibal's brother), 170
Hegestratos, 74
Helen of Troy, 7, 115
Hellas, Hellenism, xv, 21
Hellespont, 18, 52, 56, 60, 72, 73, 75, 107–113, 126–128, 131, 134, 135, 139, 180
Hellespontias, 64
helmsman, xvi, 36, 38, 102
helots, 31, 63, 74, 89, 90, 134
Helvetians, 28, 197
hemioliai, 133
hepteres, 137
Heracleo, 193
Heracles, 25, 27, 28, 55
Heraclids, 28
herald, 44, 45, 75
Hercules, 186
Hermaeum Promontory, 150, 151
Hermes, 94
Herodotus, 29, 31, 43, 52, 53, 60, 64, 65, 70
heroes, 10, 25, 112
Heruli, 216
Hesiod, xv
hexeres, 149, 205
Hiero, 145, 146, 155, 162
Himilco, 121, 122
Hippias, 51, 54–56, 59
Hipponax of Ephesus, 36
Hittites, 7–9, 12
Homer, xvi, 7, 10, 17, 32, 192

hoplites, 39, 41, 42, 56, 60, 63, 72, 76, 82, 86, 87, 90, 94, 95, 99–103, 109, 111, 128
Horace, 207
horse transport, 55, 95, 133, 149, 150
Huns, 216, 218
Hydaspes River, battle of, 133

Ialysos, 18
Icarus, 6
Iliad, xv, 7, 9, 13, 17, 32
Ilium, 9, 16, 216
Illyrian pirates, 123, 156
imperium, 170, 195, 212
indemnity, 124, 155, 159, 180, 185
India, 7, 15, 33, 133, 134
Indo-European, 7
Indus River, 133
infantry, 11, 55, 57, 63, 74, 75, 93, 94, 99, 102, 104, 110, 120, 145, 149, 165, 171
invasion, 13, 18, 43, 53, 54, 129, 145, 149, 169, 170, 171, 202, 209, 222
Ion, 17
Ionians, 16, 17, 32, 33, 42, 44, 50–53, 66, 68, 70, 71, 74, 75, 79, 98
Iphicrates, 127, 129
Ipsus, battle of, 138
Ischia, 25, 26
Israel, Israelites, 13, 15
Issus, battle of, 131
Isthmian games, 178
Isthmus of Corinth, 9, 62, 65, 87

Jason, xv
javelin, 125, 163, 166, 206
Jugurthine War, 182, 183
Julia, 182
Julian, 218
Julio-Claudians, 212

keleustes/ai (boatswains), 38, 39, 87, 108, 137
korax, 147

Kothar-wa-Khasis, 5
kubernetes/ai (helmsmen), 36, 38, 39, 87

labyrinth, 5, 6
Laconia, Laconians, 9, 10, 17, 52, 54, 57, 74, 85, 90, 100, 110, 126, 128
Lade, battle of, 53
Laelius, C., 170, 171
Laetitia, 217
Laevinius, M. Valerius, 167, 168
Lais, 96
Lake Trasimene, battle of, 161
Lamachus, 93, 95, 97, 102
Lamian War, 134
Latins, 143
Laurion silver mines, 60
legions, legionnaires, 139, 143, 148–152, 155, 159, 161, 171, 174, 179, 180, 182, 185, 187, 199–202, 205, 206, 210, 212
lembi, 156, 210
Leon, 64
Leonidas, 55, 63–67, 74
Leosthenes, 134
Lepanto, battle of, 220
Lepidus, M. Aemilius, 206
Leptines, 121, 122, 124
Lesbos, Lesbians, xvi, 16, 32, 33, 42, 49, 75, 81, 88, 127
Leuctra, battle of, 129
liburna, 210, 213, 218
Libya, Libyans, 8, 9, 29, 30, 124, 150
Licinius, 218
Lilybaeum, 27, 152–154, 160, 172
Lipari Islands, 27, 143, 147
liturgy, 38
Livius, M., commander of Tarentum, 165
Livy (T. Livius), the historian, 165, 173
London, 37, 218
Long Walls (the "Legs"), 80, 113, 125, 127

Loot. *See* booty
Lucullus, L. Licinius, 185–187
Lukku, 8
Lydia, Lydians, 17, 33, 34, 41, 43
Lygdamis, 32, 42, 44
Lysander, 111, 112, 113, 125

Macedonia, 50, 53, 55, 59, 73, 91,
    126, 130, 136, 138, 162, 168,
    169, 178, 181
magi, 64
Magnesia-ad-Sipylum, battle of,
    180
Mago (general opposed to Dionysius),
    123, 124
Mago (Second Punic War), 171
Mamers, Mamertines, 145, 146
Mandrocles, 49, 50
Manlius, L., consul, 149, 150
Mantinea, battles of, 93, 128, 129
Marathon, battle of, 32, 56–59, 76
Marcellus, M. Claudius, 163, 164
Marcus Aurelius, 215
Mardonius, 53, 73, 74
mare clausum, xvi
mare nostrum, 213
marines, 65, 68, 71, 72, 100, 104, 107,
    108, 120, 122, 127, 135–137,
    154, 155, 160, 169, 172,
    176–179, 202, 206, 208
Marius, C., 182–185, 191, 197
Mars, 145
Massilia, Massiliotes, battle of, 198,
    201, 202
Maximian, 217, 218
Medes, 18, 34, 61
Medinet Habu, 13
Megabazus, 50
Megara, 19, 27, 32, 80, 81, 85, 87, 95
Megarian decree, 81
Melos, siege of, 93
Memnon, 131
Menecrates, 205, 206
Menelaus, xvi
Menodorus, 205, 206, 207

mercenaries, 12, 16, 17, 18, 43, 44,
    90, 95, 120, 122, 130, 146, 155,
    174, 218
merchants, 22, 95, 99, 100, 101, 111,
    142, 156, 173, 174, 191–195, 202
Messana, 27, 95, 121, 134, 145, 146,
    206
Messenia, 9, 10, 27, 89, 90, 128
Metaurus River, battle of, 170
Metellus, Q. Caecilius, 194
Methone, 85, 208
Miletus, 8, 13, 17–19, 33, 42, 51–55,
    75, 107, 131, 176
military engineers, 119
Miltiades the Elder, 32
Miltiades the Younger, 49–59, 79
Mindaros, 107–110
Minos, Minoans, 4–8, 42, 80
Minotaur, 5
Mithridates, 183–187, 191, 196
Mitylene, 32, 39, 88, 111
Motya, 27, 120–122 (siege)
Mount Mycale, battle of, 74
mural hooks, 198
Mycenae, Mycenaeans, 7–9, 13, 17
Mylae, battle of, 147, 207
Mytilene, 16, 127

Naples, 210
Naucratis, 18
Naulochus, battle of, 207
Naupactus, 80, 86, 92, 100
naupegoi (ship-wrights), 87
naval siege, 163, 169, 173, 176
Naxos, 25, 26, 32, 42–44, 51, 56, 128
Nearchus, 133, 134
Nemean games, 169
Neptune, 170, 172, 206, 207
Nereids, 64
Nero, 212
Nerva, 213, 215
Nestor, xvi, 9
New Carthage, 170
Nicias, 88–103, 105
Nico (surnamed Perco), 165

Nike of Samothrace, 138
North American Indians, 4
Notium, battle of, 111
Numerian, 216
Numidia, 172

oarsmen, 7, 34, 37, 38, 39, 65, 66, 86,
    87, 95, 99, 101, 115, 120, 129,
    136, 147, 165, 168, 178, 193,
    206, 207, 210
Oceania, 3
Octavian (C. Julius Caesar
    Octavianus), 180, 204–210
Odysseus, xv–xvii, 10, 11, 23
Odyssey, xv, 5, 9, 10, 17, 24
Oeolycus, 17
"Old Oligarch," 87, 105
oligarchy, 107, 144
Olympias, 36, 39
Olympic festival, 63
Olympus, Mount, 53
oracles, 18, 28, 29, 32, 33, 44, 61, 68
Orchomenus, battle of, 185
Orem, siege of, 169
Oreus Channel, 63, 64, 68
Oricum, 167–169
Ortygia, 26, 119
Ostia, 192, 194
ostracism, 51, 59

paddle, 4, 133, 192
Palestine, 12
Panionium, 17, 52
Pantagnostos, 42
Papias, 207
papyrus, 18, 75
Parmenion, 51, 131
Paros, 19, 57, 128
Partheniai, 27
Parthenos, 68
Parthia, 201, 202, 207
Paulus, L. Aemilius, 181
Pausanias, the regent, 74, 125
Pausanias, the Spartan king, 125
peace of Nicias, 92

peace of Phoenice, 175
Peleset, 12
Peloponnesus, xvi, 8, 15, 51, 54, 55,
    69, 85, 90, 92, 96, 100, 129, 156,
    168, 169, 179, 208
Pelusium, battle of, 44
penteconter, 33, 34
Pergamum, Pergamenes, 168,
    175–180, 182
Pericles, 37, 38, 59, 74, 80, 81, 84, 85,
    88, 92, 102, 105
periplous, 86, 179, 207
Persephone, 25
Persepolis, 133
Perseus, 180, 181
Persia, Persians, 18, 33, 34, 41–45,
    50–76, 80, 106, 107, 112, 125,
    130, 131, 133
Persians, 69, 76
Phalerum, 57, 68
pharaoh, 8, 12
Pharsalus, battle of, 202
Philip II, 51, 119, 129, 130, 134, 135
Philip V, 162, 166–169, 175–180
Philistines, 12, 13
Phocaea, 33, 34
Phoenicia, Phoenicians, 9, 15, 18, 36,
    45, 50, 53, 66, 70, 71, 76, 80,
    208
Phormio, 85–87
Phosphoros, 68
Pillars of Heracles, 33
Piraeus, 60, 70, 80, 85, 87, 113, 128,
    184, 185
pirates, xv, 4, 6, 7, 10, 11, 24, 26–28,
    34, 35, 45, 130, 139, 143, 156,
    157, 175, 186, 191–196, 211, 220
Pisander, 126
Pisistratus, 32, 41, 42, 49, 51
Pithecusa, 25
plague, 85, 87, 92, 122, 124, 216
Plataea, battle of, 74–76, 85, 125
Plato, xv, 119, 122
Plemmyrium, 98, 99
plunder. *See* booty

Po River, 160, 175
polemarch, 57
polis, 15, 17, 24–26, 31, 33, 50
Pollis, 128
Polybius, 151, 161, 165
Polycrates, 32, 41–45, 49
Pompeius, Sextus, 204–207
Pompey (Cn. Pompeius Magnus), 186,
    194–197, 201–204
Pontus, 183, 187, 196
Porus, 133
Poseidon, xvi–xvii, 62, 64, 132
Postumus, 216
Potidaea, 19, 81, 84, 85, 130
praetorian prefect, 217
praetors, 192, 210
prayers, 95, 137
prisoners, 8, 14, 35, 42, 43, 45, 75, 90,
    92, 123, 135, 155, 170, 192
privateers, 42
prophecies, 93
proratai (lookouts), 87
Psammetichus I, 18
Psammetichus III, 44
Ptolemy (descendant), 185
Ptolemy I, 135–138, 175
Pydna, battle of, 130, 181
Pylos, xv, 89–93
Pyrrhic War, 144
Pythagoras, 43

Qadesh, battle of, 12
quadrireme, 119, 120, 153
Quinctius, D., 165, 166
quinquereme, 116, 120, 124, 146, 147,
    170, 171, 172, 198

rafts, 3, 192
raiding, 9, 12, 18, 49, 85, 87, 170, 213
ram, ramming, xv, 35–39, 65, 66, 71,
    74, 100, 108, 122, 128, 136, 150,
    171, 176, 177, 207, 209, 210, 213,
    222
Ramses II, 12–14
Ramses III, 12–14

raven (*korax*), 147, 148, 160
reed boat, 4
Regulus, M. Atilius, 149, 151
Rhegium, 27, 95, 123, 165
Rhine, 198, 210, 211, 213, 216, 217
Rhine fleet, 211, 213, 217
Rhion, battle of, 86, 87
Rhodes, 17, 33, 55, 72, 95, 107, 126,
    127, 131, 137–139, 175–185
Rhone River, 33, 160
Rubicon River, 201
Rus, Russia, Russians, 219, 221

sacrifice, xvi, 54, 61, 64, 112
sacrilege, 60, 96
sail, 13, 29, 30, 37, 53, 64, 65, 68, 70,
    72, 83, 85, 88, 90, 95, 111, 133,
    143, 151, 152, 155, 159, 160,
    165, 170, 185, 194, 195, 198,
    205, 209, 219–222
sailing season, xvi, 37, 79, 109, 195,
    207
Salaminia, 96
Salamis, 32, 62, 68–76 (battle), 80,
    87, 137
samaina, 42
sambuca, 184
Samos, 17, 32, 33, 42–45, 49, 53, 55,
    73–75, 81, 107, 111, 194
Sappho, xv, 32
Sardinia, 8, 15, 147, 148, 155, 159,
    162, 170, 171, 195, 201, 204, 205
Sardis, 52, 74
Saronic Gulf, 31, 54, 60, 80, 92, 127
satrap, satrapy, 45, 50, 51, 73, 75, 107,
    109, 126
Saxon Shore, 216
Saxons, 216–218
Sciathos Channel, 64, 65
Sciathos Island, 64
Scipio, L. Cornelius, see Cornelius,
    Scipio, L.
Scipio, P. Cornelius (the father of
    Africanus), see Cornelius, Scipio,
    P. (the father of Africanus)

Scipio, P. Cornelius Aemilianus (Africanus II), *see* Cornelius, Scipio Aemilianus, P. (Africanus II)

Scipio, P. Cornelius Africanus, see Cornelius Scipio Africanus, P.

Scythians, 19, 49, 50

sea power, 18, 28, 45, 84, 87, 88, 135

Second Athenian Confederacy, 128

Second Macedonian War, 178

Seleucid empire, 138, 178

Seleucus, 136

Selinus, 93, 95

Sempronius, Ti., 160

Senate, Senators, 143–145, 154, 156, 162, 168, 171, 179, 181–184, 192, 194, 201, 210, 213

Sepeia, battle of, 54

Sestos, 75, 107, 113

Severus, 215

Shardan, 8

Sheklesh, 8, 12

shell-first construction, 4

"ship of state," 33

ship types, multi-tiered
Four, 119, 121, 136 (*see also* quadrireme)
Five, 120, 121, 136 (*see also* quinquereme)
Seven, 137, 179
Eight, 136, 176
Nine, 136
Ten, 176, 177
Forty, 136

shipyards, xv, 4, 37, 137, 185

shrine, 17, 25, 28, 30, 61, 63

Sicels, 26

Sidon, 15, 50

siege, 9, 44, 56, 58, 75, 80, 81, 84, 85, 96, 98, 112, 119–122, 124, 132–134, 136–138, 145, 146, 150, 151–154, 159, 163, 164, 166, 169, 172, 174, 176, 184, 185, 191, 194, 195, 198, 201, 202, 208, 219

siege of Rhodes, 138

siege of Salamis, 137

siege works, 96, 146, 152, 153, 198, 202

signaling, 57, 66, 107–109, 137, 165, 172

Simaetha, 81

Simonides, 76

Sinope, 183

slavery, 10, 123, 205

slingers, 95, 100, 101, 121, 132, 135, 163

Social War, 183, 184

Solon, 32

soothsayers, 56, 74, 102, 106, 112

Southeast Asia, 3

Spain, 10, 15, 18, 33, 158–160, 164, 170, 171, 175, 182, 183, 195, 201, 202, 216

Spanish sword, 170

Spartacus, 186

Sphacteria, battle of, 89, 90, 134

spolia opima, 163, 212

storms, xvi–xvii, 11, 31, 33, 64–66, 72, 73, 89, 108, 109, 144, 151–154, 184, 200, 206

Successors, 134–139

Sulla, L. Cornelius Felix, 184–186, 191, 197

Sunion, xvi, 57

Sybaris, 27, 165

Syloson, 42

Syphnos, Syphnians, battle at, 44, 45

Syria, 5, 8, 136, 185, 211

Taras, Tarentum, 27, 143, 144, 165, 166, 206

Tartessos, 33

Telephos, 18

Teleutias, 128

temple of Artemis of Ephesus, 216

teredo navalis, 37

tetreres, 119

Teuta, 156, 157

thalamioi, 38
Themistocles, 59–72, 80
Theocles, 25, 26
Thera, 6, 7, 17, 29, 30
Thermopylae, battle of, 62–67, 75, 179
Theseus, 5–7
Thessaly, 8, 9, 31, 59, 62, 73, 126, 180
thete-marines, 95
Thetis, 64
Third Punic War, 175
Thirty Tyrants, 125
thirty-year truce, 81
Thrace, Thracians, 19, 50, 53, 55, 59, 73, 126, 179
thranitai, 38
Thrasyboulos, 109, 127
Thucydides, 6, 26, 36, 79, 82, 86, 90–93, 100–102
Thutmose III, 4
Tiberius the emperor, 212
Ticinus River, battle of, 160
tides, 198, 200, 217
Timaea, 107
timber, 37, 81, 183, 184, 202
Timocreon, 72
Timoleon, 144
Tiryns, 9
Tissaphernes, 107
Tjekker, 12
Tlepolemus, 17
trade, 4–10, 13, 18, 24–27, 31–34, 50, 80, 134, 139, 176, 194, 198, 219, 220, 222
Trajan, 190, 213, 215
"Transalpine" Gaul, 175
Trebia River, battle of, 160
triaconter, 6, 67
tribunician power, 210
trierarch, 38, 39, 68, 103, 104
trieres. See trireme
trihemiolia, 176, 177

trireme, 26, 36–40, 44, 49, 67, 68, 80, 88, 99, 116, 119, 120, 132, 136, 198, 220
Trojan War, 9
trophies, 8, 110
Troy, Troad, Trojans, xvi, 7, 9, 16, 26, 32, 61
trumpet signal, 121
trumpeters, 108
Tunes (city), 173
Tursha, 8
Tyndaris, 149
tyrant, tyranny, 26, 32, 41–44, 50–56, 59, 69, 75, 94, 113, 119, 121–123, 144, 145
Tyre, 13, 15, 50, 131, 132

Ugarit, 5, 12
Utica, 164, 172, 173

Vandals, 218
Veneti, 198, 202
Verres, C., 192, 193
Vespasian, 212
Vestal Virgin, 186
Virtus, 217

watchword, 170
Weshesh, 12
winds, xvi, 7, 10, 11, 24, 152–154, 165, 172, 199, 200, 217, 220
"wooden wall," 62, 68

Xanthippus the Athenian, 59, 74, 75
Xanthippus the Spartan, 151
Xenophon, 125
Xerxes, 59–62, 65, 66, 69–72, 73–74, 76

Zama, 174
Zeus, 5, 11, 17, 45, 66, 68, 88, 131
Zoroastrians, 56
zugioi, 38

About the Author

Alfred S. Bradford, PhD (University of Chicago), is the John Saxon Chair of Ancient History at the University of Oklahoma (Norman, Oklahoma). His last two publications were *Leonidas and the Kings of Sparta: Mightiest Warriors, Fairest Kingdom* (Praeger, 2011) and *War: Antiquity and Its Legacy* (Oxford, 2015). He has also published books with Praeger on piracy (*Flying the Black Flag: A Brief History of Piracy*), the history of warfare in the ancient world (*With Arrow, Sword, and Spear*), and a memoir of his service in Vietnam as an infantry captain (*Some Even Volunteered*). He is married to Pamela M. Bradford, a fine artist, whose illustrative work has graced many of his books. They have two daughters, Elizabeth and Alexandra.